THE TIDES OF POWER: CONVERSATIONS ON THE AMERICAN CONSTITUTION

THE TIDES
OF POWER

CONVERSATIONS ON THE
AMERICAN CONSTITUTION

BETWEEN

BOB ECKHARDT

MEMBER OF CONGRESS FROM TEXAS, AND

CHARLES L. BLACK, JR.

STERLING PROFESSOR OF LAW, YALE UNIVERSITY

NEW HAVEN AND LONDON

YALE UNIVERSITY PRESS

1976

Designed by Sally Sullivan
and set in Baskerville type.
Printed in the United States of America by
Vail-Ballou Press, Inc., Binghamton, New York.

Published in Great Britain, Europe, and Africa by
Yale University Press, Ltd., London.
Distributed in Latin America by Kaiman & Polon,
Inc., New York City; in Australasia by Book & Film
Services, Artarmon, N.S.W., Australia; in Japan by
John Weatherhill, Inc., Tokyo.

To
Sarah Eckhardt
and
Robin Elizabeth Black

CONTENTS

PREFACE

The ensuing conversations are reproduced very much as they were taped, though with many cuts of digressive and repetitive material, and a number of small clarifying changes. The positions taken as we talked stand unaltered; this implies that each of us might wish to qualify, amplify, or even recede from some of them, after research and reflection. To have altered them for this volume would have resulted in a mere wax image of dialogue.

We talked without books; "acknowledgment" is therefore insolubly problematic. Academic and congressional colleagues, as well as students at the Yale Law School, have undoubtedly contributed more than we can recall.

The indispensable acknowledgment is to Jane Isay, who invented and then skillfully practiced the art of editing real dialogue. Neither of us ever so much as heard rumored the existence of another editor who could have done what she has done. Thanks are due to Chester Kerr, and to all at the Yale University Press, for encouragement and for skillful performance of their tasks. Professor Ralph Sharp Brown, Jr., kindly read the manuscript and made a number of valued suggestions. Eileen M. Quinn, Carolyn B. Vitale, and Frances L. Gray carried through a most exacting job of manuscript production, starting from tapes of two hardly distinguishable Texas idiolects formed within two hundred yards of one another on Rio Grande Street in Austin.

We have been talking things over together for about fifty-four years now. We hope the segments of that talk here reproduced may start useful thoughts in other minds.

R. C. E.

C. L. B., JR.

INTRODUCTION: THE CONSTITUTIVE FORCE OF THE AMERICAN CONSTITUTION 1

BLACK: Bob, it's no secret that an introduction is normally written after the body of the book has been finished. It can't be any secret that this "introductory" conversation occurs out of chronological order, after we have, as now we do, a pretty good idea of the total contents of the book.

It should be made clear what we have taken to be the central meaning of constitutional law for our purposes here. Most Americans, when they think of "constitutional law," think of the very important protections of the Bill of Rights, and of similar portions of the Constitution—those portions protecting citizens' rights by limiting governmental action. What we have talked about, instead, are the matters which have lately come to be of so much importance and prominence, involving the actually *constitutive* law of the government —the way the government is set up and its powers distributed, without regard to the question of general constitutional limitations on the exercise of power.

ECKHARDT: In other words, this book is not, centrally, about the manner in which the courts intervene on the basis of constitutional authority to curb governmental action. It is about how government is structured under the Constitution. I don't think that limitation of power, policed by the judiciary, is at the center of constitutional law, but is sort of on the periphery of constitutional law.

BLACK: Certainly that is true as an intellectual matter, however strong may be one's emotional attachment to the Bill of Rights guarantees. The British example teaches us a great deal. You know there are a lot of people who actually don't think that Britain has a Constitution, because the British Constitution allows Parliament to do anything that Parliament wants to do, and does not impose, as a matter of law, the kind of safeguards that we are used to possessing and invoking in this country. Yet Britain has a working government—a constitution—and, incidentally, enjoys much freedom. You and I are both very firmly on record, in many places, as regarding judicial intervention in the defense of individual rights under constitutional provisions as both a legitimate and a good thing. But that kind of law is not *constitutive*. That's not the kind of law that makes the government, that legitimates the exercise of authority, that decides what offices shall exist, how the occupants shall be chosen, and what the relationships of legitimate power and authority shall be amongst them. It's this latter thing that is the essential constitution of any country. It's ridiculous to say of any country which is actually civilized and operating that it "doesn't have a constitution." It is entirely feasible to get along without written constitutional limitations on the exercise of power in the interest of individual freedom, but it is not possible to have a government, or to continue political life, if you do not have any structure of the government, no way of selecting people to exercise power and of defining the powers they may exercise.

As an example of our emphasis here, take the case of *Powell v. McCormack*,[1] on which you wrote an article approvingly cited in the Supreme Court's opinion.[2] That case had to do with the power of the House of Representatives in respect of its dealings with one of its own members, or of its deciding whether somebody was to be a member. Almost all the questions involved in the recent impeachment business have been of this constitutive kind—they have concerned the respective and interacting powers of the presidency, Congress, the judiciary. And I think it is important to emphasize from the start that it is this intellectually and politically essential kind of constitutional problem that we are going to be talking about.

ECKHARDT: I think you also illustrated the sort of thing we are

1. 395 U.S. 486 (1969).
2. Eckhardt, *The Adam Clayton Powell Case*, 45 Texas Law Review 1205 (1967).

discussing here in the Washington and Lee speech[3] you made last May, in which you pointed out that Article I of the Constitution is so salient and so pervasive in establishing a governmental structure that almost all the rest, if not all the rest, could have been left out, and a government could have been structured around Article I.

BLACK: Whether that's a correct view or not, it is an example of the kind of thought that has to do with the structure and empowerment of the government and of its different branches. I did take the view in that talk that we could have had a complete working Constitution if the Constitution had ended at the end of Article I— with the very important reservation that the President's veto power would have had to be removed from Article 1—because (since the Constitution itself would not have created the office of President) the presidential veto provision would have nothing to refer to if the Constitution had ended at the end of Article I. I said that Congress would in that case have had the power to create executive and judicial branches, and would almost certainly have done so, much along present lines. That thesis, whether or not wholly true, suggests a lot of valuable insights into the actual structure of the government as it exists. But for present purposes, the important thing about it is that it's a sample of what one thinks about when one thinks about the *constitutive* aspect of the Constitution. I didn't even consider it worthwhile to mention, in such a speech, the Bill of Rights, or the Fourteenth Amendment, or any of the other similar material, to which American constitutional law casebook editors give about 800 pages, usually, while they give about 300 to the kind of thing that has predominantly interested us in these talks. The thesis that I was sustaining there is a thesis in what I would call constitutionalism pure and simple. That is, I dealt with the question of how the government is constituted.

ECKHARDT: If you fed the Constitution into a computer, and also

3. Black, *The Presidency and Congress,* The John Randolph Tucker Lecture delivered at Washington and Lee University, May 10, 1975, Washington and Lee Law Review, Volume 32, page 841.

fed into the same computer those cases in which, in construing Article I, the Supreme Court has allowed Congress to select the means for executing its legislative power from amongst a total variety of means, and if you then asked the computer the question "What is the logical function of Article II and Article III?," the computer would probably print out something like this: "These articles contain definite though not essential limits on congressional powers already conferred by the first Article." On the whole, the significant limit on Congress in Article III—the article that constitutes the courts—is that judges are to have life tenure. Article III, as I see it, imposes no other very important limit on Congress with respect to its creating and maintaining a judiciary. The other important limit on Congress, which is that it can't tell the judges how to decide cases, would, of course, exist, but it wouldn't exist by virtue of anything in the text, and there is actually nothing in the text to that effect. It exists by virtue of a general conception of what a judiciary is all about.

The limits imposed on Congress's creating of an executive branch by Article II are more complicated, because Article II says how the executive shall be chosen, a rather complicated matter, and it also contains in effect (as a logical part of Article II, although actually the textual provision appears in Article I) the enormously important power of veto, which we will, of course, return to as a topic-in-chief later on.

BLACK: Yes, but if you take a good first look at the Constitution, what it looks like is congressional government, with very extensive powers in the hands of Congress over both the other branches, and with some reservations on that power with respect to these other two branches. It's not certain how important these limitations were. For example, even if there had been no Article III, and if Congress were creating a federal judiciary without an Article III, Congress might well have decided that life tenure for judges was a good idea. The British Parliament made that decision and stuck to it, and it's quite possible that our Congress might have done the same. As it is they must do it—or, rather, Article III does it for them—so that the problem of a Constitution without an Article III may seem fanciful.

ECKHARDT: Yes, but I think that kind of counterfactual specula-
tion has several merits. One is that, for the person coming to the
Constitution for the first time, it clears away a lot of brush and
dead wood. Take Articles IV and VI. You could just discard them
as supererogatory, because there isn't one thing in them that could
not be enacted by Congress even if it weren't in those articles. Even
the Article VI "supremacy clause," of which so much is made, is
plainly unnecessary, because nobody in his right mind could read
Article I and come to any conclusion other than that federal law is
to be supreme. There is language in Article I which says that the
States can't do this, that, or the other—language that could not
possibly occur in an instrument whose underlying assumption was
not the supremacy of national law. But even if these particular
passages weren't there, it would be rather preposterous to think that
a state law could take precedence over a power, such as the commerce
power, granted to and exercised by the national Congress. So, as a
matter of the main structure of the Constitution, you can really throw
Articles IV and VI out altogether.

BLACK: Article V, the article providing for amendment, is in a
different category but obviously neither adds nor subtracts anything
of substance. It simply provides for ways in which the Constitution
may later be changed. So that you can get right down to Articles I,
II, and III as the genuinely constitutive articles of the government
(Article VII only provided the terms on which the Constitution was
originally to go into effect).

I think that it was a natural thing for Madison to say, as he did
at the time, on looking at this Constitution (and of course he could
not foresee the future, but simply saw what was there before his eyes)
that the real danger of tyranny lay not in the executive branch but in
the legislative branch. What he failed to understand was some of the
institutional problems about Congress and the presidency which were
certain to develop when you have a multimembered, two-chambered
body with all the power, in confrontation with a single-headed branch
with very little textually warranted power.

ECKHARDT: Then considering the actual language of the Constitution without the gloss of history, if we should feed into the computer such actual language, the computer would come out with a print saying that the legislative branch is vastly more powerful than the executive branch, and it would underestimate the power of the judiciary as it has developed. I think one must therefore enter a caveat with respect to considering the Constitution literally, as a computer would do. What has happened to the branches of government, with respect to their development of power and ability to innovate and to activate under this literal structure, has been a fleshing out by time and experience.

BLACK: To that I would say two things, one of dominant significance and one that kind of leads us off into another topic. The first point that I'm making is really stolen from you, because I remember your saying this. I can therefore qualify it without immodesty as an exceedingly profound insight: This text, however widely it may be departed from in fact, always stays there, so that it's virtually impossible in a real crunch to deny that Congress has these powers, however disused they may be. None of the construction that has taken place has really taken away this primal power of Congress. Indeed, in almost all the cases, and almost all the trends of cases where the question of congressional power, pure and simple, has arisen, the Supreme Court has legitimated congressional assertions of power. And even though institutional practices may have arisen and been sanctioned by time, which greatly diminished and practically allocated elsewhere congressional power, it still remains that Congress, on the basis of the text which is still there—and which cannot be eliminated—could cut the President down to nothing but his salary, could, indeed, put the White House up for auction, if it could raise the necessary two-thirds majorities or get a President acquiescent or scared enough to sign the bill.

ECKHARDT: It could take the clerks away from the Supreme Court.

BLACK: It did abolish one whole term of the Supreme Court back in the beginning of the nineteenth century, as you know. And I don't think there's any serious question that it could do that again if it wanted to.

This text, with its structure, with its virtually total empowerment of Congress, and its placing of the other two branches at the mercy of Congress as a textual matter, is there; it can't be eliminated except by amendment so radical that I don't think we will ever have it, short of a totally new Constitutional Convention.

Kenneth Stampp, the brilliant revisionist historian of the Reconstruction period, asserted, I think correctly, that the great achievement of the Reconstruction, despite its seeming failure, was to put on the books the *words* of the Thirteenth, Fourteenth, and Fifteenth Amendments, so that, when the time came, they would be there for the judges and for Congress to use. They would serve to legitimate a change when conditions were such that change could actually take place. Now similarly I think that the empowerments of Congress in Article I, construed as they have been, modestly used as they have actually been—in contrast to what Congress might have done—are permanently there, and that fact is always standing in the wings, in the shadows, in the background, well known to all reflective participants.

ECKHARDT: The veto power is really an enormous power of the President. It says the government can't move at all unless the Congress accommodates to the President's general views of what ought to be done. This, too, is a power permanently fixed in the text. Even so, one must always go back to the basic power, the extremely great power, of the Congress. Even when acting in an area where the President has the greatest unrestrained power—the area of foreign policy—President Ford went to Congress to ask authority for the evacuation of American citizens and others from Saigon. That is a very significant thing. He could have commanded the troops and, outside an act of hostility, he could have acted without congressional authority. But he felt, I think because of the written words of the first Article, that he had to go back and get a policy determination from Congress. Actually what Congress did was debate the matter while everything was happening, and ultimately he did exercise presidential power, which I think he had; and I think probably it worked out best, because Congress was not tempted to give him official authority to engage in hostilities.

BLACK: That's a good illustration of the subtlety with which these powers actually interplay at any given time, and of the extremely subtle relation between text and custom—between the written and the unwritten Constitution. I dare say that the fact that Mr. Ford is the first unelected President—never elected either President or Vice President by the public at large—would play some part in some of his reticences.

This leads me back to my other point about this text. The two things—text and custom—have to be considered together, and they are not contradictory. My point here is that to an astounding extent, to an extent that would never reveal itself if you read books that are set up and organized as commentaries on the text, we have an *unwritten* Constitution in the United States. This is not altogether a matter of custom. It is also to a great extent a matter of law, and it extends to many of the subjects which interest us as *constitutive,* having to do with the allocation of authority. For example, you will scan the constitutional text in vain for any indication that the new States, after the original thirteen adherents to the Constitution, had to be admitted on an equal footing with those already in, although "equal footing" has now come to be a phrase that is quoted as though it were a requirement of law. In fact it would have been acceptable except as to the matter of equal representation in the Senate—and I suspect probably in the House, too, because of the specific division—it would have been entirely possible so far as the text goes, to admit States with various restrictions lying on them. Indeed, as far as the text goes, it might have been possible to admit a new State with one Senator allowed it, if that State consented,[4] and such consent could have been made a condition for admission. It was not decided as a matter of law that this could not be done until a twentieth-century case involving Oklahoma. Oklahoma was admitted, but with the stipulation that its capital should remain in a certain city. Later, Oklahoma desired to change the capital, and in some way this became a lawsuit, and the Supreme Court decided that all States were "on an equal footing," and that Oklahoma, in conse-

4. Article V, last clause.

quence, must be given the same power to locate and relocate its capital that the other States had.[5] But in so doing, the Court had no text to quote. It simply was a matter of assumed structure.

ECKHARDT: But I wonder now if we haven't perhaps said enough to give the reader some notion (or, if his only interest is in the Bill of Rights and limitation on government, some fair warning) as to what we intend to go into.

BLACK: A fresh look at that word "constitution," with its etymological connection with the verb "to constitute," suggests our emphasis. That etymology is really all that you need to recognize the fact that the basic thing required, and found in every country that is politically viable, is a system for the creating of offices, for choosing the occupants of those offices, for empowering the occupants of those offices, and then, in a federalism, a system for defining the power relations not only between the branches of the federal government, but also between the federal government as a whole, or some of its branches, and the constituent States of the Union. Those questions, and others perhaps of the same order, are the essence of constitutionalism, even of constitutional law. They are questions which must be met and solved by any political society, whether or not that society finds it necessary to have a Bill of Rights or a Fourteenth Amendment. We're talking about *constitutive* constitutional law rather than *limiting* constitutional law, and I think people lately have come to see how very important this is. A lot of things have happened that have surprised people, that require explanation or exploration. One is, and this is a pretty good example, that the presidency of the United States came into the hands of Mr. Nixon with the tradition of its being looked upon as an office of very great power, with ample means of protecting itself. The fact was that, after being reelected to that office by one of the largest majorities in history—so that behind him

5. *Coyle v. Smith,* 221 U.S. 559 (1911). It is interesting that Holmes and McKenna *dissented,* though without opinion, and that the "equal footing" idea gets no support from the actions of the Constitutional Convention of 1787; see 2 Farrand, *Records of The Federal Convention* (rev. ed. 1937), p. 454.

was not only the constitutional power of the office but also the political power that results from the fact of an overwhelming victory in an election—Mr. Nixon was totally unable to protect himself. There were really no means at his disposal as the President for protecting himself.

ECKHARDT: I don't know whether I would agree. Now it's easy to think of Mr. Nixon today as always having been weak, but I can remember when he was extremely strong and exercised power very, very strongly—for instance in dismantling elements of the poverty program without any legislative direction—as a matter of fact in the face of opposition to it. He simply didn't use money which was appropriated and available to run the program, and he got away with it. Had it not been for the fact that he made the colossal mistakes of first making the tapes and then of not destroying them, it is very likely that Nixon would be President today, and would be exercising enormous power. I think he was both more inclined to use power and more competent in exercising it than the present occupant of the White House. We get a little bit of a warped picture of Mr. Nixon because his last days in office are so firmly etched in our minds. But after you're done analyzing the President's power in terms of that which is expressly granted, or even implied, in the Constitution, you have to remember that the view that the press and the public has of the President's power determines that power to a large extent.

BLACK: Because it builds up his influence in Congress, enables him to get away with independent actions which might be of debatable legality and all that sort of thing.

ECKHARDT: It permits him, for instance, to continue to use the veto without public pressure requiring him to go along and accommodate.

BLACK: These popular views and popular interpretations are undoubtedly important to the day-by-day defining of the actual powers of any office. There does, however, always remain that text in the background.

ECKHARDT: Well, there's perhaps another example of such reaction of public opinion on power, that's the Mayaguez incident, in which undoubtedly President Ford came out much the public victor. Yet in retrospect one must recognize that what he did, if it had been done in a much more explosive situation, could have been an extremely dangerous act of war, and Congress had no opportunity to review it or to act on it. Yet almost every Congressman, including myself, immediately reacted favorably on the grounds that the President was protecting American lives. Here was a case where we had to react before we knew all the facts.

Well, it seems hard if not impossible for you and me to talk in pure abstraction. We've really introduced this book, in this talk, by sample rather than by generalization. Perhaps that's best.

BLACK: Very likely.

2 THE BUILT-IN WEAKNESSES OF CONGRESS

BLACK: I have always presented the Constitution to my classes as a masterpiece, as a document actually deserving John Adams's description of it as the most remarkable single production ever struck off on one occasion by the human mind. But just within the last three years or so we have begun to have doubts about our Constitution and its working, and I suppose our main subject here together is the exploration of those doubts, with a view to diagnosing the trouble that we're in, and trying a little to see where we go from here.

ECKHARDT: Yes, I think the doubts may arise more in areas in which actual practice, as between the executive and the legislative branches, has expanded executive authority—where there are, in fact, no clear guidelines in the Constitution. I don't think that the doubts arise with respect to what the Founders struck off at a single time. As a matter of fact, most of the areas of expansion of administrative power were not addressed specifically at all, and, I suppose, didn't have any practical application at the time of the framing of the Constitution. So we run into difficulties in interstices of the constitutional framework.

BLACK: I think that's right. The contrast has very often been drawn between the American Constitution, which is said to be a written Constitution, laying down the lines of governmental power in a fairly clear and comprehensible way, and the British Constitution, which is not written but which consists so much in certain things simply being "the done thing," to employ a phrase that they may still sometimes use. With them, certain things are not "done," and others are "done." I think that the inexactness of that contrast has been laid bare by recent events. Through the decades of our Constitution's life, a very great deal of what we have done, a great deal of what we have done wrong—and, I may say, a great deal of what we've done right—has been not so much a matter of what's in the constitutional text, or what can be drawn out of that text by inference, but simply the "done thing." Take the most dramatic recent areas, impeachment or near impeachment, the way the President is or ought to be treated, and the way the President has treated Congress. These things have been very much more a matter of a feeling, of rather silently agreed-on lines of mutual support and forbearance, than of anything you can find in the text. Nevertheless, one of the first things we need to do is to reconsider what the actual constitutionally warranted powers of the presidency are, as opposed to the powers that have been *habitually conceded* to the presidency—some of them, I think, wisely, and some of them unwisely. The power over domestic policy that the President has attained, through the elaborate process of congressional delegation, has been given him, I think, on the whole unwisely—or at least excessively and indiscriminately. The power over foreign affairs, on the other hand, I should think has on the whole wisely been given the President, though there is much room for difference of opinion in detail on that, and I dare say we'll generate some differences between the two of us. But to me all questions are open.

ECKHARDT: Congress, theoretically, has the power to determine virtually every basic policy matter that would confront government. For instance, though the President has the power to engage us in foreign commitments which may largely frame a future course relating to war and peace, I know of no place where the Congress could not limit such policy determinations. Of course, Congress has difficulty, as a practical matter, in governing the President, because very often its only enforcing power is its power over the purse, and the exercise of that power may entail a rather nonselective crippling of valuable or even essential programs.

I am not so much concerned with what some of my colleagues in Congress are concerned with, that is, the President's gaining too much power, as compared with the legislative body. I am concerned with how both these branches of government can most effectively *utilize* power.

BLACK: Then let's consider what the textually warrantable powers are of these two branches which have so recently been locked in one confrontation after another—the presidency and the Congress. Now my own short conclusion, which I think we ought to go into and maybe document from the Constitution, would be that all the power that matters actually resides in the Congress, and that whatever difficulties Congress may have in exercising this power are owing to reluctance on the part of its members—some feeling perhaps of the "done thing," as I have said—or to organizational difficulties within Congress, or to difficulties arising from local pressures on members.

On the other hand, the President has a quite astoundingly small amount of power which can be traced with any warrant to the text of the Constitution. I think a look at the text of the Constitution itself—a text which is a lot shorter than most people perhaps think— very quickly validates this conclusion. The conclusion I would arrive at is simply that the presidency lies in the hand of Congress, at any time Congress wishes to exercise its powers, and that the President has, under the Constitution as it came from the hands of the Framers, a very small number either of means of defense of his office or of powers over people and events outside his office.

ECKHARDT: But sometimes Congress seems to me like the man who comes home, and sits in his easy chair, and expounds on politics and policy. His wife permits him that position, but she actually runs the household. She has the effective power to run the affairs of the family; to a large extent the same is true of the presidency.

BLACK: Or has been. For now, let's stick with the text, and consider just what powers the President has, one by one. Most of them are in Article II. He has the power to perform a number of formal acts, or rather the duty to perform several formal acts, such as delivery of the State of the Union message or signing the commissions for all the officers of the United States. I think we'd all have to agree that powers of that order are quite unimportant. They may in some way define a kind of conception of the office as one of leadership, but they don't amount to anything significant in a crunch. The power to come and give a State of the Union message is not of much importance.[1] The appointing power is a power which lies entirely in the hands of the Senate. This is the case with respect both to judicial and to nonjudicial appointments. It is true, as was pointed out long ago in the Federalist Papers, that the Senate, as the Federalist put it (I forget which one of the three authors wrote this paper), has only the power of negation. But I think that's a little misleading, as the practice of "senatorial courtesy"[2] shows. The concerted refusal, over a long period of time, to confirm can amount at least to severe pressure for some particular appointment, and to the transfer of the power of appointment, at least in great part, to the body that has the power to refuse any appointment but the one it wants. I happen to know of a case where one Senator recently said—speaking without any intention of boasting, without any feeling that he was uttering a paradox, just stating what to him was the literal everyday truth—he said he hadn't decided yet whom to "appoint" to the appeals bench in a certain federal judicial circuit, or that he hadn't decided yet whom to make a district judge in a certain State. We both know that this expression, in many cases, reflects reality, because if the Senate won't confirm anybody except the man who is appointed in accordance with senatorial courtesy, then this gives the President the alternative of either allowing the post to remain empty, or else going along with the Senate. I think the Senate's deference to presidential appointments could have been much less than it has been, and that the body that has the power to confirm has, by virtue of its threat not to confirm, a far greater power than simply the power to confirm. It is part of the "done thing," and not a constitutional requirement, that the Senate defer as much as it does to the presidential appointing power.

ECKHARDT: Well, I don't know. I think it's about equal. I think

1. The speaker's view on this underwent a change in the course of the dialogues; see *infra* pp. 194–95.
2. See Black, *Perspectives in Constitutional Law* (revised edition 1970), pp. 56–57.

the Constitution permits an impasse, if either the President or the Senate wants to make it that way, and this has been resolved by a "done thing," to use your term. The situation you describe is usually applicable to appointments of the local or regional nature. The regional appointment may be, however, a very important one, very importantly affecting national policy, as, for instance, in the appointment of a Court of Appeals judge in the Fifth Circuit[3] just after the first *Brown* decision on school segregation. The President nearly always defers to the Senator with respect to that kind of position. But the Senate, on the other hand, nearly always defers to the President with respect to an appointment of an officer whose authority is nationwide—for instance, a cabinet officer.

BLACK: They do, but they don't have to, and here we have to do with the "done thing."

Since you mention the Fifth Circuit, President Kennedy, for example, was absolutely obliged to appoint some district judges in the Fifth Circuit who were not to his taste, because of their opposition to the civil rights movement, and to the general tenor of the Supreme Court's decisions with regard to the rights of blacks. He had no choice; he had to do that because he was confronted with a custom in the Senate which would have made it impossible for him to put anybody else in office down there, given the views of the Democratic Senators from the relevant states. When he wanted to appoint Judge Skelly Wright, who was a district judge in Louisiana, to the Court of Appeals bench, he couldn't appoint him to the Fifth Circuit bench, but had to bring him to the District of Columbia Court of Appeals in order to do it; he couldn't get it through as to the Fifth Circuit, because of the power of the Senators in the South. The Presidential power of appointment would not be of much account if the Senate ever chose to exercise all of its prerogatives.

The Senate can also exercise its power over appointments to effect indirect ends. For example, when Truman named General Mark

3. The Fifth Judicial Circuit comprises Mississippi, Alabama, Georgia, Florida, Louisiana, and Texas. During the early years of the civil rights fight, the manning of its bench was of prime national importance.

Clark, who was as unexceptionable a *person* as you could have found in a long day's ride, for the post of Ambassador to the Vatican, the appointment was plainly turned down by the Senate (although it never came to a vote there) not because of any objection to Clark, but because of the Senate's unwillingness to see an Ambassador—any Ambassador—go to the Vatican. This power over appointments can thus radiate out beyond the personality of the appointee and actually be made to give considerable leverage over policy itself.

ECKHARDT: Well, it's an interesting thing, too, that if the power does create, or does have inherent in it, an impasse, the question always arises, who benefits by the impasse, and who is most hurt by it? The President has the greater, or at least the more immediate, responsibility of carrying the government forward. Therefore, the President is under great public pressure to come up with an appointment which will be confirmed. But if the Senate simply sits stubbornly on appointments, and the President appoints one person after another, men with qualifications and general acceptability, and the Senate refuses them, the Senate is also acted upon heavily by public opinion.

BLACK: That's quite true. I'm not saying the presidential appointment power is nothing; I am simply saying that it is much less in its bedrock nature than it is often assumed to be. Even when it comes to national appointments which don't have a sectional flavor, we have seen, under Nixon, the turning down of two Supreme Court nominees, and the virtual acceptance by the Senate of the duty on its part to consider the philosophy of people who are nominated for the Supreme Court—the cases of Haynsworth and Carswell. Nobody knows why each Senator voted the way he did, but this undoubtedly played a part in the refusal to confirm one or both of those candidates.

ECKHARDT: One other important appointive power we should mention is the President's power to appoint inferior officers of government without confirmation, and his generally recognized power to run his own household. Thus, frequently, in order to avoid the necessity of confirmation, power has been moved from departments of government, from cabinet-level posts, for instance, to the White House.[4] In that way a President can appoint a Haldeman or an Ehrlichman, with really more power than most cabinet officers.

BLACK: But there again this independent appointive power is easily reducible; Congress can reassert its power at any time. Congress may, under the Constitution, vest in the President alone the power to appoint inferior officers—but it may change the rule back to Senate confirmation whenever it wants to. It's a concession to the President that Congress wishes to make, and it can always reverse it.

ECKHARDT: But how could it reverse it? By withdrawing funds?

BLACK: I don't think that last resort is necessary. It could be done by passage of a law, either over a veto or as a rider to some bill that could not, practically speaking, be vetoed. But the power over funds is underneath all this, and that could also be used.

Let's take up now the foreign relations power as another problem, just giving it a preliminary look. I think, when you read the text of the Constitution, you must be astounded at how little textual basis there is for the common assumption that the foreign relations of the United States are to be conducted, in the main, by the President. The two things that give any color to that assumption are the President's power to appoint Ambassadors, which is subject to all the same problems with respect to confirmation by the Senate, and the President's power to make treaties, which is circumscribed—in Texas we might say hog-tied—by the requirement of a two-thirds vote in the Senate for ratifying the treaty. This requirement gives a minority of the Senate a veto power which, as you know, has on very important occasions been exercised, perhaps the most important instance being the League of Nations Covenant. It's not a dormant power at all. It has to be thought of continually in the negotiation of treaties.

Those are the President's powers over foreign affairs. The power to *receive* Ambassadors is not even stated as a power but as a duty, and if one were looking at the text freshly, I think one would probably

4. See the Constitution, Article II, Section 2.

conclude that that's just a formal function that's given the President, or permitted to the President, rather than an actual power. Now on the basis of that very slim textual foundation, we have built up the *custom* that the conduct of the foreign relations of the United States is very largely, if not entirely, in the hands of the President. Here again it seems to me a question of the "done thing," rather than something that the Constitution makes mandatory or even strongly suggests. The Constitution certainly does not *forbid* it; it doesn't forbid Congress to acquiesce in the President's conduct of foreign relations. But it sure as hell doesn't command them to do so. And the power of Congress over foreign commerce, over war and peace, over piracies and felonies on the high seas, over rules of naturalization and over the purse—all these powers could easily be brought into play to give Congress a much ampler control over foreign policy than it now exercises.

ECKHARDT: Then we need to examine why, in spite of the Constitution's granting almost unlimited authority to Congress, and its granting rather limited authority to the President, exactly the opposite of what would be expected has occurred. The President has assumed more and more power, and Congress has let him do it. I would suggest that the reason for that is the nature of Congress and of the political factors that act upon it.

A legislator is acted upon more strongly by those with intense interests and long memories. Regional concerns act upon him more powerfully than do the general concerns of the nation. And for that reason he is prone to retire to the little baronetcy of his office and devote himself to matters having to do with the demands of his constituency and the pressures placed upon him, because of his position on his committees, by business interests. These things generate campaign contributions and tend to make him feel important. The press is not likely to notice his position on major issues, and even less the work he may do on bills of general importance. But his local newspapers will notice the fact that he's gotten flood insurance for an area that had been flooded, that he's gotten an appropriation for a dam, that he's stopped a plant from polluting the environment by pressure on the EPA, or that he's established a park or a new post office in his district.

Take, for instance, Manny Celler,[5] with his immense influence on the House of Representatives in the Judiciary Committee; he was beaten by an energetic young woman who decided to take him on. A race of this type is frequently decided altogether on local issues, on the personalities of the candidates and on the intensity of the effort exerted locally by one or the other. A man deeply involved in national issues may be at a disadvantage. For instance, Senator Ralph Yarborough of Texas, at the height of his power as Chairman of the Committee on Health, Education and Welfare, was defeated by a businessman who had last held public office (as Congressman) some twenty years before.

On the other hand, the President's important activities in the mainstream of public affairs are very well covered by the press. His success, or lack of it, in campaigns is to a much greater extent dependent on his success or lack of it in making good decisions and carrying them out.

BLACK: This would be equally true of all the general national concerns. Now we're talking about the characteristics of Congress, as opposed to those of the presidency, which bring about a centralization of power over national concerns in the presidency, whether or not they have to do with foreign policy.

ECKHARDT: In the British Parliament, they try to give a valuable man (like Manny Celler) a district that he can hold. True, there are some surprises from time to time, but leadership control is the rule. In Britain, a man like Manny Celler would probably have gotten a safe seat—just as Sam Rayburn was, in effect, given a safe seat, in the days before the Supreme Court cases which prevented that, or made it hard, by forcing equalization of congressional district populations. But all Rayburn's life he was scared to death they'd put Dallas in his district.

5. Congressman Emanuel Celler, for many years Chairman of the extremely powerful House Committee on the Judiciary.

BLACK. So that in a sense, the organization of Congress along territorial lines, with a firm territorial base of known extent, for each member of Congress and for each Senator, has a tendency to make the greatest motive of all, which is survival, one that pushes you away from national concerns and pushes you toward concerns with your district. This is a tendency which is strongly resisted by many members of Congress, as Manny Celler's case shows. He was a man of national concern. Herbert Lehman, when he was Senator from New York, was the best friend that the Indians in the West had in the United States Senate, although he had nothing to gain from that, there being a very small number of Indians in New York State. The Indian vote in New York State is about as important as the Viking vote which John Lindsay threw away when he came out against the Vinland map in favor of Christopher Columbus as the discoverer of America. Lehman's ethical concerns were lighted up by the plight of the Indians in the West, and he was known as the best friend that they had, whereas, as John Marshall pointed out long ago, the worst enemies the Indians had were the people who lived near them, and the western Senators on the whole, with some noble exceptions, tended to be much less friendly to the Indians than Lehman.

But that was an action against interest, or at least with no reference to personal political gain. The thing to which the interest of the Senator *must* incline is to keep his fences mended in his own State, and to do that above all, because if he fails in this, he's not going to be any good to the Indians—unless, like Sam Houston, he simply wants to go and live amongst them—because he won't be living in Washington any more. Survival dominates, and in the case of a good man it ought to dominate, up to a real point of conscience, because he shouldn't be in politics if he doesn't think that on the whole it's better for the people for him to be in office than to be out of office.

ECKHARDT: Let's consider the antithesis of the Manny Celler type. Former Chairman Colmer of the Rules Committee was really not much concerned with any ideological issue, unless it was the parochial Mississippi attitude toward blacks. He was inclined to stop bills in the Rules Committee that might have a liberal tinge, as he saw it. He had high seniority and great power as Chairman of the Rules Committee. Unlike Manny Celler and Herbert Lehman, he did not act against interest, and his Mississippi constituency rewarded him by many successive reelections. He was never a man of other than mediocre ability, and in his last period of service, during which he was Rules Committee Chairman, he was uncertain in his performance of that role. But his fidelity to local concerns, never in the least diluted by a philosophic view of the broader national interest, made him politically invulnerable.

BLACK: Man, that's putting it straight!

Now, I think we probably ought to round out and complete this. A third power we have to look at is the veto power, actually contained in Article I. It has always seemed to me that it's rather a paradox, rather strange, that the Congress has not developed a convention that vetoes invariably be overridden. Let me explain what I mean by that, why I think it's a paradox. It would be to the long-run advantage of Congress as a whole, and therefore increase the power, on the whole, of pretty much every member of Congress, if presidential vetoes were overridden simply as a matter of course. That's what would happen if the Queen tried to disallow a bill in Parliament. I don't know exactly how they would react to it within their constitution; it would be indeed a great constitutional impasse, and I'm not sure how they would deal with it, but I do know that the attitude in the House of Commons would not depend in the least on whether one favored the bill or not. It wouldn't depend in the least on whether one were a Tory, a Liberal, or a Laborite. It would be a virtually unanimous attitude that this royal veto simply couldn't be permitted. Whatever needed to be done would be done to bring it about that the Queen assent to the bill.

Now in the early days of our own history there was considerable question as to the limitation of grounds on which a President might rightfully veto a bill—not as a matter of law, but as a matter of political morality. Many people thought, for example, that he could rightfully do so only as a means of protecting his own office—that this power was not given to him to use whenever he might disagree with the policy of the bill in general, but to use only when the Congressional measure affected the presidency itself. Other people said that the veto was given to him to use only when in his view a bill was unconstitutional, and not when he simply disagreed with the bill as a policy matter. That assumption, I think, is what lies behind Jackson's message on the veto of the United States Bank rechartering.[6]

ECKHARDT: That still influences Presidential veto messages. The President, instead of simply writing his argument for or against a bill on policy grounds, frequently writes it in extremely strong constitutional terms.

BLACK: That's right, but we now don't think he *has* to; we now assume that he may veto any bill he wants to, on any ground he finds persuasive.

Now it would be possible, entirely possible, without any violation of the Constitution, for there simply to be a custom that when the President vetoes a bill either every time he vetoes it, or whenever he vetoes it for any other reason than one of these narrow reasons I have mentioned—that the Houses proceed—perhaps with the people whose consciences really bothered them staying away—and if you could get a quorum, and two-thirds of that quorum voted to override the veto, then that's all you'd need. And that would greatly enhance the power of Congress, and reduce the veto power to zero. Again it seems to me that one has to look to the *forbearance* of Congress, to the decision of Congress that that is not the proper way to act, to explain why the presidential veto has played such a considerable part in history.

ECKHARDT: But the adherence of one party in Congress to the President, if the President be of their party, is much stronger than the adherence of that party to the institution of Congress or even to the party's leadership in Congress.

6. In his message accompanying a veto of the rechartering of the Bank of the United States, Jackson extensively argued the question whether he was *bound* by a prior decision of the Supreme Court upholding the *constitutional power* of Congress to create the Bank. This would now seem unnecessary; the President is considered to be free to veto any bill on *policy* grounds, even though the action taken in the bill is *constitutionally* permissible.

BLACK: We've touched the principal textual matter which upholds the presidency, and I think it's just astounding how sparse it is. Here is this very great office, this office which has been called the "leadership of the free world," this office whose primacy is totally assumed in this country, but its textual constitutional basis for power is incredibly slender. Now when we contrast it with Congress, with Article I, Section 8, and the other powers of Congress, I think what we find is that Congress really has (if it wants to exercise it, and if it's willing to push it past the veto) power over virtually everything. It has that through the commerce clause as at present expounded and understood by the judiciary. In the virtually uncontradicted view of judges and constitutional scholars, this clause now pretty well authorizes just about any action that Congress wants to take on any subject.

There's nobody who's really against these latitudes of construction, because the people who cry out against them when they are used for purposes of effecting the desegregation of restaurants in the South are not about to propose the repeal of the Lindbergh kidnapping law[7] or the stolen automobiles act,[8] which rest on just exactly the same conception of the commerce clause.

The very same is true of the taxing power. The power of taxation is pretty much the power over everything. The maxim that the power to tax is the power to destroy really understates the case. The power to tax, if used with skill and precision, is the power to influence men and events almost wholly. You can put a tax on oleomargarine, for example—and it's been done—which makes its production uneconomic and raises its price above that of butter, and you have in effect prohibited oleomargarine, because the manufacture of oleomargarine is not undertaken for entertainment or as a hobby, but for profit.

And we now have certain well-accepted ancillary features of the

7. This law makes it a *federal* crime to carry a kidnapped person *across a state line* and sets up a presumption that a kidnapped person held more than a few days has been taken across a state line. What is in *form* a "regulation of commerce among the several states" is in *fact* a federal kidnapping law.

8. More of the same, relating to stolen automobiles rather than to kidnapped persons.

taxing system. If you ask students in Yale College, for example, to read the Constitution and then to tell you how in the world it was that this federal government of ours got into the narcotics business, they just stare at you. They know the national government is running a farm for narcotics addicts down in Lexington, Kentucky; the subject of narcotics seems to them a federal subject foursquare. Well, the way that happened, as you know, is that they put a little old one-dollar tax on the distribution of narcotics, and then, just to help out with administering that tax, they put a regulatory scheme on top of it, and required bookkeeping, so you could answer the tax collector as to how much heroin, or whatever it was you were selling, had been sold. Now since those trades don't really thrive under that kind of atmosphere of full disclosure, this, in effect, put the federal government into the center of the narcotics picture. That's how we got there, and that's how we're there now. That's something to put up to a "strict constructionist" once in a while; just ask him whether he doesn't feel that his strict-construction attitudes require him to favor the repeal of all federal narcotics legislation.

ECKHARDT: And nothing could be more typical of the States' supposed field of authority, because it deals in criminal law.

BLACK: It deals with a criminal law problem that is very much localized, very much having to do with local conditions.

If you take a great economic unit like the United States, and give a body like Congress the power to regulate all travel and commerce within it, and the power to tax all events within it, differentially as it chooses, you've given that body power over everything within the country, and that is of course just what they have.

ECKHARDT: But we've been assuming here that both the presidency and Congress *want* power. This is not always so. Much of what Congress does and much of what the President does is to avoid power and to try to attach responsibility to somebody else. You see, the power to act is also the power to pass the buck.

BLACK: Pretending not to have power is a way of passing the buck; and Congress has abundantly passed the buck.

There's another aspect of this. The powerlessness of the government as a whole is something which at certain times is agreeable to some interests—it's what they want. And I think that it's not farfetched at all to say that the paralysis of government, and the paralysis of the executive branch, that we have lately seen, however disagreeable they may have been for other reasons to Nixon, had as their net result pretty much a triumph of the policies that were proposed by Nixon. This is exactly the sort of inactive, laissez-faire, do-nothing government that he (under various euphemistic terms, such as the unleashing of private enterprise and so on) advocated all along. It's a kind of a triumph of Nixonism through the downfall of Nixon.

The bare constitutional powerlessness of the President, as opposed to the powerfulness of Congress, has been radically changed, so that if you just look at the situation quickly, it looks like the opposite is true. This has happened not because of anything in the Constitution, but through the process of continual delegation of authority by Congress to the President, in hundreds and hundreds of statutes—a process that is still going on.

ECKHARDT: This is the very sad and paradoxical situation in which Congress finds itself: The greater power resides in Congress, but the greater exercise of it has come to be engaged in by the President. Our Constitution, in the British sense, is not only the written Constitution but the "done thing." If we remain bound by tradition and the machinery of our institutions as molded by customary usage, it appears to be virtually impossible to exercise this great and pervasive power that resides in Congress.

BLACK: But, as I remember hearing you say, the permanently written character of our Constitution gives, paradoxically, a great deal of freedom. For the general power of Congress, firmly fixed in the constitutional text, includes a power to go back and start over, the power to alter and rebuild. The text preserves this power to Congress, through all the vicissitudes of custom.

ECKHARDT: In the recent troubles one of the things which we heard recurrently suggested, on which we have touched briefly, is some sort of borrowing or adaptation on our part of the British system. That suggestion centers around the problem of the easy removability of the chief political leader, around the fact that by vote of "no confidence" in the House of Commons, a Prime Minister, and indeed his entire governmental entourage, can be thrown out of office, and this requires no judgment of anything resembling criminality; it totally skips the technicalities of our impeachment process. Within the past few years some people have tended to look on this system rather admiringly, and I think we ought to talk a bit about what it would entail to substitute this system for ours.

What has made this question of utilization of the British system or adaptation of parliamentary processes to the American system a current question? There are two bases for it. Probably the question of impeaching Nixon, and then the unusual situation of the Democratic party, which is ordinarily the party of innovation, controlling Congress, which is ordinarily the more deliberative body, with the more conservative Republican party in control of the executive department. Congress must legitimate the basis for national policy, or at least it must enact it. If it lacks, in a conservative presidency, the usual external ignition source for legislation (in contrast to the situation in Johnson's Great Society era) the two institutions don't work very well. This is particularly true when the President is almost completely inactivated by loss of prestige. So then there's a desire to devise some governmental machinery totally controlled by the legislative body. That's a very difficult thing to do, and I'm not sure it's possible.

BLACK: This certainly opens up the question of the difficulties of adapting a single feature of a foreign system to our own Constitution. What Congress would attain by a vote of "no confidence," under our system, altered only by the transplantation of the "vote-of-confidence" feature of the British system, is the elimination of the President from office, but what happens then, unless we effect a further change in our system, is simply that the Vice President assumes the office. Now there are several problems about that. The first would have to do with the very situation which you have just outlined, because the enormous likelihood is (whether he be elected on the same ticket with the President or whether he be appointed, as in the case of Mr. Ford, and rather perfunctorily confirmed by the Houses of Congress, on the ground that there was nothing deeply wrong with him) he's likely to be no more a sparkplug or a leader than the outgoing President was. This difficulty, therefore, without a further change in the system, would not be answered by the removal of the President. I think we face that even under the impeachment system as it stands. Insofar as the British system involves a possibility on the part of the House of Commons of insisting upon being presented at the time of removal with an alternative leader who is thought better of and who can remedy the defects, we can't do that without a still deeper cut into our constitutional system. The mere removal of the President doesn't really answer anything like the questions that would be answered in the British Parliament.

As a kind of a side issue, I find your previous remark extremely interesting, because I think it goes far to explain why it was that, at a time when Mr. Truman's popularity was very low, at a time when —in the small way in which these things existed then—there was thought to be a great deal of corruption in government, and at a time when Congress was passing bills over Truman's veto, bills of great importance, and when he aroused a great deal of indignation by his to me courageous and entirely proper action in bringing back General MacArthur from Korea, there was never through that whole period, as far as I recall, any serious talk whatever of impeachment, and this may have been because the presidency as the leadership branch, as the forward-moving branch, was no danger to the Congress as it was then constituted, because Congress was in a position to block Truman in every way. Under Nixon just the opposite was true—the opposite dynamics prevailed.

ECKHARDT: I think it goes strongly against the grain of the American system when Congress is in the hands of the more innovative, more liberal group, and the President is conservative. It occurred with Eisenhower, but then Eisenhower had tremendous prestige, and at that time there was little pressure for innovative changes.

BLACK: Major innovations were actually being made during the

Eisenhower period by the Supreme Court—the Warren Court—notably the *Brown* decision,[9] which was an innovation directed to the very greatest of American problems. The Supreme Court at that time seemed able to handle it on its own. The dynamics of the judiciary explains some of the contentment with the Eisenhower era.

Now let's swing back to the British system. I want to attack this proposal for the institution of the British system somewhat more radically. I think one has to appreciate what that system really is as a whole. If anybody thinks that the Prime Minister, at the head of a government which has been elected by any kind of a substantial majority, is really in a weaker position, a more vulnerable position, than the President of the United States, that's because he hasn't really been there and looked at the system as it actually works. The picture drawn is of a House of Commons which at any time, if it becomes collectively discontented with the Prime Minister, may simply overturn him. The conception that this is a very live possibility, which governs British political concerns from day to day and year to year, is totally the reverse of the truth. When a government is elected with a firm majority and with a party leader at its head surrounded by a small group of influential people, it would be much nearer to the truth to say that what has been elected is an oligarchic dictatorship, with a very strong leadership in that oligarchy on the part of one man, and that the power of the Prime Minister is enormously greater than that of the President, except for the possibility (which is very remote, one that happens perhaps twice in a lifetime of any human being) that the Prime Minister may be overthrown because of some scandal, or some exceedingly wrong and disastrous policy, or some policy judged to be exceedingly wrong, like that of Chamberlain at Munich. I don't think people understand in this country what happens in England, for example, with respect to legislation. When a Tory government is in power, and the announcement is made by that gov-

9. *Brown v. Board of Education of Topeka*, 347 U.S. 483 (1954). This was the leading case holding unconstitutional racial segregation in public schools; its principle was soon applied to every form of segregation commanded by law.

ernment that there is to be an industrial relations bill of a certain general character at that session of Parliament, then at that moment it is known with near certainty that there will be such a bill passed at that session of Parliament. The members of the Tory majority are obligated to go in and vote for it. As far as the main issue is concerned, the rest is shadowboxing. Now of course there is no person in the United States, nor any group of people in the United States, who have that kind of power. There is nobody who can announce that at this session of Congress a certain type of bill will be passed, reducing further debate to matters of detail and committee work.

ECKHARDT: An important bill may generate and incubate for decades. Take for instance the Federal Aid to Education Bill, which started way back in the Truman Administration. As I recall, it was blocked so many times by a ploy—Adam Clayton Powell insisting on certain civil rights amendments that were bound to make it fail, thus complementing the work against the bill by Senator Langer, who wanted it to fail. Until Senator Taft came to support the desirability of equalization of the ability to finance education as between poor and rich states and ultimately embraced federal aid, nothing moved. That idea did not pass for many terms, and then it began to come in gradually, although it's far from perfected today.

BLACK: Yes. Well, let's contrast that with two situations, both of great importance in the fairly recent past in the American government. The first, and I'll take them in reverse chronological order, was the Civil Rights Act of 1964. Now Lyndon Johnson was totally committed to this, at great political risk to himself. He put on all possible pressure and by the skin of his teeth got a cloture vote in the Senate, but there wasn't any question of frog-marching the Senators in there and subjecting them to a division and putting the party whips on. He had to use every sort of influence that he could, and the outcome was by no means certain until the very last vote was cast and the bill was finally passed. Certainly, neither Johnson nor any party leader was at any time in a position to announce simply that such a bill would be passed, and then to send out orders to the party whips to make it a party matter.

Let's take another case, and I think this is the most striking case for those who think that the President is a powerful official compared with the Prime Minister of England: Mr. Roosevelt's 1937 Court-packing bill. It's very difficult for us to remember now the prestige and power that Mr. Roosevelt enjoyed in 1936 and '37, when this bill came up. He decided that the Supreme Court was standing in his way, and he proposed a piece of legislation to curb the Court. He put on every bit of pressure that he possibly could and in the end (to make short a very often told long story) this bill failed. The leaders went over there and told him, "Well, Mr. President, do you want it with the bark on or with the bark off?" And he said, "With the bark off," and they told him, "You're not going to have this bill." This was a message to a political leader, occupying the presidency of the United States, who was as powerful as it's possible to get within our constitutional system—you just can't have it; no, we won't pass that bill. That's pretty close to unthinkable in England.

ECKHARDT: I'm not sure that that is a good example, because it goes to a question that involves a *constitutional feeling*. And I'm using "constitutional feeling" in a sort of a British sense. There are felt restraints in the British Parliament with respect to questions like that and I think something of the same thing was happening in the United States Congress. For another instance, the very sweeping issue of the creation of TVA[10] in the Roosevelt Administration and the REA[11] Co-ops looked at that time and were criticized at that time as being socialistic engagement by government in private business.

BLACK: The reason for the independence of members of Congress and Senators is something that is absolutely basic within our Constitution, and something in which it disresembles the British constitution altogether—the firm territorial base which each Congressman has. Now to go to the British model, as you know, there is a very considerable power, it's not true as to every constituency, every time, but there is a very considerable power in the party leadership heading up in the Prime Minister, when he's in office, to influence the choice

10. Tennessee Valley Authority.
11. Rural Electrification Administration.

of constituencies in which candidates may run, and often the most influential and stable membership in Parliament will be on the part of somebody who is elected from a constituency which he visits from time to time simply as a matter of courtesy. This is what's called a "safe seat." A conservative who is high in the party council would be likely to be assigned such a seat rather than to a swing constituency. That limited but important power of designating the candidacy of members is an important disciplinary weapon in the British system. It doesn't exist at all in the United States. It doesn't exist for multiple reasons. First, as to the Senate, the State is the constitutionally designated unit, and while a Senator may, of course, be interested in his institutional position in the Senate, he lives or dies on the basis of his ability to be elected in his State. If there's a conflict between the party leadership on the one hand, and the Senator's estimate of what it takes to get reelected on the other, his constant interest has to be in his State. If it is not, and in some crucial cases maybe it hasn't been, then of course sooner or later that State is going to find a Senator who matches up with it.

ECKHARDT: The same thing is true of membership in the House. The practice of districting for House elections is of course not of constitutional origin, but it is consistently followed, and it is anticipatable that it will be followed for any measurable, foreseeable future. What this means is that the party leadership has only collateral and relatively unimportant things that it can do or not do with respect to a member, while the major political interest of that member has got to be, if he's going to stay in Congress, his own district at home.

I think a second reason is our *bicamerality*. If you could hold one of these wild horses straight, you sure can't hold two of them at the same time, going in the same direction.

BLACK: While we're on the British system, let's pin down another way in which it totally disresembles ours. With us, it is actually unconstitutional for a Congressman or Senator to hold any other federal office. In Britain, access to policy-forming posts in government is *wholly* through Parliament and through one's party leadership; only Members of Parliament are ministers, and a persistently disloyal

Member is extremely likely to be a permanent backbencher. This gives party leadership a great power.

ECKHARDT: The accommodation that is now being sought in Congress is not a movement toward the British Parliament, but a movement toward the structure of the United States Congress prior to the advent of Sam Rayburn. And that is the revitalization of the majority party caucus.[12] If we should strengthen the majority party caucus sufficiently in the House, it would move us *somewhat* closer to the British system, because the caucus, being related to the party, and being related to the party's ideological position, and having certain authority over the Committee's majority and their Chairmen, could institute a certain degree of uniformity of direction and an organization of national effort that would approach the British system. Congress would never really come near to a parliamentary system—there would be no way for the caucus to actually impose its will on its members—but it would move toward a tighter organization to effectuate a majority party program.

BLACK: No, there's no way. Let's take the case in the Senate, or take several cases. Of course there have been many, but one conspicuous case was former Senator Frank Lausche of Ohio. He called himself a Democrat and voted with Democrats to organize the Senate, but at just about that point the connection stopped. He was a very conservative man, usually voting with the Republicans, and he found that this matched up with the people of Ohio. His whole style and set of views matched up with their wishes, and he was repeatedly reelected.

There wasn't anything wrong with this, there wasn't even any violation of conscience or any question of expediency involved. I think that's something many people don't understand about politics —constituencies and representatives tend to match up ideologically. It's not so much that a man like Lausche would go in and vote against his conscience in order to get reelected. There's no reason to think he ever did that. They had found a man, and he had found a constitu-

12. See *infra*, p. 153.

ency, which matched up and suited each other, ideologically and as a matter of conscience, but in any case there was no power whatever the Democratic leadership could exert over Frank Lausche with respect to voting on any issue. Now the Democratic caucus used to be powerful to be sure, and I think we need more power in the caucus, but it never was able to command the votes of any southern Congressman on any racial issue dear to the hearts of northern Democrats. It just wouldn't have made any difference to them which way the vote went in the caucus in those times, they would have marched on in and voted in obedience to their own ideas in the main and the wishes of their constituency against the Fair Employment Practices Bill or anything else, it wouldn't have mattered how many Democrats had voted for it in the caucus.

ECKHARDT: Another example in the House, as I mentioned before, would be Chairman Colmer of the Rules Committee, from Mississippi. Now the Rules Committee, of all the Committees in the House, is supposed to be a Speaker's Committee, because it's the dispatching Committee for business going to the Floor, and it's the Committee that must determine priorities among various pieces of legislation. Colmer was, of course, entirely in opposition to the majority of the Democrats in the House at the time he was Chairman of that Committee. I remember a very interesting incident. I'm sure by mistake I got invited to a meeting of the Dixie group. Some secretary thought, well, he's a Texan, he's bound to be with our group, and I got an invitation.

BLACK: Yes, well I've been so classified many times as a result of my accent.

ECKHARDT: So, when I walked into this meeting, I discovered that the Dixies were plotting to derail the Speaker's program, which was coming up in a couple of hours. And the coup was being planned right there in the Chairman of the Rules Committee's office. The Rules Committee is of course considered the Speaker's own Committee.

BLACK: On these leadership matters, we have come up with a different pattern with each President. What we have now is kind of a mix and maybe that mix could be changed somewhat by such devices as that of increasing the power of the caucus.

But leadership in our government is a scarce resource. It's not something we can afford to gamble with. Now I have been desperately afraid, in the recent crisis, that we were going to do the most foolish thing possible, and that is (to put it plainly) to remake the written law of the presidency and remake the unwritten law of the presidency, remake the practices that go with the presidency, remake these in such a way as to make the whole set of laws and practices suitable for a President such as Richard M. Nixon. Now that's a foolish thing to do. Because if we can't do any better than elect one President after another like Richard M. Nixon, then we should go out of business. We ought to look on his term in office as the rarest of accidents, rather than as the occasion for radical revamping of the whole set of laws and practices regarding the Presidency.

ECKHARDT: Presidential leadership is really quite important in our system as it works. Let me give you an example. I was talking to Chairman Aspinall of the Interior Committee, one of the oldest and most experienced Chairmen. His attitudes were pretty typical of an old Chairman who had served mostly under Democratic Presidents. I was urging him to move on my Open Beaches Bill. Instead of explaining to me why, on policy grounds, he shouldn't or wouldn't, he went into a long statement of what was wrong with the whole shebang, the whole system. Nixon was in power at the time. Aspinall said, "Well, the President hasn't given us anything to do. The President hasn't given us the bills to act on. He hasn't set up the structure of legislation in the area of land use. What can we do?" He was really accepting the presidency as part of the parliamentary system of the United States, and he was so used to acting in response to a program generated in the office of the President that he thought the thing before him was just completely foreign to any operation that he'd ever seen.

BLACK: That accords with the expectation in the past of the American people. But if one reads the Constitution, one would see that it is in a narrow and abstract sense absurd for a President actually to campaign on any platform, because the President has no power in the Constitution to pass anything. Johnson campaigned in 1964 on a platform of increasing the measure of racial, and what I might call medical, justice, but it was not really within his power as President, aside from his temporary influence, to do anything about these things.

ECKHARDT: Let me point out the other side of the coin. If the President is completely powerless constitutionally, the Congress may be completely powerless practically, because normally the President acts as the innovating force.

BLACK: That's right at the heart of the American government. Over and over again one comes back to that point—the text of the Constitution places all the power in Congress, but the structure of the presidency is such, and the structure of Congress is such, that the power tends to flow from Congress to the presidency, and that leadership tends to be looked for in the President.

ECKHARDT: This is the real balance of power.

BLACK: That's the real balance of power. We can't change that by one little measure such as the institution of a vote of confidence. What we would do by such a measure, in my opinion, is first of all something powerfully symbolic. I think the President's prestige, and hence his capacity to exercise his leadership where he has no real clout, would be vitally diminished by putting in the Constitution a power on the part of Congress to get rid of him altogether without his having done anything wrong, simply because they didn't have confidence in him anymore. An office that's defined in that manner in the Constitution cannot be looked to for leadership, because he would be trying to lead people who can get rid of him for general reasons, just on the basis of not liking him or thinking on the whole that he's not a good President.

ECKHARDT: Let me go back a minute here to this question of the balance that exists because of the power of Congress constitutionally and the power of the President practically. I think in examining this we find that it really works well because of that balance when the presidency and the Congress are in the hands of the same party. But in order to maintain that real balance you must envisage the worst of all possible situations, when government is virtually paralyzed; that is the situation when the President and Congress are in different parties. I don't take this as a fatal flaw, but it is a flaw which can cause a long period, or at least a substantial period, of near-stagnation in government. Sometimes, it doesn't do so. The situation existed in Taft's last term, and mild reforms were put into effect with the Democratic Congress and a Republican President. But then of course there was a great surge of sweeping innovative legislation when Wilson came in, beginning his term, very much like the New Deal era. It was the era of the Clayton Act[13] and the institution of the Federal Trade Commission and many other things like that.

BLACK: One of the statesmanlike things about Lyndon Johnson was the way he operated as Senate Majority Leader under Eisenhower. What little was possible in that era, at least housekeeping and all that in this relatively calm era, was carried on to some extent with more neatness because Johnson didn't take the position of exploiting this party opposition.

ECKHARDT: Eisenhower deserved some credit for that too, not only as a man, but as a sort of an institution. He was a kind of a nonpartisan President—the closest thing to a coalition government we've ever had.

BLACK: I think that the conclusion we come to is that our political problems have to be analyzed in this country in our own terms and on the basis of our own federal situation, on the basis of our traditional politics and political ideas, and that looking with longing on something across the ocean is not really going to get us anywhere. We're going to have to deal with this problem of the presidency and the Congress, and of leadership in counterpoint with constitutional power, in terms of our own Constitution. It's not going to do very much good, and may do very much harm, to subject the President to additional vulnerabilities superimposed on those which already exist. The President is vulnerable to all kinds of actions short of impeachment and removal. The Congress has innumerable powers over the execu-

13. A 1914 Act strengthening the antitrust laws.

tive branch which could be exercised in their full force if two-thirds majorities can be mustered, but which sometimes don't even need that because they're negative powers like the withholding of appropriations.

ECKHARDT: Well, suppose though we accept the proposition from the discussion we've had, that we should not attempt to devise a system moving toward a parliamentary structure merely because our situation at the present time, which is a rather unusual one, creates some very difficult problems of forward movement in government.

THE TRADITIONAL STRENGTHS OF THE PRESIDENT 3

BLACK: The generalities we've talked about so far lead us quickly into certain specificities, and at least one of the most important general areas of policy which we must enter is that of foreign policy. The written constitutional material on the commitment of foreign policy to the President is rather sparse. Yet I suppose that most people on the street, if now asked where the Constitution places this foreign-policy responsibility, would say, definitely and without hesitation, that it places it in the hands of the President.

ECKHARDT: In the longer history of the United States, foreign policy has probably been as much directed by Congress as by the President. But in recent years it seems to me that many people have come to conclude that the salient decisions respecting foreign policy have to do with the rise of the atomic age and the question of nuclear confrontation. And for that reason it has been assumed that decisions have to be made so quickly that, as a practical matter, Congress simply can't make them. But the interesting thing is that this supposed need for instant decision has not really existed. As to virtually every choice we've had to make, a deliberate decision would have been possible, and probably would have been preferable to a decision made instantly without political input.

BLACK: I think the atomic thing comes at the end of a series, but I think that you go a little far in seeing this centralization of foreign policy in the President as a function of the atomic age. Perhaps it's this archetypal situation—the nuclear threat—that's in people's minds, and it makes them more likely to acquiesce in this centralization in the presidency of foreign-relations power right now. But remember some chronology. The primary power of the President over foreign policy started its modern development, I should think, early in the present century, before the atomic age, along with so many other presidential powers. It's always had the basis of the President's taking the initiative in the formation of treaties; it's always had the basis of his being Commander-in-Chief of the Armed Forces, capable of reacting; and it's always had a basis in his general position as executive head of a government which, it was assumed rather than put in words by the Constitution, would contain a Department of State conducting the day-to-day diplomatic business of the United States. But more high-flown judicial passages on the President's foreign-relations power really start with the *Curtiss-Wright* case in 1936[1] (a case which, by the way, did not actually involve *his* independent power, but only the power of *Congress* to delegate power to him in this field). In the *Belmont*[2] and *Pink*[3] cases (also from Franklin Roosevelt's day) dealing with executive agreements, the rhetorical characterization of the President's foreign-relations power reached a kind of judicial apogee.

Most of these foreign-policy decisions, which are said to have to be taken so quickly, might have been taken more deliberately. There was no emergency about recognizing Russia in 1933. I make bold to say that I can't see how it would have hurt us to have a debate in Congress, even a public debate, over whether to drop the first atom bomb on Japan. I don't know just what harm that would have done. We were roaming at will over the Japanese skies at the time. We could have dropped it whenever we got ready, there was no emergency on that, and no serious defense was possible. I may well be wrong on this very extreme case, but the point really is that little consideration is given to the necessity for quick action; the necessity for expediency or secrecy is usually just asserted, or assumed without discussion.

ECKHARDT: I'd have to amend my first statement, if it is construed to indicate that we only took this viewpoint after the development of the atom bomb. This is the usual ground now given for that position,

1. *U.S. v. Curtiss-Wright*, 299 U.S. 304 (1936).
2. *U.S. v. Belmont*, 301 U.S. 324 (1937).
3. *U.S. v. Pink*, 315 U.S. 203 (1942).

but even as early as the pre–World War I revolution in Mexico,
President Wilson was finding excuses for direct intervention in a very
high-handed way in Mexico, even to the extent of seizing a Customs
House in Vera Cruz, though he at least had sufficient respect for
Congress to go and ask for congressional authorization of his act. And
Congress almost immediately gave him that, because ordinarily Congress's response in the area of foreign policy—particularly if it has to
do with hostilities—is freely, even automatically given. The issue is
felt as one of being patriotic or not patriotic.

BLACK: Foreign policy can't be separated from military policy. Von
Klausewitz said war is a carrying on of diplomacy by other means, an
aphorism that certainly encapsulates a lot of truth. But there is more
to foreign policy than military policy, and I think that in some areas
in which military matters are not concerned, at least not directly
concerned, or even concerned with any visibility in an indirect way,
the power of the President has nevertheless hypertrophied to an enormous degree. Take the two cases I mentioned a while ago, the *Belmont*
and *Pink* cases. In these, by virtue of the President's supposed power
to recognize Russia in 1933 (a power, by the way, which is nowhere
mentioned in the Constitution, which is present if at all only by inference from his power to appoint or receive Ambassadors), the Supreme
Court seemed to be holding that the President had a very broad
power to enter into executive agreements without the concurrence of
Congress—agreements altering property rights, and in other ways
changing the law—as *incidental* to recognition. A subsequent case[4] has
cut back on that a little bit (though not in the Supreme Court) to the
extent of holding that an explicit congressional statute will prevail
over a subsequent executive agreement, let's say with respect to the
price of potatoes. But there still remains a current idea (without perhaps sharp legal shape) that the President has some power to *commit*
the United States by agreement without any concurrence by Congress.

ECKHARDT: Well, he has the power to commit the country tentatively, but the Congress always has the power to withdraw that tenta-

4. *U.S. v. Guy W. Capps, Inc.*, 204 F. 2d 655 (C.A. 4, 1953).

tive commitment. Unless of course a treaty binds the United States which has been agreed to by the Senate with a two-thirds vote.

BLACK: Now the difficulty of a commitment appears at many points. For example, our present difficulties with regard to the Middle East very largely revolve around the difficulty of our making a binding commitment, whatever its tenor may be, whatever degree of force or contribution it may involve our committing ourselves to. We have one clearly correct way of doing that, committing ourselves as well as any nation can do, and that is by *treaty*, in the normal manner, negotiated by the President and ratified by the Senate. Why do you suppose we seem to be shying off of that mode and using every other possible means, however uncertain, however inapt to bind the country, these other modes may be?

ECKHARDT: It's because we apprehend that a democratic process which gives prior information to another nation puts us at a disadvantage. We attempt to put ourselves in a position to deal in the same way that, for instance, a totalitarian nation would deal, the position to make immediate decisions and engage in a kind of flexible bargaining. This is pretty much reflected in our attitude about Kissinger's authority to deal for the United States as a sort of free roving agent for United States policy, without much responsibility to remain within traditional governmental restraints.

BLACK: When you refer to Mr. Kissinger's role you're undoubtedly illuminating at once another category of foreign policy—it's a very old one, a most venerable category. A country, in this case the United States, in effect offers its good offices for the purpose of stimulating or mediating negotiations between other people. Now no commitment of the United States is necessarily involved, up to that point. We can offer our services, just as Catherine the Great offered her services for the settlement of the American Revolution, and there's no necessarily inherent commitment of the United States to guarantee the result of the settlement. I suppose that the answer to the question of the constitutional rightness of presidential actions, through cabinet officers, in that manner, is that organizationally and structurally he's the one who *can* do it.

I don't think there's much of a constitutional problem there. But to go on, that kind of activity, intervention by facilitating negotiation, leads to the point where *commitment* is asked for. Obviously, in the end, whatever settlement is reached in the Middle East, it's very likely to be expected by both sides that the United States, probably in conjunction with Russia, will enter into some kind of a commitment to maintain the frontiers that are agreed upon, and to support the other arrangements. Now our standard way of doing that is by treaty; that is the way that's explicitly sanctioned by the Constitution. The real danger of proceeding in any other way is that a subsequent Administration—or a subsequent Congress—may, perhaps legitimately, not feel itself to be bound, as it would feel itself bound by a treaty.

ECKHARDT: There is of course a severe limitation of commitment, when the commitment is tantamount to making war, or committing the United States to a course which inevitably would involve hostilities. Now there the President, under the Constitution, is not authorized to make even a tentative commitment.

BLACK: I think you'll find that international lawyers would not be unanimous in agreeing with you there. I do agree with you. I think that our Constitution really provides one mode by which the United States can make that kind of a supremely serious commitment, and one mode only, and that is by treaty, and that other forms of agreement are simply not binding, not constitutional, for such a solemn purpose as that.

There is a rather subtle point—half-political—which must be made here. Even if the better *arguments* favored the conclusion that the President, by executive agreement and without congressional concurrence, could commit us to limited or unlimited war, there is certainly *room for argument*. If such a commitment is to be made, it should be made by means that leave *no* room for argument as to its binding force, or as little room for argument as possible. I think only a treaty can do that.

ECKHARDT: Let me ask you this: Do you think that we can do that even by treaty? After all, a treaty is a commitment made by the President with two-thirds approval of the Senate, and the Constitution limits the war-making power to the decision of Congress itself, including the House.

BLACK: I think there we run into the question that applies to all commitments. Of course Congress can break a treaty. We have broken treaties before. We broke the Chinese Immigration treaty in the '80s,[5] and the Supreme Court held that Congress could validly break a treaty *as far as our own law was concerned,* and leave the country open only to the charge of being a treaty-breaker, and to whatever diplomatic reclamation might take place at the hands of the offended nation. What you're saying comes to this, that there is no way in which we can bind ourselves to do anything in such form that we actually will be physically forced to do that thing when the time comes.

ECKHARDT: Of course there's no question but that Congress can, for instance, delegate authority to the President to do things which may inevitably and perhaps rather gradually result in a war situation. The Tonkin Gulf resolution was not a direct declaration of war, but it granted authority to the President to make certain decisions without congressional restraint. It in effect delegated war-making powers to the President. I don't think there's any question but that Congress can do that. It did very much the same thing in Franklin Roosevelt's time, when it authorized the President to engage in activities in the Atlantic that would check the submarine warfare of the Germans, as a result of a really rather weakly supported contention that we had been fired upon by a German submarine. Actually, as I recall, a U.S. destroyer sighted a German submarine, being depth bombed by a British aircraft. The destroyer was giving information concerning the submarine's position to the aircraft by radio. Finally the submarine, in desperation, loosed a torpedo at the destroyer. And then Congress granted certain authority that permitted the President to engage in activities leading toward direct hostilities with the Germans in the Atlantic—of course well before Pearl Harbor.

BLACK: Sure, but this again is not so much a matter of commit-

5. Chinese Exclusion Case, 130 U.S. 581 (1889). A Chinese was excluded under an Act of Congress passed subsequent to (and in clear violation of) a treaty with China.

ment, because I don't think anybody would have contended at the time that any commitment had been made that we could not get out of—in other words, no one would have said that Congress could not at any time it wanted, by a normal passage of an act, either by two-thirds majority over veto or with the presidential signature, have withdrawn this delegation, and made it unlawful to arm the American merchant marine, or even for the destroyers to escort them in convoy, although the latter point is somewhat more doubtful. But it's doubtful only because one wonders whether it needed to be delegated in the first place—whether, in other words, it was not already comprised within the President's authority as Commander-in-Chief to order the Navy to escort our own merchant ships.

We've talked about the problem of commitment, and I think that in all probability the only plenary moral commitment which the United States can make, the only commitment which would be binding upon it, the only commitment which a subsequent Congress would without question be morally bound to follow, would be one made by treaty—at least when it comes to making war, or any other activity of that magnitude and high seriousness. But another thing we have is the problem, which is exceedingly important, of *economic* foreign policy. The formation of trade relations is the second branch of foreign policy, a branch which has always been extremely significant.

ECKHARDT: In this area, just as in every other area of policy-making, Congress has the ultimate decision. The difference from the war-making power is that the Constitution speaks directly to the latter power, and says in effect that not even a tentative commitment that actually results in immediate hostilities is within the President's power. Within every other area it seems to me the President may move in an executive way subject to the reversal of Congress, but in the area of making war, the President has absolutely no authority to engage in it without prior congressional sanction.

BLACK: Before we take up war, let's look at these other questions of foreign policy. There is a considerable conflict between the executive and some components—strong components—of the legislative branch over the appropriate trade policy with respect to Russia—specifically with respect to the formation of the so-called most-favored-nation position of trade with Russia. You can clear away some dead wood by noting that this phrase has a kind of sound that makes it misleading. It does not mean that Russia will be *the* "most favored nation." It means that Russia won't be discriminated against, in comparison with other nations with whom our relations are normal. And that's all that it means. There are a whole lot of countries that are in the most-favored-nation position, not just one.

ECKHARDT: The most-favored nation is the average nation. Britain, France, Norway, Belgium, and of course a very large number of others are in the most-favored-nation position. It is the normal position. The only proposal as to Russia is to put Russia in that *same* position, that is, to treat Russia on a footing of equality with our *normal* treatment of trade partners.

BLACK: I think this phrase, "most-favored nation," has a kind of a superlative quality about it which has given a lot of ammunition to the opponents of this policy. I am a strong proponent of this policy. I think that the flag of pacification, and even of softening of Russian policy with respect to some critical matters, may very well follow trade, rather than trade's following the flag. But what we're talking about now is *where the authority resides* to form such a policy, and I suppose the answer that you are giving, and that I would have to give, is that it resides ultimately in Congress—or at least that Congress has a veto power in this respect, but that it's very difficult for Congress so to organize itself as to be able, through the decades, to form one policy after another of this kind, so that the policies form a consistent whole and constitute a kind of general foreign policy of the United States.

ECKHARDT: When the question of tariffs, for example, arises, every member of the Congress is thinking in terms of certain industries within his area. A Congressman from the southeast is concerned about textiles; he doesn't want textiles to come in. Another Congressman in an area where hardware is manufactured doesn't want the Japanese to send into the United States hammers and saws that may sell for four or five dollars, to compete with hammers and saws made

in his area that sell for twelve dollars. So every Congressman has
a constituency that will oppose certain areas of free trade, and in the
aggregate, on the basis of "you scratch my back and I'll scratch
yours," Congress is essentially restrictive in trade, whereas the presidency tends to be a free . . .

BLACK: Now I wonder why that is. I haven't any doubt that that's
the political truth, and yet in view of the benefits which economic
theory seems to propose from trade, it's rather strange that there
wouldn't be an even stronger set of local interests around the country
in favor of the expansion.

ECKHARDT: That's true in certain areas. For instance, when we
were dealing with the Commerce Committee's energy bill, Congressman Rogers and Congressman Heinz supported an amendment to
that bill prohibiting petrochemicals from being sold abroad, on the
grounds that those petrochemicals should be first available to proces-
sors in the United States. I thought this would be to do something
entirely opposed to the best aspects of a market economy. We ought
to manufacture that which is best manufactured in the United States,
and will sell at a good price overseas. But their concerns apparently
were for some manufacturers in their areas who felt they'd been
shorted on certain petrochemicals that they needed. Ultimately, the
amendment was voted down. And it was voted down, I suppose, because a great number of manufacturers of petrochemicals in the
United States were very concerned that it not be passed. The amendment would have been very much in opposition to the commercial
advantage of a larger segment of American industry. In voting it
down Congress responded intelligently in the trade area.

BLACK: But that, I take it, is something of a rarity. Take your
hammer case. The man who might buy a cheaper hammer from
Japan is not concretely and immediately aware of that, and has a
much smaller individual interest, perhaps not rising to the threshold
of his becoming politically active, as compared with a man who is
manufacturing hammers on a large scale and has a trade association
that's keeping him informed as to what's going on in Congress, and
who will in fact lose a great deal if the cheap hammers come in from

Japan. The benefits of an expansion of international trade are in the future, they are to some extent conjectural as to the identity of the beneficiaries and so on, whereas the benefits of the status quo are always visible. There they are; they've got it; they've got the income from the hammers right now.

But what I don't see, and I think I'm trying to query fundamental things that are always assumed, is why this pressure, the pressure from hammer makers, bears more heavily on Congress than on the presidency. Take a thing like the authority of the President to negotiate and put into effect tariff reductions. This undoubtedly was granted by Congress not only for negotiating convenience, but also in part because it was well known that many tariff reductions simply could not be passed one-by-one through Congress—that although the President might negotiate them, if all he did when he finished negotiating them was to present the Congress a new tariff schedule, it would be defeated beyond any doubt, because there would be so many interests that would come in, so many trade associations that would come in and protest. So Congress gave the authority, delegated the authority, not only to *negotiate* but also to *act.*

ECKHARDT: Exactly. This is a very interesting point. There are areas in which Congress understands its own weakness, and no member of Congress really wants to give each of its members authority to undermine trade policy. For instance the Ways and Means Committee, under Wilbur Mills, has been rather favorable to presidential authority in the reduction of tariffs. Now individual members, if permitted to vote, would undermine the whole structure, and this is one reason why Ways and Means has established a peculiar position for itself on trade bills. It actually does this also on tax bills. It ordinarily gets a rule from the Rules Committee that doesn't provide for any amendment, because we have a kind of an institutional wisdom that the members of our institution will whittle away at any given bill to satisfy parochial interests to the point where the total interest is sacrificed.

BLACK: We have got our hands here on something of very high interest. We have an instance in which, as you read the position—and

I see no reason to disagree—Congress has abstained from the full and concrete exercise of its own undoubted power over the taxation of foreign trade, and has done so not merely because of the convenience in negotiation when the matter is in the hands of the President (because negotiation might take place and still be subject to Congressional ratification) and certainly not through indolence, but more through an appreciation by itself of the political disabilities under which it stands.

What I can't see right away is why it is assumed to be true, and seems actually to be true in practice, that the President—who after all is subject to election by the same people who elect Congressmen—would not have to respond to the same kind of localistic and particularistic pressures which move and must move the Congressmen—in the President's case multiplied by 435 (the number of districts in the House) or 100 (the number of Senators). Why isn't the President similarly bound hand and foot by pressure, as it were, from the hammer manufacturers? Why is it that the President is not equally obstructed by such sentiment?

ECKHARDT: I think he is equally acted upon, but he is acted upon by so many divergent and interrelated interests that he must necessarily reconcile these interests in favor of a common interest. One example occurred on our Committee on Interstate and Foreign Commerce the other day, relating to the Federal Energy Administration. There was a provision, in a pending bill as originally written, prohibiting, except with administrative authority, the shipment abroad of oil-drilling equipment. In this instance our Committee itself recognized the overriding public interest, but here is an example of the difficulty of considering that overriding interest. If one were simply to respond to certain oil drillers in the United States who feel that they don't have enough drilling bits to explore in the United States, one might well block out shipment of this equipment abroad. But when the matter is considered with regard to the general public interest, it appears that the shipping of such drilling equipment abroad may bring in more fuel resources, that can be used in the United States at a cheaper rate, if enough oil is developed in other countries as the result of drilling with that equipment. Furthermore, this has to be considered: Don't we gain more in terms of foreign trade if we manufacture and sell the kind of goods that we can manufacture best? On the other hand, if the Japanese can make hammers or saws more cheaply, why not buy hammers and saws from the Japanese?

BLACK: You are stating there the classic philosophy on the merits of foreign trade. I must remark that this philosophy has received a jolt lately—it is certainly a philosophy as to which caution is indicated by the Arab oil embargo, because we did just exactly what you say. We left the production of oil to those countries where it could be produced cheapest, on the theory that that was economically wise, without realizing that in doing so we were placing ourselves largely at their mercy.

But I don't think it is so much a question between us as to what the policy ought to be; it's more a question of who forms it, and why it is that Congress has so largely delegated to the President this power to form the economic policy of the United States with respect to foreign trade. It seems there is continual pressure to lodge in the executive the power of forming that policy—rather than in Congress, where it would appear that the Constitution very firmly puts it. There are no *vested* interests in a *future* development of trade, which might be produced by, let's say, a lowering of tariffs. On the other hand, the people who will be hurt by such lowering of the tariff are in business now. They know who they are. Their interest is not diffuse, and I repeat my puzzlement as to why their collective dissatisfactions are not communicated with effect just as much to the President as to the Congress. This is something I know nothing about. To what extent is the foreign economic policy which the President forms after delegation, such as that in the Reciprocal Trade Agreements Act, a function of a kind of overall Olympian public interest, and to what extent is it in turn a function simply of particular pressures playing on the negotiators and on the presidency?

ECKHARDT: This is affected at least in part by the fact that the President responds to a national constituency. If it is conceived that to sell wheat to Russia may ultimately result in a certain desirable interdependence between Russia and the United States that a dependence by each on products produced by the other will reduce the dangers of military confrontation—the trade between the two countries is conceived not totally in terms of a narrow interest, but of a much broader one.

BLACK: It seems to me that, in connection with this topic of foreign policy, you are saying something very serious about Congress and the presidency: You are saying, it seems to me, that the President can and will respond to the long-range interests of the country better than Congress will. That is to me a sad conclusion, if it is true. It would constitute something very near a totally satisfying rationale for a continued growth in the power of the President, and would in fact equate that growth, by a very easy equation, with the more efficient serving of the overall interests of the nation in the long run.

ECKHARDT: I am not saying that Congress shouldn't make the ultimate total decision, but it must make the decision *even with respect to its own procedural defects,* and must hold a rein on its own procedural defects.

Now I am not saying, though, that the delegation of authority should be final. The first wheat deal with Russia is a good example. Ultimately I think that the President reflected too much the interests of the large grain dealers who were making a considerable profit from the sale to the Soviet Union. In the long run the President's activity with respect to the wheat deal had some very good results in international relations, but it also tended, as we now see it, to favor certain interests. These defects are now being corrected and should be corrected. Congress, in granting authority, also must recognize that the same pressures exist, perhaps in a greater magnitude, on the President, because the presidency may be acted upon by extremely large special interests.

The same would be true with respect to oil. The President, in setting up the Federal Energy Office, created an agency that I think came unduly under the influence of the major oil companies, and that then set prices for oil that constituted not a control but the granting of an imprimatur of governmental authority to price increases.

BLACK: You are saying now, as I understand it, that a considerable measure of delegation of power from Congress to the presidency is inevitable and even beneficial. For example, the Reciprocal Trade Agreements Act, with its authority to lower tariffs within certain limits, with power to act vested in the President, produced results which probably would be *generally* approved by Congress, but which the Congress—in its organic capacity and by virtue of the mode of its own constitution and of its relations with its own constituencies— would probably not have been able to do by itself. In that sense you would see delegation as both inevitable and beneficial, but you would suggest that one of the ways in which we can begin to bring this tiger under control is by some more vigilant insistence on *accountability*.

How would we do that structurally without putting the whole thing at large in Congress again?

ECKHARDT: Congress's best role is standard-maker, rather than delineator of specific answers with respect to the rate of tariff on a particular product. In recent years Congress has tended to delegate too much authority in standard-making, but I don't think that means that the presidency should be weak or that Congress should fail to utilize the facilities of the presidency to bring together a considerable amount of specific expertise in an area. Congress should refrain from exercising detailed control where interests vie with each other, but it should exercise more authority with respect to some kind of objective standard applicable to the problem. That's the area in which Congress acts best.

Congress as a representative of the people (and of course it reflects people's interests) has really not been interested in the details of international affairs and it is not very competent to deal with them, because its interest is too weak to make it knowledgeable as to these matters of detail. It has tended to avoid detail, but to be inordinately concerned about major effects of foreign relations. For instance, the question of going to war, the question of creating a world in which the United States has certain economic influence over other nations in a broad sense, are of great interest to the people and to Congress, but the details by which this is accomplished constitute a matter in which

Congress just doesn't want to be involved. The people at home don't understand it and don't respond to these issues.

Presently, for instance, there is a strong anti–foreign-aid attitude on the part of the people at large and in Congress, which exists contemporaneously with the conflicting concept of a one-world situation, that we are part of that world and that we ought to influence it. We in Congress don't want to take these matters up in detail, and tend to be paralyzed by these contradictions, so Congress has in effect given the President, over a long period of time, almost a free hand in foreign relations.

BLACK: Eckhardt, you seem to me to be, in one case after another, preaching counsels of despair and prophecies of doom. What you are saying in one context after another is that Congress is just disabled from doing anything very important. This matter of a Middle Eastern treaty, for example, is not a matter of detail but an absolute cornerstone of United States foreign policy. We are committed to that region heavily in a physical way, we are pouring aid to one side, we have gone to Egypt and tried to make a friend out of somebody on the other side. The end result of all this activity—and this surely isn't a matter of detail—ought to be a commitment of some kind. I don't suppose we ought to commit ourselves to go to nuclear war on this account. I think people will have to be satisfied with less than that. But we might very well be called on to commit ourselves to military supply, to contribution of an economic character to the region as a whole, perhaps by implementing the idea, which I have heard you express, of a great project that could engage the energies of both sides. More unhappily, we might possibly even have to commit ground forces in a limited number. The thing that, in the end, people are going to want from us over there has got to be a binding obligation resting on the United States to do certain things in the event of certain other things happening. It isn't really Congress we are talking about, but the Senate—we are talking about the possibility of a treaty. This kind of thing is classically the subject matter of a treaty. I do not, regardless of all the doctrinal argument that has been expended on it, believe that the President can do this by sheer executive agreement.

ECKHARDT: We are talking about more than the Senate's involvement. When we are talking about money, we are talking about the whole of Congress.

BLACK: I agree it would be unwise to enter into a treaty of this kind without some distinct understanding, perhaps even one would solicit a resolution—something of the sort—that the Congress would appropriate the necessary money. But again we are dealing there with two different things. One thing—and this is what I'm talking about now—is the creation of a moral obligation which *all people in this country* will have to concede rests on the United States. Whether the United States will actually fulfill that agreement is another thing, and it may be that the mode of not fulfilling it might be not to appropriate the money necessary to fulfill it, and if we didn't appropriate the money there wouldn't be anything that anybody could do, as far as I know. So you really have to divide this question up: First, what it takes to create what you and I as lawyers would agree is an obligation uncontestably resting on the United States, a contractual obligation as firm as international and constitutional law can make it; then we face the question of whether we are going to turn around and break it.

ECKHARDT: We may be leading to a Middle East treaty, but there must be considerable preliminary steps to such a treaty. There always have been. And, of course, those steps have always rather paradoxically contained kind of preliminary assurances that are understood by all concerned, but that have a certain tentativeness about them. It may be that we are on that kind of a track.

BLACK: Frankly, I doubt it, from what I hear and read. I don't hear much talk about a treaty as the way in which this crisis will be ended. It seems to be looked on as something that is expected to be ended by privately-given "assurances" of various kinds, without a treaty. I don't think these are binding.

ECKHARDT: Ideally there should be a treaty and, in addition to a treaty, commitments by whatever validating authority may exist in all the nations involved in carrying it out. In most instances, such a treaty calls for an expenditure of money—commitments along the lines you were discussing. You were mentioning that I at one time said that one way to play down the animosities that exist there would be some gigantic project in the Middle East, that would involve both the Arab countries and Israel. Of course it would take considerable money to carry it out—such a project, for example, as putting a pipeline across the Near East to go through both Israel and the Arab countries. Both a treaty and Congressional action would be needed to perfect such a thing.

BLACK: But that action would have to take place over a number of years to come, and the question whether it was continued (assuming that the agreement was clear) would be simply one of congressional morality. There wouldn't, properly speaking, be any honest decision left to be made—only the decision whether to stand by the binding agreement that had been entered into. That is why I am so insistent on breaking apart the questions of the formation of the obligation, and of the action of Congress to implement it. There is no way you can force Congress. Suppose you did get a unanimous vote in the Ninety-third Congress to the effect that certain money later would be appropriated; this wouldn't force the Ninety-fourth Congress, or the Ninety-fifth Congress. You really haven't added anything to the treaty. As far as *obligation* goes, treaty obligations are as binding as any obligation can be, more binding than the obligation you would get from a unanimously passed concurrent resolution that stated an intention to appropriate money in the future. You still wouldn't have to appropriate it. But the use of informal diplomacy and the exchange of understandings that are partly secret and without the concurrence of Congress, and specifically without the constitutionally required concurrence of two-thirds of the Senate, greatly *enhances* the probability that we won't do what the "agreements" say, because it gives another talking point to those who don't want to when the time comes. They are not then in a position of advocating the *breakage* of an *obligation* which is uncontestably binding on the United States. They would have one more thing to say, in addition to their practical arguments, and that is that we are not really bound.

ECKHARDT: It would have been a good test of American attitudes toward the situation in Vietnam had the matter been reduced to a treaty, and had the issue been confronted squarely in the Senate. There was a lot of talk about whether or not the SEATO treaty dealt with it, but the SEATO treaty didn't. All the SEATO treaty said was that we will have fervent hopes that no treaty nation will be invaded by another country without the nations signatory to the agreement coming to the treaty nation's aid—but that the ultimate decision with respect to support of the treaty will have to depend on the constitutional process of each nation. This adds nothing and subtracts nothing with respect to the constitutional authority of the President to engage in war. It leaves it right where it is. I think the Vietnam experience is an excellent example of the disaster inherent in the formation of apparent obligations by which the country is not constitutionally bound.

BLACK: It at least underlines a great danger in making commitments which seem to other people to come from the United States, but which, when you really get down to the wire, in this country are not by any means universally conceded to have constitutionally binding force.

ECKHARDT: The value of constitutionally binding force, or at least a constitutional process, is that the action taken by the United States is validated—not that it cannot be altered (it always can be)—but once validated, political support of the action is to a much greater extent assured.

BLACK: Yes, that's right. All honest people have a respect for commitment made in an authorized manner which they don't have for commitments not so made—they will act in accordance with a commitment made in an authorized manner, where at the moment of implementing the act they might not have acted that way without the prior commitment. We are in a kind of political quandary on this question of commitment. The only party that seems to have the organic capacity to go out and make these commitments is the President. We see that process going on now, obviously, in the Middle East. On the other hand, the only method by which we can actually bind the United States in a manner which will be undebatably satisfactory to everybody who is sane is by the process of a treaty, ratified by the Senate.

ECKHARDT: Let me put it another way. If the President feels that he has to achieve acceptance by some formalized process from Congress, then he will not give a commitment that is not likely to be ratified. It's not so much that the nation is any more bound by a treaty legally with respect to its future activity—

BLACK: Though I think you would concede that it is more bound by a treaty.

ECKHARDT: Yes, but I think the more important thing is this. If the President must follow such process as that of treaty-making, he must achieve a kind of consensus and agreement from a broad segment of government and from the people. Therefore he may be better assured that these decisions will be supported later down the line. Now this is not so much a moral commitment on the part of government as it is a broad-based moral commitment on the part of the people. Furthermore, if we were required to take specific action through the processes of government before we purported to make a long-term commitment, the commitment might be a lesser one.

BLACK: Yes.

ECKHARDT: Let me give you an example. Suppose early in the Vietnam war, President Johnson had asked for price and wage controls, kind of an OPA operation; if he had received that assurance, if he had been able to pass it through Congress, there would have been an assurance that a large enough body of American people were in support of his Vietnam objectives to carry it through. But when he sugarcoated the war, and people were not really committed in any way to sacrifice, he had less assurance of continued support through the conflict.

BLACK: In considering the traditional and present *strengths* of the presidency, we have almost necessarily mixed military and foreign policy. Let's now move on to the institution which gives muscle to the President across a whole range of substantive fields—the veto.

ECKHARDT: The topic is crucially important. From what we said some time back one would imagine or might come to the conclusion that Congress could itself institute a total program, for instance, a total economic program, or a program with respect to certain social services, or reforms of a positive nature, and do it quite independent of the President. This would be somewhat difficult, even were it not for the veto power, because Congress is institutionally geared to respond to broad economic and social programs developed by the President, or to respond to certain specific interest groups or local groups. It is not too well geared to formulate a total economic program. But the veto power is a very powerful obstacle to Congress's establishing any broad program, even if it were itself capable of doing so. I suppose that initially the Framers must have been thinking of the veto power as a means of preventing a sort of runaway activity—legislation which included catastrophic mistakes or accidental mistakes that needed to be erased by the executive department.

In practice as well as under the literal authority, the veto power reaches much further—the veto power can prevent *any* new program from being put in effect by Congress, thus virtually forcing the President's own policy on Congress. I doubt that the situation that now exists was really envisaged in the beginning—the President freely using the veto as a general negative power and refusing to accept many congressional programs. For instance, he can force a policy of reliance on the marketplace rather than on governmental controls to determine the price of oil. In this situation, the President does not provide a program and when Congress attempts to step into the gap, it is virtually impossible to move against the veto power.

BLACK: We ought to expand on that a little, because most Americans—and until just a short while ago I was certainly of their number —rather carelessly looked on the exercise of the veto as a series of mere unconnected episodes. I have been impressed lately by the *systematic* effect of the veto. It is an enormous alteration of what, as you point out, might otherwise have been thought to be the moving force of the system—that is, creativity in Congress. Let's be concrete. A President, who will rarely have less than a third of the members of his own party in at least one House under our system, because that's the way our politics tends to sort out, can prevent the enactment of any legislation unless a stable, reliable two-thirds majority can be commanded in both the House and the Senate on the same occasion and at the same time, within a matter of days, to override a veto.

That means that when it comes to questions of economic policy, Congress, as you point out, can formulate a beautiful economic policy. It might even be that the exceedingly difficult feat of marshalling adequate support to pass such a policy in all its parts in both Houses could be accomplished. But you go through all this work, and all this committee study, and all this organization, and then the President in ten minutes, having previously decided to do so, can slap a veto on it, and all this work has been in vain. This reacts backward on the process; the need to guess as to whether something will be vetoed is a constant drag on congressional initiative.

ECKHARDT: Let me give you an example. The President is in favor of complete decontrol of the price of oil. Now it is arguable as to whether this is good or bad. According to his contentions, it would create more production of oil in the United States and therefore greater self-sufficiency. On the other side, of course, moving from $3.85 a barrel to, say, $14.00 a barrel is terrifically inflationary. Without arguing the merits, suppose—and this is the situation that does in fact now exist—Congress should desire to put some kind of control on price, and suppose within a Subcommittee like the one I serve on (Energy and Power) a majority of the Democrats say, "Look, we've got a program," and they present it to the Chairman of that Subcommittee. He says, "If we try a program which is devised in a manner not in accordance with the President's views, on August 31 all controls will go out of effect and all prices will go to the world price. Therefore, you would be well advised to try to devise a program that the President would not veto." It may well be that anything between a well-thought-out price control program and a complete deregulation might be worse than either, so you are put in the very difficult position of not being able to put into effect, as a Congressman associated with other members of your party, and with a strong majority of Congress, what you think best for the economy. Even a strong majority may be forced to substitute for their program an entirely different one to avoid a veto.

BLACK: I'd like to point up that this is a perfect illustration, because the question of whether or not to impose controls on the price of oil is not a question that involves constitutionalism. Such a step in either direction would obviously be constitutional. It is a sheer policy decision. Secondly, it has nothing to do with a defense of the executive office; the President in vetoing legislation of this kind is not protecting himself or the dignity of his office or indeed the independence of a third branch, like the judiciary. Thirdly, and this has a kind of tangential importance and interest, there is nothing obviously wicked about either one of these steps. It isn't the kind of thing where a person steps into the breach to prevent an outrage of some kind, which may be a value of the veto envisaged by the Framers. You have to do a lot of study about it and balance off a lot of things.

Oil price policy forms a component, and at the present time an extremely important component, of the economic policy of the United States. The fact is that no matter how much we talk about Congress, and how much we flagellate Congress, Congress cannot do anything about it against a resolute President, unless it can muster (and this is usually impossible) immediately commandable two-thirds majorities in both Houses. This veto power is one of the most important systematic characteristics of the American Constitution.

ECKHARDT: Charles, let me also point out how fallacious the idea of a veto-proof Congress is at this time. Initially it was thought, and asserted in the media, that a Congress that had more than two-thirds Democrats would be veto-proof. But a Congress that looks veto-proof when elected can easily be shown not to be so. Let me show you how that really works in our system, which lacks any strict party discipline exercised on Democrats (or Republicans, for that matter). Let's assume that Democrats and Republicans are equally likely to veer from their party position. About a third of the House are Republicans, and I will use an exact figure for an example. Say 145 members are Republicans and, say, 290 are Democrats and, say, that 10 percent of the Republicans, because of their districts or because of their predilections, vote with the Democrats on a particular issue. One could assume that the probabilities of breaking from the party line on the Democratic side would be equal. Of course, as a matter of fact, they are even greater, because the party is more diverse, regionally and politically. But let's assume that it is just a question of probabilities; and 15 people break from the Republican Party. One might expect then, upon the same percentage basis, 30 Democrats to go to the Republican side. But to retain a veto-proof position there would have had to be an even trade—30 Democrats for 30 Republicans. In addition to that, with the Republicans you have a relatively small party, whose members are thirsty for power and for effectiveness in the only area in which they can be effective, negatively, and support of a veto is the most effective power available to them. Also, the veto is explained by the President and his views publicized. His program is, or seems, very definite. On the other side, you have a much more amorphous program developed by a great number of persons with different viewpoints which has been put together by compromise and stuck together with scotch tape, so to speak.

BLACK: Both differences you are pointing out are systematic, pervasive, and can be expected to persist through all time, as long as the Constitution is in its present form. This numerical reason for the improbability of override is geometrically increased by the fact that in each case it applies simultaneously in both Houses. Thus, if there is one chance in four of override in each House, there is only one chance in sixteen of override in both. You probably have more accurate statistics than I have; the last time I looked I think I saw that Mr. Ford had vetoed fifteen bills, and four of the vetoes had been overridden.

ECKHARDT: That sounds about right. There may have been more vetoes than that. I doubt that any more have been overridden. One veto you would have thought to be an inevitable override was the veto of a bill that would have created additional jobs in areas of heavy unemployment, and yet that failed by some thirteen votes.

BLACK: Now there we have another case where it is just a matter of economic policy. Once again the Congress, which is so much criticized for failing to formulate policy, plainly could not do so because of the veto.

ECKHARDT: Another very good example is that not long ago we failed to override the President's veto on the farm bill; of course, some of the avant garde northeastern liberal Democrats voted to sustain the veto. Then we got a bill that had to do with the cities and unemployment. One of the rural southern members, a freshman, not conservative, not pro-Republican (I don't know how he finally voted) got up and said—and I thought it was rather revealing—he said, "I may vote to sustain the veto just out of pure damn cussedness," because he was sore that the northeasterners would not support his group in overriding the veto on the farm bill. This is an innate weakness of a congressional body.

BLACK: I want to put up to you an idea that I have entertained as a possibility, and see what you think of its actual chances—if not today at least some time in the not geologically remote future. It would be the easiest thing in the world, as far as the Constitution is concerned, for Congress simply to follow a convention of overriding vetoes where they did not concern the integrity of the presidential office, the constitutionality of the measure or, of course, something very wicked. This would not require any member of Congress to violate his conscience because it has been held, I think properly, that the two-thirds vote required is two-thirds of those present, provided there is a quorum, so the people who are against the measure on the merits, and agree with the presidential veto on the merits, could simply stay away on the occasion when the override vote was taken. Now I have wondered why such a convention has not arisen, because it is pretty plain that the power of Congress as a whole would be vastly enhanced by such a convention as this, and yet they have never done anything but vote on the merits. What do you think of the possibility of such a convention's arising?

ECKHARDT: I think it could arise in this kind of situation. Recently we passed a bill that would extend the authority to control the price of oil from August 31 to December 31—merely an extension of existing authority—to give Congress time to act. The President vetoed it.

When we compromised and sent him a bill to extend the time only to November 15, he did not veto this latter bill. Had he done so, Congress might well have started the kind of convention you envisage. The short extension was institutionally necessary to give Congress time to act. In fact Congress did eventually act within the deadline. The bill providing the extension was purely for the purpose of giving us time to deal with the general question of oil pricing. It was not ideological, it was neutral with respect to whether there should be deregulation or regulation. If there is any situation in which we should be able to develop this convention it is one involving protection of the institution. In such a case Republicans might, as you indicate, merely absent themselves. Perhaps anticipation of this possibility persuaded the President not to veto the simple extension bill.

BLACK: Well, a convention, of course depends for its efficacy on acceptance, and there is no possible constitutional way to do this. But conventions somewhat similar have developed firmly, for example, senatorial courtesy with respect to judicial appointments. It doesn't work every time but it usually works. The result is that the Senate as a whole finds its influence vastly enhanced. This is in the interest of every member of the Senate because, while he may disagree with a particular determination, the institution within which he lives, and which gives him power, is built up correspondingly. Now that certainly would be true of a convention of veto override. I am encouraged by your thinking that this is a live possibility. I had just about thrown my hands up on it.

ECKHARDT: Yes, I think it is a live possibility in a case like the one I described concerning the bill to create the extension of time to permit Congress to act. There is a different situation when the issue is ideological. We might be able to override the veto in order to give the Commerce Committee an opportunity to come out with a pricing policy respecting oil. There might be a very good possibility of overriding a veto on that point simply on institutional grounds very similar to the institutional grounds behind the convention of protecting the Senator's designation of a court appointee. But when eventually the subject is a bill which deals with the options of price deregulation or price control, it would be very difficult to keep such institutional discipline mounted to overriding a veto—a discipline controlling, for instance, southwesterners whose interests are in taking regulations off oil prices. We have to go a much longer way than we have at present to bring about party discipline achieving that objective and, frankly, I don't think we can do it under our congressional situation.

BLACK: I think that on this the Congress and the country ought to fish or cut bait. It is absolutely plain that congressional formation and enactment of comprehensive, major, overall congressional policy, in opposition to the policy preferences of the President, is not feasible under present conditions of the veto. In the main the President by this veto is in a position to sit back quietly and say, "Come forward with what I want, or just about what I want, or I won't sign it," and he will be supported normally (statistically, normally) in *one or the other* of the Houses of Congress, which is all it takes. If a convention like the one I have suggested is not developed or the Constitution is not amended (which is a step I always shrink from) we might as well all settle down and stop expecting that Congress will play a leadership role in the development of, let's say, economic policy.

ECKHARDT: I think everybody ought to be brought to understand this, because Congress is put, in the situation that I described, in a very unfavorable public light. At the present time the President has gotten by with pulling off four pages of the calendar and saying that during all these months Congress was doing nothing. I happen to serve on five Subcommittees. You can get an idea about how much time is involved when one meets in one of those Subcommittees three to five days a week. And that's about what we've been doing on the Energy and Power Subcommittee to draw up a bill that ultimately might well face, and almost surely will face, if we follow our own convictions as to policy, a veto. Now, we should not be placed in a position, in the view of the public, of simply dragging our feet, at a time when we are laboring to produce something acceptable to the members' views but must at the same time try to effect a type of compromise that will get by a veto. If we don't effect those compromises we run the very serious risk of being said, quite unfairly, to have done nothing with respect to the major problem of our time.

BLACK: Sure. If this discussion did no more than underscore the systematic and pervasive effect of the veto on our entire legislative institution, it would have served its purpose. I am inclined to think, the more I ponder the powers of the presidency, that this veto is the real one. The others are rather flimsy stuff that Congress can pretty well control.

ECKHARDT: That's right. Maybe this is a little like the Electoral-College system, which you and I agree we ought to keep, because it has worked and because there have been so few times when the possibility of its not working would create a threat. There are not many times when the Congress and the presidency are in the hands of different parties, and even fewer times when (in a period crying for affirmative action) the presidency is in the hands of the party which is perhaps the less innovative and more conservative, and the Congress in the hands of the more innovative and the more likely to press for innovatory legislation. And perhaps to try to change the system would not be as desirable as simply to live with it. Let Congress develop its adversary program; let it demonstrate that it has a solution; and then wait until the next presidential election.

BLACK: Maybe we should wait and see a bit; it has worked a long time and maybe it will keep working. But it wouldn't be a change in the Constitution itself for the Congress to develop (if this is a possibility) the convention of overriding vetoes on sheer questions of policy where there is just a plain disagreement, let's say, as to what a sound economic policy for the country may be.

ECKHARDT: I have the idea that the convention couldn't be established as a *general* convention. What might happen is in a situation where it becomes obvious that there is no presidential leadership, and that there is a potential congressional leadership offering real programs—in such a case it is conceivable that persistent vetoes followed by persistent response by Congress with innovative and reasoned programs could ultimately create a climate of public opinion that would cause Congress to develop such a convention or custom as you suggest.

BLACK: The only reservation I have about this is that, as you pointed out, the veto itself is such a discouragement to Congress's forming clear and coherent policies. We are not really testing the ability of Congress to form policy and get it into coherent and organized shape in the *absence* of the veto. We are testing its ability to do that when it stands continually in the shadow of possible veto. Those things are two different things. This discussion shows that you can never conduct a pure experiment in politics, and we will have to wait and see what may develop if there comes to be a stand-off. That's when the real test comes—when you can't get anything through.

ECKHARDT: That's true. Then, of course, at that point let's take the situation of a New England Congressman, who is in a situation where home heating oil goes to an inordinately high cost level. Does he then vote to sustain the veto or does he not?

BLACK: He's a Republican, with a Republican President?

ECKHARDT: Yes, he is a Republican in Congress and his President is forcing him to continue to support vetoes which are unpopular. He can't answer his constituents' demands, and he begins to mutter in the cloakroom to other Republicans, saying, "Look, the President is going to destroy our possibility of winning in the next congressional election." You can conceivably get an override on that basis, actually from defections within the President's own party.

BLACK: The veto remains a big shadow overhanging any congressional initiative.

ECKHARDT: That may not be all bad. It means that so long as the President is acting within reason, the veto system will be sustained, and Congress cannot play at congressional one-upmanship with the President. After all, Congress can devise solutions which it knows won't work but which look good, and it may put them up to be knocked down, in order to put itself in a better political light in the next election. That kind of thing was illustrated by Congress's giving President Nixon the power to put into effect broad price and wage controls. Nobody thought that the President would do it. That sort of thing ought to be discouraged.

BLACK: I remember how surprised I was when he did put on some controls because I don't think the public had been aware of the fact that these powers actually existed. I certainly was not.

ECKHARDT: Of course, he was in the ideal situation. If price controls worked, he was a hero, but if they didn't work, Congress had devised an extreme non-free-private-enterprise way of solving problems—a solution which he always really rejected in principle, and which now was proved to be a failure. That's about what the Republicans did say, in the event, about wage and price controls.

BLACK: I would wonder if the use of the veto might not be curbed somewhat if the leadership in Congress were more forthright about withholding some of these things that the Administration wants for its "free-enterprise" supporters in the form of governmental assistance.

ECKHARDT: To assume that this would work is to assume that the President has something that he is willing to ransom. If an Administration doesn't want to do much, if it wants to dismantle controls and leave everything to the natural forces of the economy, there is nothing to ransom.

BLACK: But does this Administration, for example, want the next general appropriations act not to contain any money for the shipbuilding and ship-operating industries? Of course, they don't. Once they get to dealing with these people they forget all about free enterprise and start changing the subject, and I am sure that it's true over a considerable range of subsidy and help which takes the form of money. In that sense it is probable that even the most conservative Administration has got a lot that could be held up for ransom.

ECKHARDT: But the thing is that you don't have anybody who is willing to demand the ransom money because you don't have enough Congressmen who are willing to say, "Look, we don't care if the shipbuilding industry in our district stops or not, we are going to force the President into a position on a broad economic issue in order to achieve it."

BLACK: And then the ones who don't come from such shipping districts don't have as intense and concentrated an interest in a particular single matter as the person from the district with a big shipbuilding industry has in maintaining it, so when these intensities get to playing with one another and the trade-offs are made, it is rather unlikely that a long-range policy would prevail even amongst the majority of Congress of kidnapping something like ship subsidies for the President to ransom by signing an oil control bill.

ECKHARDT: Sure, there are unspoken trade-offs. "I'll protect your cotton subsidy and you protect my shipbuilding interests."

BLACK: I am always amused by this pervasive network of right-wing subsidies, just as I am amused by the reaction of the strict constructionists to the question of how the federal government got into the narcotics business. Similarly, the free enterprise man tends to change the subject when you mention the shipbuilding industry. Not perhaps if he is an academic, who doesn't have to get elected, but if he is a politician, a highly conservative politician, you can be pretty damn sure that he is strong for ship subsidy, which absolutely contradicts the idea of "free enterprise."

ECKHARDT: Take the price of oil that we were discussing a minute ago. There is a great fight against government's controlling the price of oil directly, but the government has controlled the price of oil *indirectly* since the early 1930s, when the East Texas oil field came in. It was controlled by the Texas Railroad Commission. They regulated the number of days a well could pump, and this kept the price of oil *up*. After Texas ceased to produce about half of the United States' oil and the United States half of the world's, we limited foreign oil imports so as to maintain the price. So price has always been controlled either by the flow out of the Texas oil wells or else by the inward flow of foreign oil. *The very same people* who instituted those programs through government, and stuck to them for decades, now oppose government's taking an active part in keeping American prices from going up to OPEC prices.

BLACK: Sure, your true-blue "free-enterprise" man is opposed only to controlling prices *downward*. The venerable tariff system is really another illustration. You don't find a principled and consistent opposition to all protective tariffs amongst people who are in active politics and who talk the rhetoric of "free enterprise." It is not a very likely coincidence; it may happen in a very few cases but not many. They always start special-pleading at that point.

ECKHARDT: You've got an absolutely up-to-date example of that in the President putting an import fee or a tariff on oil of $1 on February 1, 1975. At that point domestic oil went from about $11 to $12, the rise exactly equalling that tariff. All that increase of $1 went into the pockets of those who produced the oil.

BLACK: I am not sure just how we got here from the veto. We seem to have wandered a little bit, but I think for systematic purposes we have about wrapped up the question of veto. Above all, it's the systematic rather than the episodic character that one needs to think about. Where the solution may be—in the way of amendment, or convention, or perhaps even in presidential restraints as part of a series of trade-offs—is all conjectural. But the first step toward some kind of solution along one or more of those lines is the realization that we are dealing here with the irreducible minimum of presidential power and with an institution, the veto, which has enormously important effects, drag effects, side effects, throughout the whole of the legislative process.

ECKHARDT: Let's say one other thing. It emphasizes that our system operates as a system of interplay between the presidency and the Congress, and that when this doesn't function, it becomes virtually impossible for our system to work as it was initially envisaged.

BLACK: There's just one other thing about the veto—a minor point intellectually but of some importance—the pocket veto. That, of course, has nothing to do with the whole theory of veto. A student of mine, Richard Zuckerman,[6] has been working on this subject under me in seminar, and I have his work on it, so it is fresh in my mind. There isn't an acceptable rationale any more for the pocket veto, except possibly between Congresses. It is reasonable enough for a bill to die at the end of one Congress if it has not gone through. But the Constitution says that the pocket veto is effective only if Congress by their adjournment *prevent* the return of the bill, and it seems to me

6. Yale Law School, Class of 1975.

entirely plain that if the Houses of Congress just appoint an officer to receive bills during some week or ten days of recess—a thing which they have done—then a short adjournment does not *prevent* the return of the bill. The bill *is* returned, and can be voted on by the same Congress that passed it. Remember that the pocket veto means that there is not even an opportunity for the difficult business of override, and the President doesn't have to give any reasons for his veto. This may have been all right in 1787, but nothing can be said for it today.

ECKHARDT: There ought to be ways that can be corrected.

IMPEACHMENT, IMPOUNDMENT, AND EXECUTIVE PRIVILEGE 4

ECKHARDT: We've been talking about the close relationship between Congress and the presidency. The most extreme problem occurs when one part of this machinery—the presidency—becomes inactive, by virtue either of acts on the part of the President that may constitute grounds for impeachment, or of a lack of confidence so deep as to make the presidency ineffectual. Sometimes this latter situation can occur, as we have said, simply from the fact that the President is in one party and Congress is in the other, and the system has bogged down. To a certain extent that existed under Nixon, entirely aside from Watergate.

The question is, what can be done in these crisis situations? What can be done, first, in a typical impeachment situation, where the President is accused of being guilty of a high crime or misdemeanor, and there's some sufficient basis for considering impeachment; and, secondly, what can be done in the situation in which the government flounders because of the ineffective operation of the presidency?

BLACK: This question really branches off into two: there is the process of impeachment, and the question of how the government is to operate during crises of confidence in the presidency, of which the impeachment situation is simply the end case. The second of those probably fits more into what we've been talking about up to now. I find it a hard question to deal with, because I'm driven into this dilemma. The easy solution would of course be the "vote of no-confidence" device that we've already discussed, and that would require a constitutional Amendment. This would enable us to get rid of the President and get another one. A fundamental objection to this (one which I have already stated) is that the subjection of the

President to easy removal at the hands of Congress, while it might have some tendency to solve these crisis situations, would so weaken the presidency, as a matter of prestige, in a *normal* situation, that the cure would be worse than the disease. What you have to do is try to develop some leadership in Congress, some creative leadership which does not depend on a discipline of members which, as we have said, Congress simply cannot administer.

ECKHARDT: I don't think it can be done in a way that will permit Congress to exercise the sole or even the chief innovative force, and I don't think it should be done in that way, because I think the institution of the presidency is one which brings to the forefront of political endeavor the sweeping questions affecting the public at large, questions like civil rights. But there ought to be some way by which Congress can be set in motion, some machinery by which Congress can meet economic problems, and other broad problems, and can be called upon, particularly in unusual circumstances, to fill the gap for a period of time. Probably the best hope for that is the majority party caucus,[1] a strengthening of the majority party caucus.

BLACK: When we reached the point where the Judiciary Committee was well into its impeachment hearings, and the tapes were already out, one thing became entirely plain, even before the resignation— we were not going to have strong leadership from the presidency within the near future, however the impeachment business might eventuate. It seems to me that we cannot look for strong leadership from Mr. Ford. So we have partly seen, and we're going to see more fully, what Congress can do—how far it can go in approaching, within itself, the American version of the kind of initiative that is required. However, perhaps we ought to talk first about impeachment itself.

ECKHARDT: I think we ought to talk not only about the constitutional bases for impeachment, but about the importance of the issue, and how it comes up, and how Congress responds to a situation in-

1. See *supra*, p. 33, *infra*, p. 153.

volving acts which may possibly be grounds for impeachment.[2] First, the Framers were very much concerned about not utilizing impeachment as a bill of attainder, which would in effect give the legislative body such a supremacy that it would not be different from the supremacy of Parliament.

BLACK: I think that's a very important point, and I think it leads us into the question of the permissible grounds for impeachment, a very complicated and difficult and also an extremely interesting topic. With respect to the Constitutional Convention of 1787, the most weighty piece of evidence, by far, of what thoughts the Framers had about impeachment is a colloquy which took place between Madison and Mason on the eighth of September, 1787, in that Convention, and I ought to mention that that was very close to the Convention's end. The question actually pending was whether to transfer the power to try impeachments and to remove from office, from the Supreme Court, in whom it had been lodged by the report of the Committee of Detail, to the Senate, where it is now located. This proposal, which of course prevailed, was brought in by the Committee of Eleven, which did much of the final revision of the substantive provisions of the Constitution. Mason spoke up and said that because (and I'm of course not quoting, but paraphrasing) that exactly because of the unavailability under our Constitution of the bill of attainder,[3] it was necessary that the grounds for impeachment be broadened, and in addition to the grounds of treason and bribery, which were in the draft, he proposed to add "maladministration." (This proposal of Mason's was not strictly relevant to the proposal for empowerment of the Senate to try impeachments, but the Convention often proceeded without full formality.) Mr. Madison objected to this on the ground (and it's very important that this got no dissent) that "maladministration" was too vague, and would put the President

2. It should be said here that this dialogue was recorded just before the writing of Black, *Impeachment: A Handbook* (1974). No attempt has been made to eliminate the overlaps natural in such circumstances.

3. The "bill of attainder" is explained in the text just below.

simply at the pleasure of the Senate. Mason then withdrew "malad-ministration" and substituted the phrase which is now in the Con-stitution—"other high Crimes and Misdemeanors." There was general agreement, and that's where the matter stood.

Now it seems to me that one lesson that was gotten out of that was that of all things the Framers did *not* intend to include, or, rather, intended *not* to include, "maladministration," with all it implies, was one of them. This very clear piece of evidence rejects that, and it's the clearest thing we've got. But the other thing which hasn't been noticed very much up to now is that Mason saw that the constitu-tional prohibition of the bill of attainder was also a limiting concept on the power of the Senate to remove the President, and I think we ought to just talk briefly about what a bill of attainder was and is. It is a piece of legislation which finds certain conduct retrospectively to have been wrong, and punishes it in some way.

ECKHARDT: They punish it either by exaction of a criminal penalty, or by removal of authority.

BLACK: Or removal from office. Now the leading case in modern times is the *Lovett* case,[4] in which the Supreme Court held that a provision that no federal money should be expended on the salary of two named persons, on the ground (which appears in the debate) that these persons were suspected of having Communist sympathies, was a bill of attainder and therefore forbidden by the Constitution. Now it's very hard to give concrete and specific meaning to the phrase "other high Crimes and Misdemeanors," but there are two things, it seems to me, that we do know about it. One is from the Constitution itself, and that is that it does not mean a bill of attainder, or anything that is equivalent to a bill of attainder.

ECKHARDT: But on the other hand, it also does not mean simply a defined crime.

BLACK: No, well we'll get to that of course, I agree fully with that. But we have to kind of box these things in one at a time. To impeach simply on the ground that Congress retrospectively disapproves of

4. *U.S. v. Lovett,* 328 U.S. 303 (1946).

presidential conduct is the equivalent of a bill of attainder. The other limiting thing which emerges with rare clarity from this debate is that "maladministration," which was at the time a ground for impeachment in many of the state constitutions, is not available as a ground for impeachment.

ECKHARDT: If you say "maladministration" you may come pretty close to some of the high misdemeanors involved.

BLACK: Yes, I don't think there's any problem there. I think the word "maladministration" would include virtually all that we would include within high crimes and misdemeanors. But it would also include a lot more. It would include, for example, *inefficiency* in office; "maladministration" might well comprise serious inefficiency. I don't think it's possible that "high Crimes and Misdemeanors" include mere inefficiency.

ECKHARDT: But maladministration might also include the failure to comply with constitutional limitations, which could either be impeachable or not impeachable, as a high misdemeanor.

BLACK: Sure, again I think that a great deal which we would include within "high Crimes and Misdemeanors," if not everything, would also be included within the phrase "maladministration." The problem is the *outer* part of these concentric circles, because what this bit of history at the Convention seems to forbid is our simply taking "high Crimes and Misdemeanors" as *coterminous* with "maladministration," and treating it as though the latter were what they had said. Because that obviously is not what they meant. It's maladministration in trumps recklessly and deliberately to violate the Constitution; it is probably also in many if not all cases a high crime or misdemeanor. Had it been adopted, however, the term "maladministration" would have included, as a matter of ordinary colloquial usage, a lot of things which I think we'd all agree are *not* included in "high Crimes and Misdemeanors," and therefore these two items of history, the "bill of attainder" history and the "maladministration" history, set bounds to the concept, "high Crimes and Misdemeanors." From that point on, everything is pretty vague and uncertain. We do know that mere maladministration, mere inefficiency, is not enough for impeachment, and we know that an impeachment must not resemble too closely a bill of attainder.

ECKHARDT: The relationship between all politicians is rather close, and it becomes extremely dangerous if some type of subjective judgment with respect to maladministration or any kind of malfeasance in office is the standard of judgment.

BLACK: Well, one thing about it, too, is that you can always "stack charges" on this kind of thing, in the civil-service phrase; there's no President who ever lived or could possibly live who could run the enterprise the President runs without there being found within it, on full investigation, a large number of instances of less than ideal administration. Mr. Truman would have been impeached and removed beyond a doubt, if the necessary political animus had developed, and if it had been an accepted rule that inefficiencies, weaknesses in administration, less than ideal running of the presidential office and of the government, were to be grounds for impeachment. But I dare say that would be true of just about every President, except possibly the first President Harrison, who died a month after he took office. All the others must have made a lot of mistakes at one time or another.

ECKHARDT: Suppose, for instance, you were to subject the question of the bombing of Hiroshima to the rule of maladministration in office. It resulted in tremendous tragedy, and may have been one of the greatest mistakes ever made.

BLACK: I think "maladministration" was properly rejected in the Convention, but this does not mean that some other things which would be maladministration may not also be within the narrower circle of "high Crimes and Misdemeanors." Let's pin one thing down before we get to that difficult circle. I think on this we can entirely agree, without any reservation, and that is that it's just an absurd idea that a President may be impeached and removed only for an *indictable crime,* a crime, that is to say, that could be punished in the normal process of law. I've given elsewhere the example of a President who moves to Saudi Arabia during his term so that he can have four wives, and who proposes to run the government from Mecca or

Medina by radio, by wireless. I think this would not be an indictable crime, if he'd gotten a passport in normal order, but I wouldn't question for a moment that this kind of reckless disregard for the responsibilities of the office would be an impeachable offense. It's more than maladministration, it's a wanton, reckless act, without deference to any arguably sound view of the public welfare. I would think a President who announced his determination, and adhered to it, of appointing nobody to any federal office, including all Cabinet officers, who was over the age of nineteen, would be impeachable.

ECKHARDT: Suppose he refused faithfully to execute the laws. For instance, suppose he deliberately appointed only Republicans to a regulatory agency where the statute clearly says that there shall be a balance of Republicans and Democrats. There you have another category which is not that of *crime*, but which involves the distinct breach of positive law. This could be an impeachable offense, and there again you'd have the category, which is even more definite than the ones that I've been talking about, where plainly the criminal law would not apply. We don't have that easy an out in defining high crimes and misdemeanors within the meaning of the Constitution, because any constitutional interpretation which leads to absolutely howling absurdities has got to be rejected. And I think the conclusion that a President can only be removed for breach of the criminal law as it stands in its application to ordinary citizens is one that leads at once to complete absurdities.

BLACK: It's not bounded by the statutory crimes, and the only thing I would add that could help us technically is to apply the concept "eiusdem generis,"[5] as we lawyers call it, to the entire phrase, "Treason, Bribery, and *other* high Crimes and Misdemeanors." That means, if there's any question about this, it's resolved by the word "other." It has to be taken to mean offenses of somewhat the same tenor and seriousness as treason or bribery.

---

5. "Eiusdem generis" means "of the same kind." In a phrase meaning several *specific* things, and then a more general category, it is sometimes a good rule of interpretation to take the general category as comprising only things "of the same kind" as those specifically named.

ECKHARDT: But we don't want to—we can't construe it as being limited to *only* these type of offenses which are criminal, else the phrase "or Misdemeanors" would not have been added.

BLACK: That's right.

ECKHARDT: Certainly it didn't mean that you could oust a President for illegal parking. It meant a *high* misdemeanor. It meant something that was such a basic violation of constitutional concept of the office as to be of like magnitude with a crime of the type described.

BLACK: Yes. I don't think that we want to press the notion of its having to be exactly the same type of offense as treason or bribery, on any very definite descriptive level. It really has more to do with two things: one is the magnitude of the offense, and the second is the character of the offense, as in some way either constituting a major infidelity to the government, or some corruption of the government, or some corrupt use of the office. That's a big category, and it gives ample room for everything which as a practical matter ought to be an impeachable offense. I'll give a couple of examples; as you can see, they're not entirely imaginary. If I were to find that a President of the United States had used assets which he'd acquired through previously having held another high office, and had used the prestige of his presidency to shield himself from investigation, so as to perpetrate with impunity a half million dollar tax fraud, that seems to me to be a crime which is of very much the same sort as bribery— that is, it's corruption with respect to the office—it's the use of the office for some corrupt, in this case financial, purpose, and I would regard that as very certainly an impeachable offense. I don't mean that as judgment on any one case, because as we lawyers know, you want to know all the circumstances in the case before you make a judgment on that case. But I would find in that general direction, the use of the office for personal financial or other corrupt aggrandizement, an impeachable offense. I think that despite the precedent of the Bay of Pigs—and it is a troublesome one—the use of the office for some kind of murderous and totally unauthorized attack on a foreign country might, in many circumstances, constitute an impeachable offense The President is given his powers as Commander-in-Chief not for the purpose of using them in any way that he wants to, but with some responsibility to the national interest and to international law. This is delicate territory, because he must have a very wide discretion, but I think it's possible that in that area he may go beyond the bounds of allowable discretion.

ECKHARDT: Well then, even if the Constitution had not added "Misdemeanors" and had referred only to "Treason, Bribery, and other high Crimes," there would still be a necessity of a sort of common-law definition of what constituted other high crimes, but it would not leave an open-ended discretion with respect to what these impeachable offenses were.

BLACK: I think that all us lawyers, whether we be constitutional lawyers, or lawyers specializing in other fields, realize, and I suppose a great many laymen realize, that it's not a unique thing to have to give some precise legal content, fitting a particular case, to language which is in itself rather sweeping and vague. We do this, for example, with the due-process clause of the Fourteenth Amendment, and we do it in many other cases. We do it in interpreting the Antitrust Act, with its sweeping prohibitions of certain rather vaguely defined conduct. I think that there is no question, and it must be faced frankly, that within certain limits, the deciding authority, the court, does make the law. In that sense, the House of Representatives in impeaching, and the Senate in deciding on removal, are charged with very much the same responsibility as that which rests on the Supreme Court when it concretizes and applies to a particular sort of official conduct the Fourteenth Amendment's prohibition against deprivation of life, liberty, or property without due process of law. We're no more at sea in the impeachment case than we are in the Fourteenth Amendment case. We have a firm boundary with the bill of attainder, which must not be approximated or equalled in what we do; we have a fairly firm boundary in the decisive rejection of the word "maladministration." We have, on the other hand, every reason to believe that no such absurdity was intended as the limitation to ordinary indictable crimes. Within these interstices, the Senate and the House simply have to make responsible judgments. I've always told audiences to whom I have spoken on this subject, that probably the best way to form the attitude for making such a judgment is to ask yourself whether the particular offense which you are considering is one which you can be pretty certain you would have considered impeachable if it had been performed by a President whose policies you *generally* approved. Somebody like John Kennedy, from the standpoint of supporters of John Kennedy, and so on.

What the Senate is called on to do, and what the House is called on to do, is to construe this language in such a manner as to make that construction acceptable as a general thing, and not simply acceptable because it's a talking point, a good way to get one person.

I would like to say one thing about the concept of negligence. There has been a great deal of talk about it. To my mind the general law furnishes a very good distinction on this. I can't conceive that it's practical to hold any official, including the President, liable for everything that his subordinates do, or to hold him for ordinary neglect of inspection here and there. It seems to me that's expectable of any official, and is not within miles of what is implied by such a solemn phrase as "Treason, Bribery, or other high Crimes and Misdemeanors." I do think, however—and this is a distinction which I know is familiar to you, right out of tort law—that there can be a negligence so wanton and so reckless as to equate virtually with intentional wrongdoing. If a man drives a car at seventy-five miles an hour, knowing he has no brakes, through a crowded town, then it's immaterial whether he intends to hit somebody or not; he has so behaved as to exhibit his *indifference* to whether he hits somebody. Now I would think a President might be so lax in superintending his subordinates, so disregardful of warning signals, that a negligence which we could call really criminal negligence could come into play.

Eckhardt: Let me also suggest that you may put together a group of facts and circumstances that would constitute an impeachable offense, by showing negligence in delegation of power to subordinates, persons known to be willing to engage in illegal activity to the advantage of the President.

BLACK: I wouldn't disagree with that as a general matter. You would probably agree that the final judgment on a question of that kind really has to be made on the particular facts that emerge in evidence. It is very hard to quantify these things in advance.

ECKHARDT: Negligence and intent do merge. There couldn't be a better example of this, if one puts the worst light on President Nixon's discussions with Haldeman that came out in the transcripts. One could draw the conclusion that the President was hearing these things reported to him and responding extremely mildly to shocking revelations of what had happened, and by so doing was giving his tacit assent to further acts of the same kind.

BLACK: That's possible, that's possible. I haven't read these things with the care with which they were read by the people who actually had to be judges in this, the care with which you would have had to read them if it had become your duty actually to make a judgment on them. It seems to me clearly possible that this is the solution to the negligence dilemma, because if you just talk about negligence in the abstract, you can state absurd cases on either side—either that ordinary negligence, such as almost anybody is likely to commit, would make the President impeachable, or that on the other hand he could just go and plow his way through a morass of corruption and crime and not notice, and would be safe from impeachment if he did nothing about it.

ECKHARDT: What about a wink or a nod?

BLACK: A wink or a nod really just poses the question of proof, because they may obviously be an express or an implied-in-fact command or acquiescence.

I would like to go on to one other puzzle that has surrounded this language, and that is the problem of a difference of opinion on the constitutional powers of the presidency or, to put it another way, the problem of defining those areas in which the President's exceeding his constitutional powers, or behaving in a manner as to contravene the Constitution, can be looked on as a high crime or misdemeanor. I would insist rather strongly here that these would have to be areas in which there is virtually no room for honest difference of opinion.

We have a pretty good recent example, and that is the action of President Nixon in impounding funds which had been authorized to be spent on programs of which he disapproved. I have expressed myself in print as believing that his constitutional position on this was wrong. As a matter of ultimate constitutional law I think he was at fault with respect to his obligation "to take Care that the Laws be faithfully executed" when he deliberately set about to cut off money, depending differentially on whether he approved or disapproved of the program concerned. I do think, however, that in the precedents in the past, and in the ambiguity of congressional directions on this matter, there was room for honest difference of opinion, and I should consider it not an impeachable offense to have done this.

ECKHARDT: The first thing that must be considered is, "What is impoundment?" It is crystal clear that there are some acts of impoundment which are authorized by implication in some legislation. There is a second level where one statute, say, calling for budget balancing in general terms could be construed to impinge on another statute, which appears to direct that funds be spent in a certain way. It would be extremely difficult to establish a clear constitutional violation in that set of circumstances. But there could be a case in which specific grants of funds—divisible, say, among States—have been directed by the statute in certain amounts, and you get closer to the question of an intentional constitutional violation when the President simply refuses to put into effect the formula that has been specified by Congress.

BLACK: For the failure to give money to identifiable entities, whether they be natural persons, municipalities, or States, there is a milder remedy than impeachment, and we ought not to think of running right away to impeachment to satisfy this need. I don't see why there shouldn't either be provided, or—where it already exists—utilized, a judicial remedy for settling the question of the right to this money, as between the persons in the federal government who are to disburse it and the persons or entities who are to receive it. That is an adequate remedy, and I believe that there ought to be some conception in this field of the exhaustion of other remedies before starting on such a drastic course as impeachment.

The second point I would make—and this might be generalized as to some of these other matters as well—is that the remedy for this kind of thing rests above all with Congress—that if Congress desires to make it absolutely clear that certain money is in all events to be disbursed, then it has a means of doing so. I think it somewhat unfair, and politically unwise, for Congress to *refrain* from taking that step in the legislation, and then to charge it as a fault to the President that he has not taken his cue from some less specific directions, or no directions at all.

ECKHARDT: Suppose instead of Congress defining the duty, say, the Attorney General of the State of Texas brings an action which is carried through the courts and is ultimately decided by the Supreme Court in favor of the State of Texas. The President still says, "I insist that the authority of impoundment does not arise out of the statute, but out of my constitutional authority as President." He might make that insistence, and he might be sincere and he might make a contention that the right arises from a constitutional power of the presidency (incidentally, I don't think the President has any such constitutional power).

BLACK: No, I don't either.

ECKHARDT: He might make it in good faith. If he makes that contention and ignores the Supreme Court decision, has he committed an impeachable offense? If he hasn't committed an impeachable offense, how can a constitutional mandate ever be enforced against the executive?

BLACK: There are several answers to that. I would think that the time would come when a decision of the Supreme Court in such case would have to be regarded as settling the *law*, so that a constitutional opinion to the contrary could not be as a matter of law considered to be *bona fide*. Such cases would occur, and you have probably stated one. Further, Congress in future legislation could make it so clear where his duty lay that the President might then be in a position of proceeding at his own peril when he just flatly refused, on grounds of ultimate executive authority, to make a disbursement. Here it might well be that the concept of a good-faith mistake would no longer apply. Another possible solution is the one that has been used, as far as I know, on many occasions where presidential authority was questioned. That is an action in the courts against the *subordinate official* responsible for the disbursement, to get the money from him, and then holding him in contempt and punishing him for contempt if he didn't obey the order of the court.

ECKHARDT: I think that we've pretty well covered the reasons that led the Committee to drop the charge based on impoundment.

BLACK: All this brings me to examining the generality that I have heard expressed in public to the effect that executive power has grown too much, and that we now must call a halt, and therefore that we must start impeaching more freely. In the case of Nixon, there may have been entirely adequate grounds for impeachment and I am not addressing myself to that one case, but on this line, it seems to me, Congress almost always has a very great deal that it can do before it starts impeaching. As we have perhaps implied before, it is a part of political wisdom (and it really is a part, in a way, of the definition of "high Crimes and Misdemeanors") that Congress try to do what it can in milder ways before it treats the actions of the President as criminal.

ECKHARDT: Yes, a good example of that is anti-impoundment legislation. It gives authority to Congress through its agents to identify areas in which Congress takes the position that the impoundment is in violation of the statute, and then if the President does not expend the funds, either House may declare that those funds should be expended. The President's refusal to spend the funds after that time, it would seem to me, would be entirely improper. But even then, before impeachment should be resorted to, injunctive and mandatory processes can be started to get some kind of adjudication finally determining the right.

BLACK: As long as you have proper parties to such a case—and that would be a case where there are identifiable persons or entities to whom the money was to be disbursed. It seems to me that this idea of congressional action is one which is applicable pretty much down the line on these impeachable offenses. Congress has recently passed a so-called War Powers Bill, which in the most complicated and

Catch-22 sort of way is very easily susceptible of the construction that it frees the President even more than he had been freed before. It was indeed so interpreted tentatively by the Secretary of State, when he conjectured that it might authorize the reopening of the Cambodian bombing. By matching sections up, I think what one discovers is that the bill positively authorizes or at least pretty well immunizes the President for what he might do for sixty days, which, of course, is the crucial sixty days. In ten minutes you can put the country in such a situation that war is inevitable, and the Congress really has no practical alternative. Now I have suggested and you have suggested, in our separate forums, that some attempt ought to be made by Congress to define the circumstances under which the President may commit the United States forces to war for so much as ten minutes, and those in which he may not—and the latter is probably the more important. I have been met on public occasions with the claim that you can't do that, that there is no way to define these things in advance. But that is a counsel of despair, because if there is really nothing meaningful that can be said about this, if there is no possible definition of even a partial area in which the President would be behaving wrongfully if he committed United States forces, obviously you cannot expect *him* to know. You can't fault him *after* the event if there is no way in the world to state *before* the event what he can do. Congress could, I think, usefully act in this area, could do a great deal more than it has done in the so-called War Powers Resolution which was passed recently, and I think it should do that. That is the step Congress should take in resuming its power over war and peace, instead of just inveighing against the President, or finally impeaching him for doing something which by now has ample precedents on the part of many of his predecessors, however unfortunate those precedents may be. Congress ought to step in and put a stop to this, and *then* if the President acts in a manner that contravenes legislation, his conviction on impeachment would meet one of the most important and crucial elements of fairness: he would have had warning in advance, warning of what the other branch of government considers unconstitutional and wrong.

ECKHARDT: When Congress gets in this area, it operates in very dangerous waters, like a sea mined with torpedoes, because it can give away power, it can delegate some of its own war-declaring power to the President, but it can't take from the President his constitutional authority to direct forces, so anything it does can diminish its constitutional authority, and nothing it does can enlarge it.

BLACK: I am not at all sure of that as a constitutional proposition. The President has the duty to take care that the *laws* be faithfully executed. It is not clear to me that Congress can make no "law" having to do with the disposition of the armed forces. I think it is *practically* a dangerous sphere for Congress to enter, but I recall that there was a draft act passed in 1940 which forbade the use of the drafted soldiers outside the western hemisphere. Now that was an Act of Congress, and I don't think anybody questioned its constitutionality. They just argued about whether Iceland was in the western hemisphere.

ECKHARDT: I don't question that either.

BLACK: Then Congress can act in such a way as to limit his power. We can agree that there are some ways, and Congress could at least explore them.

ECKHARDT: The important, practical thing about defining the limitations of presidential power in the statute is that it is the only way you can then call upon the President to report immediately to Congress, so that Congress as a practical matter can act so as to disengage or to declare its lack of having given authority to engage troops.

BLACK: The War Powers Bill that was passed does that.

ECKHARDT: It does more than that. It purports to define a kind of gray area, and it says that within this gray area the President may act for sixty days (I'm paraphrasing all this).

BLACK: It also provides that Congress can pull him out.

ECKHARDT: It doesn't say that Congress can pull him out. Let me put it this way—Congress can pull him out by a concurrent resolution, and the concurrent resolution is presumably not veto-able; if it were veto-able, of course, it would have no real effect. The implication is that the Act grants authority which is conditioned on a subsequent event or subsequent action by Congress. If that be so, then some authority beyond the authority which the President had in the beginning must be implied. Now I argued this on the floor when this Act was up.

BLACK: We had better get a couple of things straight. It should be made clear, if it is true, that there is no way in which Congress can limit the President with respect to the initial commitment of forces to a hostile situation. If it is true, then we ought to admit that, and cease to criticize him for anything he does, because if Congress can't state the principles which ought to govern, can't even state extreme cases or partial areas in which such commitment would be wrongful, then I don't see how we can expect the President to know where it will be wrong. One of the real resistances to putting this into words is that everybody is afraid his ox is going to be gored. People who attack the Cambodian bombing on constitutional grounds, when what they really objected to was the bombing on the merits, don't want to tie the President's hands to the point where he cannot send forces into the Middle East, if that should become necessary in his (and their) view. Very few people are really willing to impose on the President this kind of across-the-board abstinence, and without any question as to the merits of the war that he might be getting us into.

ECKHARDT: When we passed the War Powers Act, we passed it to fit the situation in the Vietnam war, and Congress is naturally taking the position that the President was at fault and that Congress was not at fault, and therefore that Congress needs more legislative, legal machinery to protect itself. That is very questionable, because, without the War Powers Act, Congress could have done even more powerfully everything the War Powers Act permits. For instance, it could have cut off funds.

BLACK: In order to do that so as to be veto-proof, it's got to wait until the next time that funds are needed from Congress, and that usually isn't very long. I have thought consistently that a great deal of the opposition to the Vietnam war in Congress was really play-acting, that Congress had all kinds of powers it could have used at any time to bring that conflict to a fairly prompt halt. I would recur there to your suggestion of a concurrent resolution.

A concurrent resolution does not have the force of law, and for that reason it is not veto-able, but if Congress had really wanted to get this country out of the Vietnam war, it might at least have passed a strongly worded concurrent resolution stating the sense of Congress to be that we ought not to be in that war, and that we ought to get out as soon as possible. The effect of that resolution would have been enormous. It would have been very difficult for a President to go on drafting people, for example, after a thing like that had been put on the record by the American Congress. But they didn't do it.

Unfortunately, the Vietnam war, as long as we stayed in it, was simply an expression of democracy at work. Every poll, close to the very end, showed that the majority of the people wanted to fight it and win it, at least the majority of those with an opinion. I think Congress was reacting to that, and at the same time trying to pass the blame on to the President.

ECKHARDT: Let's keep on war powers for a minute. We come to about the same conclusion in this area of exceeding constitutional authority as we did with respect to impoundment: after all other remedies have been exhausted, and after authority at the highest level has determined that the activity of the President is a wrongful, persistent breach of the Constitution which cannot be stemmed in any other way, this may bring Congress legitimately to impeachment.

BLACK: It stands to reason, given the general nature of law and of politics, that it is sensible to use the milder remedies first; it is sensible with respect to a proceeding which is even quasi-criminal or has any of the flavor at all of criminality. Perhaps even in many civil proceedings, but certainly in any proceedings that are penal in nature, you ought to try to give the maximum notice you can under the circumstances. You can't always do it, and I think it would be a great mistake for Congress to codify the whole law of impeachment or of impeachable offenses, because if we got a really bad President such a code would become, in the Shakespearean phrase, his perch and not his terror. He would find ways between the planks to do what he wanted to.

But I think Congress could act usefully at many junctures and in many ways to clarify its own position, and then, as a matter of good political sense, and sound action under law, it could proceed with much greater sense of fairness to find conduct that contravenes this expressed understanding to be within the "high Crimes and Misdemeanors" phrase. Beyond that, there are some areas in which specific statutes could be passed, and either signed by a President who is in agreement with them or passed over his veto, which would make certain actions on the part of the President unlawful.

ECKHARDT: That's what appeared in my offered substitute to the War Powers Act—a clear warning to the President that overstepping these authorities, after Congress had expressed itself by concurrent resolution, would be considered most seriously as to whether the President had faithfully executed the law.

BLACK: You stated explicitly that such resumption would be a gross abuse of power, raising serious questions under the impeachment Article.

ECKHARDT: That's the kind of warning we have been talking about.

Let me bring up one other area in which the President is deemed to have attempted to subvert constitutional authority and law, the President's insisting on executive privilege in the extreme case, the case in which he is himself being impeached or tried under impeachment. He refused to produce evidence that the trier of fact or the impeaching authority thought necessary in order to determine relevant facts concerning impeachment. Now clearly Congress has to be the ultimate authority to determine what is material. I can't imagine it being ultimately determined by a court.

BLACK: No, I don't think the courts have any part to play in impeachment, none whatever.

ECKHARDT: But suppose Congress determines that certain facts—and suppose it is a reasonable determination—are relevant to the proceeding, but the President insists on his constitutional authority under the doctrine of separation of powers not to reveal information that he considers to be within executive privilege. Now, when the showdown is clear and final, and at the point where Congress has insisted on having material which it has clearly identified, there is no longer any question of whether or not an alternative might conceivably be a reasonable compromise and thus acceptable. I think he properly exercises his own judgment as to what is appropriately considered an in-house conversation[6] concerning a matter not related to the subject matter involved, but ultimately Congress has got to decide that issue when it is acting in impeachment proceeding. If Congress then declares that the President has been in contempt of the subpoena, it seems to me that the President's persistence in preventing the trial of the case on the evidence that Congress has determined to be appropriate, is in itself an impeachable offense.

BLACK: I would reply to that in the affirmative with greater alacrity if the *relevance* of the material were the only consideration. There are two grounds of executive privilege. One is the maintenance of secrecy as to material the secrecy of which is important to the United States, and the other (and I think this is a very weighty interest and one of great importance) is the maintenance of integrity of the consultative process, so that people who are talking to the President will not constantly have to fear that everything they say may at any time be revealed under some kind of subpoena and consequently put on parade, so that they will not discuss things with frankness. Now, I think that it's a kind of dry question whether the second of these reasons ought to be respected by Congress in an impeachment hearing, because I don't think it possible that the Congress will in fact respect it, and I don't think there is any authority on it.

On the other hand, I do think that the ultimate national interest in secrecy, as to national security material, presents some very difficult issues. Let's suppose that somebody, of about the credibility

6. The case of *U.S. v. Nixon,* 418 U.S. 683 (1974) was decided after this dialogue. While that case must be regarded as establishing, for now, that the protection of the confidentiality of presidential discussions is not absolute, at least where "national security" is not involved, great constitutional questions of this kind are never wholly closed off; we have therefore thought it best to let our earlier exchange stand.

and character, say, of John Dean, charged that during the airlift in the Middle Eastern War of October 1973 and during the alert declared therein, the President, in multiple ways, acted improperly, perhaps that he denuded the United States of its defenses, let's say with SAM Missiles, and also that he consciously and deliberately used the alert as a means of bolstering his own political position. I take it that both of those things would be offenses that one would begin to think of as possibly impeachable, gross abuses of power. Now let's suppose that a House Committee investigating these charges were to subpoena the records of every conversation that the President had on this subject with anybody, including Golda Meir and Moshe Dayan, during the period in question, and also the complete military records of the tactical disposition and capabilities of all our forces and weapons during that period. I think it might well be that a President would have to refuse that subpoena, and that Congress would then have a most difficult question—the House of Representatives, that is, would have a most difficult question. There wouldn't be any question whatever about "relevance" and that's why I say that relevance is not all that is at stake. No question whatever but that all this stuff that was subpoenaed would be strictly relevant to the charges, not the slightest, it's exactly what you need to evaluate such a charge. The question would rather be whether it was protected by a privilege *even though relevant,* which, of course, is the usual thrust of a privilege. A privilege protects the disclosure of material even when it is relevant; the question of privilege need not even arise if material is not relevant. At least if you can make a guess in advance that it is not relevant, you don't have to judge on whether it's also privileged, because it doesn't come in anyway. So, I take this case as one where the material is clearly relevant. Wouldn't you think there is a problem there about what a President ought to do in those circumstances, even in an impeachment inquiry?

ECKHARDT: Sure. I think he should refuse to produce the information.

BLACK: Then do you think he should be impeached for that? For his refusal?

ECKHARDT: Well, that depends. The House might consider this an impeachable offense, might consider the importance of determining the issue of the President's fidelity, and the issue of whether or not he committed a crime or misdemeanor by denuding the country of its defenses, as a much more important matter than some historic condition of military tactics and strategy.

BLACK: Historic conditions when they are that recent can have a hell of a lot of bite. The Russians would sure like to know what all our weapons could do, and how many we had, and where, a year ago.

ECKHARDT: If you want to make the extreme case, let it also include certain information about the location and disposition of nuclear submarines.

BLACK: Certainly. That's all quite relevant to the question whether the United States has been denuded of necessary defenses.

ECKHARDT: Some of these very arguments would be raised by the President. He could not even say what would be revealed, because in saying that, he would give some information that might be vital to our defenses.

BLACK: I find this a terrible dilemma because it's also a danger to the United States to leave in office a President who habitually will denude the country of its defenses. Let me make clear, this is an imaginary case. I have no reason to think that it happened. It's just a hypothetical case.

ECKHARDT: The question poses difficult questions of balance, but when you consider it step by step and procedurally it's not something that can't be taken care of by our processes of impeachment. I would assume what would happen is that the House would weigh these factors and would come to a conclusion one way or another. If the case were put very strongly by the President, it's most unlikely that the House would insist on using the failure of the President to produce these materials as grounds for impeachment. Everybody with final power can of course act wrongly. The Supreme Court can act unjustly, though it may be the final arbiter of a question.

BLACK: More people are involved in the case of the House, and it's also unlikely that the courts are ever really going to ask for this kind of information, or that despite all the general and loose talk about executive privilege being totally absent, a court would hold that the President could not withhold information like this.

ECKHARDT: Suppose the House does decide that this is an impeachable offense, and, therefore, brings an impeachment. It's the Senate then that ultimately determines these issues. The Senate would hear facts that would not include the substance of the material invited—except that the Senate might set up certain *in camera* processes to examine what was actually involved. And I see no more reason why, for instance, designated persons representative of the Senate for having this information in their heads should be more dangerous than, for instance, half a dozen generals and clerks in the Pentagon. So, I don't think the question is all that hard. It's one in which the President might act entirely properly in refusing to produce the information, even to the extent of resulting in the bringing of impeachment in the House.

BLACK: I suppose in the end there would be other things that would come into play in the President's mind. There might be reached a point where in effect he would just have to go into civil disobedience, he would have to say, "I cannot reveal this material, it's incompatible with my duty and I must take the consequences whatever they may be." On the other hand, the judgment would have to be made by the Senate—and this is probably the most difficult possible judgment, but I think it is one that might very well have to be made finally in good faith whether the refusal itself is really in good faith.

We have traversed a good go-round, the question of law of impeachable offenses, and I think that we might move on to a question on which I'm not sure we'll find agreement, the question of *burden of proof* in the case of impeachment. Now there has been a lot of ink spilled on the question of whether an impeachment process is or is not "criminal." I think that is mostly wasted ink, because it is a matter of a label, and it doesn't really make very much difference what you label this procedure. The question really is, "What standards of establishment of fact and law are to be applied to it?" Now as to the establishment of law, that is to say, as to the determination whether some given offense—assuming its being proved—is impeachable, I think we've said enough and there's no real problem about that except what is inherent in any legal process of construing a rather vague standard. But there still remains the problem of the *proof* of the facts, the proof not only of physical facts, but also such crucial facts as the state of mind of a person who is doing a certain thing—with what intent and what animus an act was performed. The law has to inquire into these matters every day, and in a criminal case we do say that the "reasonable doubt" standard must be applied—that the guilt of the accused must be established beyond a reasonable doubt. Now I think—entirely leaving the question of whether we're going to call impeachment a criminal proceeding—we'd still face the question of how high a standard of proof of the facts of the case the Senate ought to apply when it comes to try the issue. I think we may not really be at one on that.

ECKHARDT: You can't entirely divorce this question from the question of the seriousness, with respect to processes of government, of the act in the first place. Whether the act be a criminal offense or a high misdemeanor, it must be of an extremely important nature, and it must have a bearing on the processes of government in a very destructive way, so as to impede the processes of government. This might not be the sole test, but it must be at least part of it. Having established a quite high standard as to the *offenses* to which impeachment would apply, I would then say that *proof* of those facts should be simply on the basis of a preponderance of the evidence. The reason I say that is because I see no reason for using proof "beyond a reasonable doubt" in any case criminal or civil, except for one fact, and that is, that we have a strong predilection against taking away from a man his life or his liberty in any event. And I don't feel that same compunction with respect to taking away a man's office.

BLACK: Well, I think I do. We are in clear disagreement on this. I would not insist on the standard of reasonable doubt—that is, that the charge be proved beyond a reasonable doubt—largely because I don't think that standard has proven to be meaningful, and I don't think that in its ordinary colloquial sense it actually does prevail in a great many criminal trials. I do think that a standard perhaps like the one necessary to reform a written instrument—that is, *clear and convincing evidence,* or, say, a *decided* preponderance of the definite evidence—should be required.

I have two reasons for that. The first is that I don't think that it is true that you are not depriving the individual of something of great value. The impeachment not only deprives him of his office, it may also go further and commonly does, and disqualifies him from any further holding of office, which is a definite punishment well known to criminal law. It inflicts upon him a great dishonor. The other one is political. The man in the office of the President has been elected by the people for that office. *They* are parties in interest in this. By the regular constitutional means—and I brush aside public opinion polls and all that sort of thing—by the regular means provided by our Constitution, the people of the United States have chosen this man to be President. There's a strange attitude one hears—I think we're still fighting George III in a sense, because the President is often referred to, even in some Supreme Court opinions, as though he were some kind of hereditary autocrat, while democracy is seen as being represented by the Congress. This comes closer to being the reverse of the truth than correct. It isn't quite the reverse of the truth, but the fact is that the most meaningful political choice that most people make in the United States is their choice of the President. Now it seems to me unfortunate that he should be removed from office in contravention of this exceedingly important democratic choice unless there is a very strong preponderance of the evidence to the effect that he committed the impeachable act.

Another reason is really practical, and it wouldn't work every time, but I think it often would work, and that is that while impeachment and removal themselves are not party political matters—and I think they shouldn't be, and I myself do trust to the honesty of the people who are conducting them, that they will not be when they reach the impeachment stage—it nevertheless is far more likely that the stage at which impeachment is considered will be reached when the Congress and the President are at loggerheads politically. The two examples of near-removal that we have in our history were exactly like that, and I think that is true because the *initial* investigative processes are likely to probe much more deeply when the opposition party is in control of Congress. Now what this means is that very often people will be judging the evidence, judging the weight of evidence, who are in political opposition to the President. They are, to be quite frank about it, almost all people who would be disqualified in a court of law on the ground that they have a definite antagonistic relationship with the person who is being tried. That can't be avoided. But it seems to me that it's wise for such people to give to themselves (and they are the only ones who can do it because nobody can second-guess them on it) a very high standard of proof, and not the kind of standard that prevails in a civil trial, where, for example, you hear two witnesses and you decide which one of them to believe.

ECKHARDT: I suppose it is very difficult to distinguish between burden of proof and the level of the offense as originally established. For instance, when we were discussing this question of gross negligence, and when we were discussing this question of the wink or the nod, with the intentional delegation of authority but without explicit knowledge of what the delegation would lead to, and when we were saying that this would have to be of an extreme nature, something more than the common level of negligence, that it would have to be quite clear that there was, in fact, complicity in the act, we were touching on the question of proof, but in another context. We also were defining the level of the offense. Perhaps what we're really saying is the same thing, but approaching it in different ways. However, I would still say that once you require the offense to be at a very high level of seriousness, I would prefer not to talk about burden of proof, because I think there is a very grave danger that Congress, particularly the Senate (because the Senate would ultimately try the case) would do what criminal courts, or district attorneys, frequently do, simply slide off of the important allegation of a very serious offense back to something of less importance but still deemed to be an impeachable offense.

BLACK: Let's suppose that there were two counts, two articles of impeachment which are equivalent to two counts in an indictment. The first one was an allegation that a President has distinctly authorized the payment of hush-money to people who were about to go on trial for an offense of burglary in order to stop their mouths and prevent them from revealing the truth about this incident—a very serious offense. The other was that he had used too much money for a wall at his home. The second of those was clearly established and had no problem about it. And suppose that the proof on the first one stood as follows: that there were no tapes. (It will always remain a mystery, I think, why there were any tapes in the Nixon case; I don't know why in the world they were ever made.) Let's suppose a normal situation where there were no tapes and the person, one person, let's call him John Dean, or any other imaginary name, testifies that the President said, "Pay these fellows the money," and another person testifies, there being just the three people present, that the President didn't say this, that this subject didn't come up in this conversation.

Now on that state of proof, as to this first serious count, in a civil case the jury would be told to decide which of these two people it believed and to decide the case on the basis of a 50.0001 percent probability, one way or another. I had rather see the Senate go to this second offense and face the issue of its substantiality or of its pettiness, than to see the Senate make up its mind as a jury would as to which of these two people is telling the truth just by "demeanor evidence." And, despite all the talk about "demeanor evidence," we both know that there is nothing in it, that there really isn't any way to tell which of two people is telling the truth, that we pretend that there is just because we have to decide cases one way or another. I'd rather see the Senate pass over that count, and treat it as unproven, and then address itself to the question of whether this other offense was substantial enough. I'm trying to test whether you really believe in sticking to the standard of proof that prevails in a civil law suit, for purposes of impeaching and removing the President. That's a question quite distinct from whether it is a criminal procedure, because we impose greater standards than this even in some civil law suits. For example, if you want to reform a written instrument on the ground that it doesn't correctly embody the intention of the parties, you have to come in with more than just contradictory testimony.

ECKHARDT: Now let me go back to these facts you stated. This may be somewhat shocking, but I don't necessarily find the facts that you described, if proved, grounds for impeachment. For instance, had the President said, "I made a mistake, I set up a force that I thought was necessary for the security of the United States; it got out of hand. People engaged in activity that was clearly criminal. In order to protect these persons who, I thought, were acting honorably and in accordance with what they considered a presidential directive, but extralegally (they really felt it was extralegal with respect to ordinary law, but that ordinary law was suspended by a presidential directive), I found myself in the very difficult position of having to do what could be done to protect persons whom I alone knew to be without culpability. Yes, I paid hush-money, I may have been wrong." Now I'm not sure that is really an impeachable offense.

BLACK: Well, I think with all respect that that's a little diversionary, because I can make up an offense which would clearly be impeachable with the same proof problem about it. Let's suppose that one person testifies that the President said, "X's mouth has got to be stopped, and I don't care if you have to kill him." And in the morning that person is found murdered in a ditch, and another person was present at the same conversation and says, "That's absolutely absurd, nothing like that was said on that occasion by the President to anybody, this is sheer fabrication." Now again you have the testimony of two witnesses, and you have what beyond any doubt would be an impeachable offense.

ECKHARDT: I would impeach and remove, in such a case, on the preponderance of the evidence, because I think that if on balance the evidence falls against the President it would be extremely dangerous to have a man in the presidency who is held guilty of such an offense even on an ordinary "preponderance" basis of proof, and I feel that the interests of the public in removing such a man from the presidency are greater than the interests of deliberation and caution in protecting a possibly innocent man, and in preventing possibly precipitous change in government, which itself would be bad from the standpoint of policy.

BLACK: I think we'd have to leave this with a state of disagreement and pass on to what I think is the last stage in the question of impeachment, and where I think we probably can agree, and that is the function of the judiciary in impeachment process. It seems to me that it's a politically incredible proposition that a President who had been impeached by the deliberate processes of the House of Representatives, Articles of Impeachment drawn and voted up by the House, who had then stood his trial in the Senate, with a two-thirds majority required for conviction, and who was then convicted and sentenced to removal from office, should then be put back in office by the Supreme Court of the United States. That seems to me out of all question a political absurdity.

With what legitimacy could such a man govern? If the Constitution explicitly and clearly commanded such a result, then I think we would all be scurrying around to try to find some way out of it, as we do out of the Amendment[7] which says that everybody is entitled to keep and bear arms; we try not to make that applicable to sawed-off shotguns. But the Constitution doesn't command any such a thing. It's to be drawn out of the Constitution only by the remotest and most conjectural kind of inferences. What the Constitution says is that the Senate should have the power to try all impeachments. As to any further judicial or other activity on it, nothing whatever is said. I just can't conceive that the courts have any useful role or any constitutional role to play in this process at all.

ECKHARDT: Well, I can't either. The question of the grounds for impeachment must be determined with something like judicial standards, and it may not be anything like a bill of attainder. Then one comes, I think, to this question: "But what if Congress violated this standard; and isn't Congress so politically motivated that it is likely to do so?" But I don't think it necessarily follows that the judiciary must be involved. It would create an impossible procedure, an impossible

7. Amendment II.

result, to permit the Supreme Court, for instance, ultimately to overturn the Senate, because the President must have a relationship much
more closely with Congress than he need ever have with the Supreme
Court, and his relationships would be utterly destroyed by the fact
of impeachment and conviction.

BLACK: His relationship with Congress would be destroyed, his
relationship with the people would be destroyed, his prestige as a
leader in foreign affairs would be destroyed, everything about him
would be destroyed; it's simply the kind of absurd result which you
reach in constitutional law only if the words of the text grab you by
the throat and force you there. The first maxim of constitutional construction, where any room is left for construction, is that it has to
make sense, it has to make some political sense, and judicial review
of an impeachment doesn't make any kind of sense.

ECKHARDT: Besides that, of course, the whole question would remain in the air even if the Supreme Court did purport to overturn
what the Senate had ultimately done. I can't conceive of the Senate
ever accepting the validity of the Supreme Court ruling.

BLACK: The unspoken major premise behind all this judicial review nonsense is that there is no way to get due process of law except
by going into court. It is thought to be absolutely hopeless to get due
process in any other way. I think the Constitution, not unreasonably,
confides to the House and Senate the job of bringing about that due
process of law be observed. Somebody, after all, has to make the final
determination.

ECKHARDT: Moreover, though both you and I have likened this
process to ordinary civil and criminal cases, neither one of us treats
it as an ordinary criminal or civil case. It's an entirely separate category, a different authority for determining a set of facts which result
in removal from office.

BLACK: If we cannot, in a solemn case which is confided explicitly to them by the Constitution, trust the House of Representatives,
operating first through its Judiciary Committee and then on the Floor,
and then the Senate, operating as a court on special oath, with the
Chief Justice of the United States presiding—if we can't trust these

people to behave fairly and make an honest good-faith attempt to resolve these questions in a lawful manner, then why in the world should we think they can be so resolved somewhere else?

ECKHARDT: Doesn't nearly two hundred years of American history, with only two cases concerning impeachment of the President ever being brought anywhere near to culmination, tell us something, don't they tell us that Congress is certainly not quick to jump to the use of impeachment as a political process?

BLACK: It's very evident that it is done with a very great distaste and anytime we get a Congress that doesn't behave that way, a Congress that would do it with alacrity, we are pretty well lost anyway. It seems to me plain that this responsibility is confided *finally* to Congress.

*

5 THE LIMITS OF THE JUDICIARY

BLACK: Americans in recent times have had a sense that we are in some way at a deep crisis in our constitutionalism, and that all facets of our government should be put under examination and talked about, with a view to considering what part they can play in what quite honestly will have to be a work of rehabilitation. Now the judiciary plays a very great part in our government, both through its inevitable role as the interpreter of statutes passed by Congress and through its peculiarly American role as reviewer of the constitutionality of both congressional and state legislation, as well as of other governmental activity, including administrative activity on both state and national levels. Although we are not now especially feeling any pain with regard to the judiciary—although the other departments of government, particularly the executive department, are taking most of the flack—I think we really need at this point to reconsider quite deeply the use that we are increasingly making of our judiciary.

I would start with the thesis that in recent times, amongst many people of good will, the process of reasoning by which we let the courts into the business of passing on the constitutional validity of governmental action has been turned entirely on its head. Let me just say briefly what I mean, and then you might comment on it.

We need to be reminded continually of one simple scheme of reasoning. It may happen, in an ordinary lawsuit of any kind, that one of the litigants relies for the support of his position in the lawsuit on some action of some branch of either the state or federal government. The simplest case perhaps would be reliance on an Act of Congress. It may be that his adversary in the lawsuit will claim that the Act of Congress is unconstitutional. The Constitution is a *law*, since it says on its face that it is a law, and it is clearly a superior law to other enactments. It must therefore prevail over other governmental acts, including an Act of Congress. An Act of Congress which is repugnant to the Constitution must therefore be treated as void.

The fact that the lawsuit has been brought, as lawsuits regularly are, into a court, has meant with us, and I think quite legitimately, that when this situation occurs, or when any one of the innumerable variations on it occur, the court decides the question of constitutionality, because it reaches it in an ordinary lawsuit, and has no alternative to deciding it. The Constitution is a part of the law, and a court which meets a question of law under the Constitution in a lawsuit must decide that question. That is the simple line of reasoning that underlies all justification of judicial review for constitutionality, from Federalist No. 78 and even before, right down to the present day—or almost to the present day.

The one essential in this reasoning is the thing that is beginning to undergo a radical change, and that is the concept of the lawsuit—what it takes to make an ordinary lawsuit. It seems to me that a very serious thing has happened in recent years to this plain and entirely legitimate pattern of reasoning. I can put it in simple terms, but I think accurate terms, by saying that there is a very strong tendency not to look for the existence of anything that you or I could recognize as a lawsuit, as a prerequisite to a court's considering a constitutional question, but rather to insist that some kind of a lawsuit *must* be devised and endorsed by the courts if a constitutional question is at issue. Now this is why I say that this new line of thought stands the doctrine of judicial review on its head. One is no longer saying that the courts, in those cases where constitutional questions inevitably come up, have to decide those questions, but rather that if there is a constitutional question at large in the nation, then some kind of a lawsuit must be devised to bring it about that the courts decide that question.

ECKHARDT: The thought is that constitutional abuse must be rectified whether or not the judicial process properly is invoked by a specific case.

BLACK: The new thought is that it must be rectified *by the judiciary*. I consider it an entirely illegitimate conclusion from anything in our Constitution, or from anything in our traditions, that whenever a constitutional question arises—even where there is no personal interest on the part of any litigant in the outcome—we must somehow bring it about that this question be decided in court.

I can give you examples of this. I think the watershed case was the case of *Flast v. Cohen*,[1] which was decided some years ago, I believe in 1968, and which held that a *taxpayer* had the "standing"[2] to bring a lawsuit to enjoin the expenditure of federal money for the support of parochial schools. I am not concerned now at all with whether or not such an expenditure was *constitutional*. I am concerned with the kind of a lawsuit in which that question arises. The simple and perfectly obvious fact is that nobody really expects to pay more or less taxes on the basis of there being expended, or not expended, money for the support of parochial schools. That's not the way the government runs; that's not the way the budget is made up. The taxpayer in that suit cannot have made any showing, even to a small degree of probability, that he would be out money, if that money was spent. He is accepted as sort of a representative of the public, to bring this issue before the courts. To me that radically changes the entire structure and thrust of judicial review.

ECKHARDT: What about the same attitude concerning *Baker v. Carr*[3]—how is that any different? A single voter's interest in the districting of a state legislature is a relatively dilute interest.

BLACK: I think that *Baker v. Carr* was a borderline case on the "standing" issue. I would be willing, with some misgivings, to accord

1. 292 U.S. 83 (1968).
2. "Standing" is a shorthand term for the requirement that, in any lawsuit, a litigant must have something to gain or lose, depending on the outcome. The doctrine has many ramifications, and the word even has another, more technical meaning not necessary to be considered here.
3. 369 U.S. 186 (1962). It was held that a voter had "standing" to bring suit to force equalization of population in legislative districts, or at least to force the administration by the court of some remedy for the mass population inequalities that formerly existed.

standing in a case of that type, on the ground that the voter is a member of a large class which, because of very substantial differences in
voting power, will probably suffer through lack of proportionate influence in the government. I don't think that the jump from that kind
of conjecture to federal taxpayer's standing is warranted. This taxpayer is not in any position that distinguishes him from a member of
the general public, and we all know that he's suing, in truth, only
because he's discontented with the way the government is run, and
not because he himself is suffering any injury, however small.

ECKHARDT: But don't you think that *Flast v. Cohen* rested on cases
like *Baker v. Carr*, perhaps drawing the wrong analogies?

BLACK: I think that there is a discernible difference on the standing
issue alone between the cases of *Baker v. Carr* and *Flast v. Cohen*.

ECKHARDT: I am not disputing that. All I am saying is that it
seems to me that the movement toward liberality in "standing" at
least found a steppingstone in *Baker v. Carr*, which might have been
a good ways short of *Flast v. Cohen*, but at least directed the development of the law of standing toward almost unrestricted liberality.

BLACK: Yes, as a historical matter, as a matter of intellectual history, that might well be so, but I think when we reach *Flast v. Cohen*,
we reach a terminal point. It seems to me that whatever may be the
case as to *Baker v. Carr*, however much they had to *stretch* the concept of standing to cover *Baker v. Carr*, the concept is no longer being
stretched, it is simply being disregarded, given nothing but lip service,
in a case like *Flast v. Cohen*.

ECKHARDT: But what about an environmental case in which, for
instance, someone who hunts in the area, simply enjoys nature in the
general area where a power generating plant is planned to be built,
goes to court to enjoin the building of the plant or to enforce certain
regulations of the EPA?

BLACK: I think we have a different question there from standing.
If a man can establish that it is his custom and wont to frequent a
certain part of the world, and that he has the legal right to do so, and
that an act of a defendant will interfere with his enjoyment of this
right, then he has a standing at least as great as that in *Baker v. Carr*.

In many environmental cases there is simply no warrant in *substantive* constitutional law for concluding that the Constitution of the United States in any way speaks to the issues that are drawn. These are usually questions as to what is the wisest and best balance to strike between certain environmentalist concerns and certain economic concerns, reaching all the way to the relief of poverty in the big cities. Such concerns are all legitimate and worthy, but they are concerns between which the Constitution, as far as I can see, doesn't choose.

ECKHARDT: Of course there are also the *statutory* environmental cases, particularly those arising under the Clean Air Act. The statute specifically states that its purposes are for the protection of the persons in the nature of the man who is hunting.

BLACK: Of course, that's a quite different question. Where Congress has enacted, first, that a certain choice is to be made between so-called environmentalist and other interests, and where it makes this choice within its own constitutional powers, and where, either by explicit designation or by implication, Congress makes the political decision that for its own purposes it wishes to create a class of private attorneys-general to enforce the statute, then the case is entirely different. In that case, the legislative branch has decided that this is what is wanted. I don't think the great bulk of the present expansion falls along those lines.

I do think, however, that as to some environmental issues another breaking point could be reached. I'm not familiar with the field in any detail, but I think the point could be reached where issues might be committed to the courts which are so thoroughly political, and so totally unamenable to settlement by the processes of law, that the courts should decline them on an entirely different ground, on the ground that no justiciable issue is presented. I think, for example, that if a judge were ever to be called on to decide what the best use is of the air in a certain locality, or whether it's better to have a power plant or to have an unpolluted river, he ought to decline to settle that issue, because it is not a legal issue; it is a pure political or policy issue and nothing else.

Let me give an example of the attitude that I think is beginning to prevail. The question of the Alaska pipeline came up. In the Congress of the United States a determination was made on this. It was perhaps unfortunately phrased in terms of an exemption from the standards of the environmental protection.

ECKHARDT: I don't think it was quite that. I think what we actually said in that case was that the initial determination favorable to the Alaska pipeline was approved, as a matter of statutory law. I didn't like that much because I thought once we set up the process to make a determination about environmental impact, with an environmental impact statement, we ought not vary it, just as a matter of policy.

BLACK: We hit here another area which at least on first impression seems to be an area of disagreement between us.

I would start all over again and say this, that if ever I heard of a question that ought to be decided by plenary deliberation in Congress and nowhere else, it's the question whether that pipeline should be built. It involved everything from the migratory habits of the caribou to the relations of the U.S. with the countries in the Middle East; it involved the location of industry in the U.S. I don't think a court has very much that is useful to contribute to this kind of a thing.

ECKHARDT: We not only circumvented the court action, but also circumvented the administrative action, plus court review. Now this is what had happened, as I recall, in that case. A court had thrown out the decision of the EPA favorable to the pipeline, because the EPA decision had ignored an old statute that said that a right-of-way for a pipeline shouldn't be greater than a certain number of feet in width; the court never got to the question of reviewing whether or not EPA followed correct standards with respect to the whole environmental question. Then, in the meantime, we came in and authorized the Alaska pipeline, reversed the silly statute that required the ridiculously narrow width. That was a perfectly right thing for us to do. But we also said you don't have to submit the question of whether proper process was followed to determine environmental issues. The original decision of the agency was statutorily approved, whether those processes were properly followed or not.

BLACK: With that procedure, probably the determination of what was right in the case fell between two stools, that is, nobody finally took it up as a plenary matter and considered it.

ECKHARDT: It became wholly a political question instead of a question for determination upon facts measured under preexisting legal standards.

BLACK: Insofar as this procedure with its confusion resulted in there not being any plenary consideration anywhere, then nobody could regard that as good. Of course, it's unfortunate if no consideration occurred. I think, to be sure, that that may not be altogether unconnected with an overreliance on courts. But what struck me at the time was that a great many editorials, and a great many comments that one read, attacked this determination not on the ground that it was wrong, but on the ground, rather, that it had not been made by a *court*—as though Congress were in some way cheating or breaking the rules of the game if it took a vast geopolitical question of this kind, having to do with ultimate concerns of the country, and finally decided it in Congress, without reference to any other body. Now, if Congress did that without adequate consideration, of course, that's quite irresponsible. But, I would still reiterate that the place for the decision to be made was distinctly and definitely in Congress, and not in a court.

ECKHARDT: By the way, sometimes Congress at least proposes, or one House of Congress may propose, a burden upon a court that is typically of congressional origin. An example of that was in the Product Safety Bill. That bill set up an agency to control product safety, and then, in the original Senate version, it provided for suits by individuals to call upon the agency to write a standard in an area that was within the reasonable scope of the bill. Under the bill, the court could then issue a directive to the agency to make a standard in that area, and then could review that standard as to its adequacy. Now, the first part of that I thought was all right.

BLACK: By the first part, you mean the part to the effect that a court could order the standard to be set up?

ECKHARDT: Not that it *be set up,* but that the commission *address* itself to the problem raised, and *either* set a standard *or* say why it wasn't doing so. This seemed to me sound, but to go further and use the court as an instrument for policy-making seems unsound.

BLACK: All along the line, we see erosion of the limits that have very soundly been set, by the very nature of the judicial process, on the use of that process. The recent *De Funis* case,[4] for example, was moot,[5] if ever I heard of one that was moot. It was not a class action; it was a suit by one man, who was already in the University of Washington Law School, for admission to the University of Washington Law School. He was actually about to graduate, and the Dean of the law school was willing to file a stipulation that, in the very unlikely event that he should fail his last term, to which he already had a contractual right, he would be allowed to return and finish his law school work and get his degree. So, he had absolutely nothing to gain, no relief whatever could be administered for his benefit, in that suit. It was all finished as far as he was concerned. The amazing thing to me is that four Justices of the Supreme Court refused to treat that case as moot. Fortunately, five actually did, and the appeal was dismissed on that ground. This was a case so clearly moot, a case so clearly with nothing at stake as regarded the litigant before the court, that De Funis himself, at the end of the lawsuit, at the time when he was already in this absolutely safe position, was just like any other member of the public who was asking the Court to issue a manifesto on the exceedingly difficult constitutional question of whether a state law school may follow a preferential admissions policy by way of compensation to the minorities, a question that's very very hard to handle.

ECKHARDT: He had a little more going for him, though. After all, he had expended his time and effort to get the case determined, and there seemed at least some reasonable justification for a court completing the process.

---

4. *De Funis v. Odegaard,* 416 U.S. 312 (1974).

5. A case is said to be "moot" when the situation has so changed that no relief is needed or possible, so that the litigants stand to gain or lose nothing, whatever the decision. The discussion of the *De Funis* case, in the text, will make the point clearer.

BLACK: It seems to me that that is exactly the way we lose sight of the analogy of the constitutional suit with the ordinary lawsuit. If a man were suing for a breach of a contract, suing for specific performance of a contract to sell land, and it was shown at some point in the lawsuit that the land had already been sold to him and that he was in peaceful possession of it, but for some reason he wanted to continue the lawsuit and get a judgment, then a court in the contract suit would simply dismiss this case, without any doubt of the rightness of this step. It would do that whether or not an interesting question of law was raised.

ECKHARDT: The court in the contract case would be wasting its time to determine the issue, because the determination now would be merely to satisfy a whim of the litigant. But it seems to me that the application of certain standards to the question of standing has a very good practical basis. If a person who has no real interest in the facts is permitted to establish the precedent which may be for all time, then a person who does have a real interest in the facts may be deprived of a right to try his case properly, and also to persuade the court that the case is important.

BLACK: It seems to me again, though, that we are losing sight of the *original justification* for this quite extraordinary American phenomenon of judicial review. We are speaking as though the questions governing whether the court should take a case were strictly prudential, whereas the bedrock legitimacy of judicial review (and it certainly has a wide scope over an enormous range of cases) rests on the presence of a lawsuit which is substantially similar, in adversity of interest and in the magnitude and substantiality of the interest affected, to other lawsuits, and is not a lawsuit brought into being simply because it is desirable that a court decide some question of law.

ECKHARDT: Let me just raise this question. Suppose that somebody brings a case like *Baker v. Carr,* and the case goes through the Court of Appeals, and an application for a writ of certiorari is acted on and then the plaintiff moves out of the district. Now, he had a very dilute interest in the case in the first place. It really is kind of theoretical to say that the fact that he now has moved out of the district really makes any difference. So, shouldn't the court decide the case anyway?

BLACK: Usually, those cases are class actions[6] which as you know raise very different procedural points. Once again, I am troubled by the standing question in *Baker v. Carr*. I'm not sure of where I would come out on it on total rethinking of that question, and I sure wouldn't want to reason from it to less substantial grounds for lawsuits. After all, as Justice Holmes said, all law as it becomes more civilized, becomes a question of degree. Of course, as to this standing question, there's got to be a question of degree. Now, somewhere along that line, unless we are prepared to convert the courts into organs of general government ready to act at the suit of any citizen to set things right, we've got to draw a line.

It worries me to think that we are just about ready for that use of courts, as to constitutional questions, or at least many people are ready. This is a trend that I very much deplore. It is of course possible to have a government in which the real governing authority is a body of tribunes who are selected at one remove from the democratic process, and this would characterize our judiciary, our federal judiciary in particular. It's entirely feasible to run society that way. The federal judges ran the New Haven Railroad for a long time. You could put the whole country into receivership and have it run by some real good United States District Judge. I think before we do that, or move much farther toward it, we ought to stop and take thought, and consider what that is likely to do to other institutions of government, and why it happens that we have gotten to this point at this time.

ECKHARDT: I must say it seems more reasonable for the Sierra Club to come into a case raising the question of environmental issues than someone who just happened to picnic on the land occasionally. The interest in the Sierra Club is a lot more real.

BLACK: To me, the answer to that question would depend again on whether Congress had made the determination that it was wise

6. A "class action" is a suit brought by one or more (almost always more) "named" plaintiffs, on behalf of the "class" of all similarly situated.

to have some of these questions settled in court. But I think there is a limit even on that. A lot of people make a mistake in this because they think that what bounds the possibility of judicial action is merely *procedure*. You can make up a lawsuit *procedurally* to bring about any result. It would be the easiest thing in the world, for example, as a matter merely of procedure, to join the members of Congress—of the Senate and House—as a class too numerous to name, as parties defendant, and to place them under an injunction to pass an appropriations bill, or to pass a bill giving me a pension for life. There is not the slightest procedural difficulty in this. The difficulty would be that a court at this stage of the game would say, or should say, that the question whether I should have a pension is a political question, and that the court will not in any case interfere in that depth with the operations of another branch of government.

We have to separate the question of whether we can think up an ingenious procedure by which a result can be brought about—which we always can, given the flexibility of modern procedure—from the question whether the subject is one on which the courts ought to be acting.

ECKHARDT: Maybe it's at that point that the cases should be cut off, and not at the level of standing. It strikes me that there is something salubrious about permitting generous rules of standing where the issue is one of common concern to a great body of the public, like the question, for instance, of the right to fair districting. I would think that if we go along with the courts' liberality on standing, but crack down at the level of whether or not the type of issues raised are issues the court can deal with at all. . . .

BLACK: I can't go along with that, because I think that there are some constitutional issues which are better left settled in Congress—which traditionally have been left settled in Congress—and I think that undoubtedly one of the most important of these issues, and indeed in some way the dominant issue in all government, is how money should be spent. That's one of the many reasons why I think *Flast v. Cohen* was such a breakthrough case.

Go back to the so-called American System in the days of Henry

Clay. There was a very serious question whether it was within the constitutional power of the federal government in those days to collect money mainly from the customs, and then to use it to effect internal improvements—canals, highways, and bridges. That was the "American System." So serious was this question that several Presidents —I think four—actually vetoed a bill directing expenditure for something like a highway or a bridge, on the ground that this was not within the constitutional power of the federal government. This sounds archaic to us now, but we have to remember that that was the locus of the line of dubiety at that time, and it's by no means certain that a Supreme Court would have upheld the expenditures if the question had been presented to them.

When we talk about the spending of money, simply spending money, as important as it is, I think what we have developed up until very recently in this country is a kind of a double track of constitutionality. When a governmental practice falls with some identifiable impact on a person, or even on a class of people, as in *Baker v. Carr* (which is the farthest verge of this concept to me), we have seen this situation as appropriate for judicial review, precisely because it is closely analogous to, or even identical with, an ordinary lawsuit. When nobody is hurt, but only money is being spent, a lighthouse being built, or a pension being given to a widow, or anything of that sort, we have confided solely to the political process the question whether this was constitutional or not. I think that was a good system.

The one we're moving into is apparently quite a different one, where every governmental action that has any importance—regardless of its impact on any individuals or even on any identifiable class—is to be subjected to judicial scrutiny on constitutional grounds. And if we don't have a lawsuit for that purpose, then we must make one up, or feel that some cheating is taking place. I repudiate that concept altogether. It clashes with another conception of the judicial function at its best. It seems to me, in the broadest civilized conception, that a court is a place to go for the redress of grievances, for relief from some kind of injustice. This presupposes some kind of a *sufferer,* either an individual sufferer or a class.

ECKHARDT: What was the style of the case that came up in Texas, also similar cases from other states, involving the contention that a tax-collecting system, for the purpose of financing schools which ultimately resulted in disproportionally high taxes to certain taxpayers, and disproportionally lower quality of schooling for certain children attending in certain districts, constituted unequal treatment and was violative of the Fourteenth Amendment?

BLACK: I don't know the full style. That's the *Rodriguez* case out of San Antonio.[7]

ECKHARDT: Now that seems to me to raise an extremely difficult question because, on the merits, the case exhibits an evil crying for remedy. But it seems almost impossible to afford that remedy judicially, because what it calls for is not only a revision of local school laws and local school taxes, but also state taxes. On what grounds was that case reversed?

BLACK: I have forgotten exactly the grounds on which it was reversed, but I think that it marks another danger in this relaxation of the standards of standing to sue. Probably there was nobody in those cases who really was in a position to make out that he or even a class of which he was a member was actually going to be hurt by what was being done.

Now the trouble with a case like that is that when a court takes it without actually any justiciable standards to administer, without any but the vaguest and most conjectural kind of constitutional norms to apply, and when, through a combination of these reasons, it declines to give the relief that was wanted—as the Supreme Court I believe did in the end—this has the appearance in our system and in our psychology of *legitimating* the practice as a general matter.

ECKHARDT: In the *Rodriguez* case, the real difficulty was the difficulty in fashioning any remedy on the basis of a policy ground enunciated by a body equipped to make a policy decision, which the Court certainly was not.

7. *San Antonio Independent School District v. Rodriguez*, 411 U.S. 1 (1973).

BLACK: To my mind one of the main elements of plain non-justiciability is the total inapplicability of legal methods or techniques.

ECKHARDT: Now just a moment there. Some of the same elements exist in the segregation cases, and yet I think you would agree that the courts should have reached far . . .

BLACK: This comes down in my mind to a question of substantive law. Standing and substantive law are complexly interconnected. There is no legitimate question whatever that the Fourteenth Amendment, in the light of its history, ought to be read to command, without equivocation, without the possibility of exception or reservation, that there be no discrimination against black people as such. The Constitution states no such unequivocal command concerning school finances.

ECKHARDT: And that a remedy be instantaneously put into effect? I mean it is utterly impossible to prescribe a remedy that doesn't take some time.

BLACK: That's right. In the *Brown* case it was my own position—and I must avow that I was of counsel in the *Brown* case, in *Brown II*,[8] where the remedy was under scrutiny—that the remedy should have been much more rapid than in fact it was. In fact the Supreme Court took its cue from certain equitable ideas about the possibility of delay for what amounted to "balance-of convenience" reasons. It did actually delay the relief a long time. I don't think, however, that up to a point there was any intellectual or legal puzzle as to what ultimately should be done in those cases.

ECKHARDT: These two positions aren't necessarily contrary. *Brown* —the progeny of *Brown*—could have immediately required that the black child living within the attendance district of the school should be immediately admitted to it.

BLACK: The court didn't do that. In my opinion it should have done it, and it would have been thoroughly warranted in doing it. It was, in my view, I'm sorry to have to say, simply a failure of nerve on

8. *Brown v. Board of Education of Topeka,* 349 U.S. 294 (1955). This was the decision (following the original *Brown* decision, *supra* p. 29) which adopted the requirement that desegregation of schools go forward "with all deliberate speed," rather than right away.

the part of the Court, rather than any difficulty about imagining what a remedy could possibly be.

ECKHARDT: That wouldn't have been a difficult problem. Some schools would have been overloaded but they would have immediately rearranged their attendance districts. Of course there was another problem with delaying relief, and that is that in the South there was much more of a salt-and-pepper arrangement of population distribution within the school districts than there has come to be in both the South and particularly in the North. A lot of problems that have been brought about in connection with the remedy called bussing have come about because of that delay. The salt-and-pepper design in the South began to yield to white flight. So the problem got to be much greater. And in the North there had always been segregated areas geographically, and of course up to the present time we still treat those segregated areas as protected on the basis of political unity.

BLACK: De facto segregation presents a large number of puzzles which are really a meal in themselves. In the *Brown* case situation you should have been sent to the school that would have been your school under the whole set of dispositions of law, if it had not been for the maintenance of the segregation regime. The fact that the Supreme Court didn't make them do that right away was in my view not an intellectual but a volitional thing—they lacked the nerve and fell for the fallacy that difficult things are always better done slowly.

ECKHARDT: At the very least, a black child who wanted to go to a school in his neighborhood to which a white child living next door was going should have been given immediate relief to go to that school.

BLACK: I don't think that up to that point the case presented anything like the complexities of the *Rodriguez* case, or the complexities of other cases, where it comes to be quite unimaginable how a court can afford any sort of relief. So I wonder now, while you and I are not perhaps entirely in agreement as to the desirability of this trend in the courts, whether the disagreement is as deep as it looks like. You no more than I would be content with a gradual formation of a new kind of government in which the judges took charge of important questions of policy. I think the reason the people are turning to this and going for it so strongly is that they have lost faith in the other branches of government. I have been running into this in class for some time. A few years ago, the question of long hair was of great interest. Certain high school principals were trying to get people to cut their hair, and keeping them out of school if they didn't cut their hair. Now this is an example of the kind of petty tyranny in school systems which is likely to inculcate in a human being a lifelong disre- spect for law, which he perceives as being used as an instrument of lawless power, of petty prejudices. It's a horrible thing. Very far from being order-keeping, it's order-destroying.

Now I had students in the Yale Law School who were interested in this problem and who wanted to write papers on possible redress against it. But I found the very greatest difficulty in getting them at all interested in any procedures other than constitutional litigation. First, for example, talking to the principal about the matter. Sec- ondly, and only if he proved recalcitrant, going to the school board, or having the matter raised in a PTA meeting. If the school board didn't act, then maybe you could go in to the city council, or lobby the legislature for a law prohibiting this kind of petty tyranny in the schools. None of these things interested them in the least. They didn't care about these low tracks. Even having to go into the lower federal courts was just a kind of a necessary delay, which they rather re- sented. The one thing they wanted was to get to that Supreme Court, and have the issue resolved whether the Fourteenth Amendment allowed you to wear your hair any way that you wanted to.

ECKHARDT: Let me give you a contrast to that. Recently, in the Spring School, there were four young boys who came to school late and were sent to the assistant principal, who detected the smell of marijuana on their persons. So he then began to question the boys, and questioned them separately, and put considerable pressure on them until he got someone to inform against the others. So the principal then suspended the boys for three days with a notice that they were suspended for "drug abuse." The parents were understand- ably concerned that their children should have a record of being suspended for drug abuse, which could mean anything from heroin to marijuana. So they got them a lawyer, and they presented the case to the school board, and the school board reversed the whole thing and expunged the record entirely.

BLACK: I have a feeling that some of my students would feel cheated by such a result.

Let me mention just one more thing. I recently had conversations with a couple of well-regarded and exceedingly able and meritorious federal judges, and I raised with each of them the same sort of issues that we've been talking about today, concerning the overuse of the judiciary to decide all sorts of questions, whether or not these questions arise in proper lawsuits. One of them said to me, "But these questions have to be *decided*." Now you see there's always that hidden major premise you want to look for. And the hidden major premise there is that these questions not only have to be decided, but *have to be decided by federal judges*. In the case under discussion, the very reference was, I think, to a judgment in a case brought on behalf of several Congressmen to have something issued—I don't know what you'd call it, certainly not a declaratory judgment or even an advisory opinion, maybe a manifesto—to the effect that Archibald Cox was wrongfully fired. Cox was not a party to the suit. He wasn't asking for reinstatement; he had gone on back to Harvard. Some people were curious as to whether it was lawful to have fired Cox. The question whether he was to be fired had already been decided. But behind the statement, "These questions have to be decided," is the assumption that they must be decided by federal judges.

When an issue doesn't fall within the bounds of something like the traditional lawsuit, particularly when there's no identifiable harm to any person or class of people to be observed, then I would rather see it decided finally, even if it's a constitutional question, by Congress, than to devise some kind of simulacrum of a lawsuit for the purpose of procuring a decision by the federal judiciary.

ECKHARDT: But you don't mean finally, in the sense of its not being reviewed if some person is directly affected.

BLACK: Of course not. Then you would have an entirely different situation. If, for example, it should turn out at a later time, as some people predict, that the financing of parochial schools could be shown to have resulted in a very harmful decline of the public schools, so that the children who went to public schools were getting a terrible education, and all these facts could be established to the degree of probability that we ordinarily require in lawsuits, why of course I would then say that there were people who were being harmed.

ECKHARDT: Children would then be suffering a harm personal to themselves, or to a class of persons in the same situation. Whereas a taxpayer, if he is suffering at all, is suffering a harm which is common to the entire populace, who presumably can seek a political remedy.

BLACK: These things do hang together and they do make political sense. Where the harm is diffuse and does not fall on some one person or on some identifiable minority, then the political remedy for it is really the right remedy. It's the one that ought to be used, and it's the one that's promising. Where a small class of deviants, or a racial minority, are in some way especially hurt and vulnerable, they don't have very much of a chance for political solution.

ECKHARDT: I've always lamented the use to which the courts have put the term "political question." They don't define the terms we've used just now. If a group of blacks object on grounds that senatorial districts covering Houston and Harris County have been gerry-mandered so as to prevent any black from representing Harris County, it is impossible to get relief by addressing the question politically, be-cause it can't be effectively addressed politically.

BLACK: That's part of the reason. Another part of the reason is that it may be amenable to intellectual attack by the methods of law. The question whether it's a good idea to have a lighthouse on Mon-tauk Point is not amenable to the ordinary methods of law, to the kind of methods in which you and I are trained. When I worked on the revised edition of a little book of mine called *Perspectives In Constitutional Law*, I thought over the political-question doctrine and really turned it inside out. It seems to me that the political-question doctrine makes sense only in these terms: Almost all governmental questions are political, but there are a few that are justiciable, comparatively few. In absolute numbers, a whole lot of questions are justiciable, but the real business of government, as it goes through Congress and administrative agencies, involves about 99.44 percent political questions. The question whether you should be paid $42,500 or $43,000 a year is a purely political question.

ECKHARDT: Suppose some disbursing officer refused to pay me the statutorily mandated amount.

BLACK: You could sue for the difference because it becomes a justiciable question, a question the law can attack intellectually. There's a statute that says one thing, and something else was done, and if you then can show that you suffer from this, that's fine.

ECKHARDT: That was the residual question of the *Powell* case—whether or not he should get his pay. At the time the Supreme Court decided it, the case would have been moot on other points.

BLACK: He did get his pay, didn't he?

ECKHARDT: Yes.

BLACK: Certainly the case was not moot on that point, and was a perfectly reasonable and typical lawsuit. Sue for your pay under those circumstances.

ECKHARDT: That raises again the interesting question of mootness. It would have been a really bad thing if the *Powell* case, had it gone to virtual conclusion, had then became moot. Suppose, for instance, Congress said, "Look, Mr. Powell, we'll give you your pay. We've already got enough out of it, we kept you out of Congress, now take your money." Something would have bothered me about treating a case like that as moot.

BLACK: Well, I wonder what it is. That's the question—what is it that bothers you about that?

ECKHARDT: If that can be done in that case, various devices relating to dragging out lawsuits and then offering whatever part of the remedy which still is not moot could constitute a basis for the denial of rights in the future, without any judicial determination.

BLACK: But dismissal for mootness wouldn't be a judicial precedent —it wouldn't speak to the merits of the case at all.

I'm very concerned about the decision of any case where nothing is involved. That goes in my mind beyond the judicial forum.

For a congressional analogy, take the case of the "faithless elector,"[9] which came up in January 1969. As you know, at that time my position on that case was that the Congress, in effect, should say there's nothing involved here and therefore we won't decide this case. This is a solemn and tremendously serious constitutional question, but if Richard M. Nixon is going to be elected no matter how we decide to classify this elector, it's a question absolutely without practical importance. Look what actually happened. The question was raised in the House of Representatives Chamber, and the two Houses then separated and deliberated—I think for *one hour* each, or was it two—it was one or two hours—I forget what the time limit was, then they came back and solemnly announced their decision on this question.

This is the mode of procedure which would be regarded as absolutely frivolous in any court with respect to such a question. Consider what would have happened if that vote had been the decisive vote in a presidential election. Every mind in the country who had anything to contribute would have been energized. Every member of Congress would have had to search his mind thoroughly. As it was, it was a skylark.

ECKHARDT: I voted against considering it, in effect.

BLACK: Yes, I know you did. Now let's go back and consider *why* it is that the polity as a whole has so lost confidence in the political process that they just really don't want anything decided except by judges.

ECKHARDT: One thing that contributes to it is a great desire of Congress not to decide nuts-and-bolts questions or technical questions or questions that involve nice decisions of law. They are inclined even to delegate that to someone else, an administrative agency, and to leave the nice decision of law to a court. One way of doing this is

9. I.e., a member of the Electoral College who declined to vote for the candidate to whom he was pledged.

by the use of vague terms in statutes. Now I'm not against the use of terms of art of broad range in some areas. For instance, I think that the antitrust law is properly cast in such terms. Section 5 of the Trade Commission Act uses the term "unfair or deceptive." That is a broad term, but it is a good measure of the limits within which the Trade Commission may make or seek cease-and-desist orders. But I am concerned in certain other areas about the delegation either to the President, to the courts, or to agencies, of broad areas of policy determination. I think that's a cop-out on the part of Congress, and Congress frequently attempts to do that.

BLACK: Another thing may be that we have had an overkill, for some period, on the use of judicially devised means for *avoiding* decisions on difficult issues. Then the pendulum swung from that, and the sense and the nonsense of these methods of avoiding decision got mixed together. The task of the judiciary itself ought to be to go back and try to untangle those things and take a stand on more solid ground than I can believe *Flast v. Cohen* and similar cases to be based on, for the exercise of the judicial function.

But Congress perhaps could help. It's just possible that Congress, through the use of the device of the concurrent resolution—in this case the use of that device as an act of *conscious abstention* from exertion of its full legal authority—might at least trigger a process of reconsideration in the courts of some of these advanced decisions on standing and other such matters. Then the courts themselves might begin a process of overall reconsideration of the question whether the pendulum, with respect to justiciability, to standing, to mootness, and to the whole progressive commitment of what ought to be political questions to the judiciary, ought not to be reversed and some backing and filling done.

ECKHARDT: Incidentally, it always makes me shiver a little bit when I see a court say, "Congress in its wisdom has done so and so," and I remember walking from the Longworth Building to the House Floor to vote, asking someone on the way, "What is this amendment?"

BLACK: But have you seen any analyses recently of the workload of the Supreme Court? The fact is that *all* public men are overworked and have insufficient time to consider the questions that come before them, and it's entirely true that in Congress there's not much time, but there isn't as much time as there should be in the Supreme Court or in other courts either. I won't name any names, but you and I have had occasion within the last few years to read a transcript—the whole transcript—of an argument, with comments and questions from the bench. You know that that transcript doesn't reflect any more consideration than you could give to something in the car in the tunnel on the way to the House.

ECKHARDT: I guess we always understand our own deficiencies better than we do those of other agencies of government.

BLACK: Would some power "the giftie gie us" to see others as they are, perhaps the Court would not admire the wisdom of Congress so much, and perhaps Congress. . . . Now these are all people who are trying to do their best. Busy public men on both sides of the fence are trying to do their best. The question is, "What's a wise division of function between them?"—and not, "Who has a lot of time?", because nobody has a lot of time.

I have another, much more serious problem about the current reliance on the courts. We have seen a great deal of success in judicial action in the last twenty years, beginning roughly with the case of *Brown v. Board of Education*. I take the liberty of doubting whether this success can be continued because, it seems to me, the problems which we face for the *next* twenty years, in all probability, will be of a qualitatively different kind—of a kind that probably won't lend themselves to the judicial remedies.

ECKHARDT: *Brown v. Board* and *Baker v. Carr* responded to areas of greatest reluctance by Congress to act—in the first case, the reluctance of a majority to do anything really meaningful for a minority in a legislative body in which the minority was virtually unrepresented; and in the second, of a legislative body to do anything that would possibly shake the security of its existing members.

BLACK: Well, those were the two triumphant cases of the use of judicial power during the period of the Warren Court. In the third area, the area of free speech, although again it is an area very suitable for judicial intervention, it is hard to be sure what the effect of the judicial remedy was. In any case, the United States of America now enjoys a freedom of speech which is just about as great as you can expect in an imperfect world. People are entirely free to get up and say virtually whatever they want to. The only serious problem that I've heard anything about with respect to freedom of speech in the last decade is the problem of extreme rightists who are heckled and not allowed to speak by people on the left. These three great areas, free speech, racial oppression, and (with some dubiety which we don't have to explore right now) legislative apportionment, were good areas for judicial activity.

But the point I want to make now is that I see the next decade as containing the *poverty* problem as the great justice problem—the dominant strategic question about justice—and it is my thesis that the courts have very little to contribute toward the solution of this problem.

ECKHARDT: Perhaps this tough problem is not unlike another tough economic problem which we addressed in the first quarter of this century, at least with respect to the difficulties in finding a court-fashioned remedy. I'm speaking of antitrust. It seems to me that we perhaps did make a mistake in attempting to delegate to the courts broad economic determinations under the Sherman Act, the Clayton Act, and other related antitrust Acts. We called upon the courts, without the intervention of any agency or any other body exercising quasi-legislative authority, to determine issues calling for broad economic remedies, with virtually no guidelines—to prohibit monopolizing and to prohibit agreements in restraint of trade. We did also provide an optional way not through the courts, and that was through the Federal Trade Commission. It seems to me that perhaps this latter procedure may suggest a way toward legislative, administrative, and judicial processes that might fit the poverty situation.

BLACK: But when a judge has to frame an antitrust decree, the one thing he does not have to do is the one thing which is going to be needful with respect to the remedy of the injustice of poverty: to appropriate large sums of money—and I mean billions and billions of dollars—in such a manner as to reflect not only the felt equities and merits of individual lawsuits but also a nationwide set of priorities. The courts haven't got the power or the resources to effect this large-scale reallocation of money, and of all that money represents. That is what is required for the doing of justice with respect to the evil of poverty, the evil that now chiefly oppresses black people, as well as poor whites. Secondly, I think that judicial action is legitimated by the presence of something which you can call a legal norm, and I cannot conceive how, out of the Constitution as a whole or any part of it, a satisfactorily legitimate set of legal conclusions concerning the allocation of resources in this country, so as to relieve the injustice of poverty, can be deduced, worked out, or arrived at by any methods which are legitimate within law.

In the present instance, in contrast to antitrust, we don't have any Acts of Congress which give even general norms that the courts can appeal to. We are not likely to have any, because they don't seem to be apt in the case of poverty. What we need for the poverty evil is a total overhaul of priorities of allocation of resources. I think that to look to the courts to do that is plain folly. I don't think they can do it, or that in the end they will do it. We can see in some vague way how justice commands some relief of this, some movement toward relief, but I don't believe a judge is in a position even to say what the goal ought to be ten years from now.

ECKHARDT: In some areas, the court cannot do that. But what about this: The court very properly determines that it is not admissible to try a person accused of crime who is poor without affording him a lawyer.

BLACK: I don't have any doubt that in some cases, where poverty is correlated one-for-one with something which is in itself an injustice for other reasons, such as not having a lawyer, there is some aid the courts can give. But this is so peripheral, so ancillary, and so much like a Bandaid for a serious wound, that I don't think it proves very much. The very case you give, *Gideon v. Wainwright*,[10] where the

10. 372 U.S. 335 (1963).

court held that a criminal defendant must be furnished a lawyer, did very little, for example, to change the enormous disadvantage under which a poor man operates when he faces a serious criminal charge. And I feel a sense of danger from cases like that. Actually they do very little; they illustrate, in the very puniness of the amount of good that they can do, the powerlessness of the judiciary in the face of poverty. But, because they are viewed as landmark liberal cases, they may have the effect of lulling us to sleep and, further, of encouraging yet more reliance on the judges to correct something which in the end has to be corrected, if it is going to be corrected, by the kind of reallocation of all our resources that only Congress can bring about.

ECKHARDT: I am not arguing against Congress doing something about these problems, and I don't disagree with you that Congress is best equipped to do it. But in many instances beyond *Gideon*, it is perfectly proper for a court to apply the goad. For instance, in that San Antonio case involving the question of support of Texas schools, the lower court went too far and got reversed. But suppose the court had simply told a plaintiff that, if he were required to go to one of the schools which had inferior financing, he might say, "To heck with that, I am going to the school across the district line, in a more affluent part of San Antonio, and I am going to get the quality of education that I ought to be permitted to get." Now, I would not find it undesirable for the court to say, "You can do that, and this limitation with respect to district attendance lines improperly deprives you of equal protection of the law, and of due process." That wouldn't disturb me, and it might ultimately goad the State or the federal government to do something about the whole problem.

BLACK: You may be right about that. The goading function of the courts will have to be tried; I think we have to try everything concerning the evil of poverty. But it does seem to me that to look to the courts for anything that will really begin redressing this hideous imbalance is a false hope, for two reasons. First, the law doesn't *intellectually* provide the means for the redress of poverty, except where it ties in with other guarantees, like the due-process guarantee and the right-to-counsel cases. Secondly, and much more important, *practically,* the courts can't appropriate money in any quantity.

ECKHARDT: But there have been cases somewhat similar in which Congress has acted and has appropriated money, and the executive department has not actually used the money for the purpose appropriated. Suit was brought then to determine whether or not that money should have been expended. Now the court could not actually enforce its decree against the President of the United States. Yet there is, usually, an understood accommodation between branches of government, and the President did in every instance, I think, release the funds after those orders.

BLACK: When it comes to judicial power, I fully agree that at many points the courts can help, when special circumstances exist. One could aggregate a large number of special cases in which the judicial power may be useful in an ancillary or goading way, but the problem as a whole is one that has to be met and solved by legislative means.

ECKHARDT: The idea that the mere fact of massive injustice makes judicial relief appropriate is totally false. However, it seems to me that there are areas where the courts have properly acted in recent times, where they would not have acted before. For instance, in those cases where Congress has defined objectives, and has indicated who is entitled to the benefit of these objectives, and has defined this latter class to include the general public, the courts have begun to decide, under broad standing provisions, that they may enter in behalf of a person who formerly would not have had standing, and in a case that would formerly have been considered as raising a political question. They may, for example, require that an agency act in accordance with law, or that a dam not be built because an agency had not properly acted in accordance with law, and I don't disagree with that approach. That is an exercise of great judicial power, and it is an exercise in connection with the general welfare and not with respect to individual hardship. But it seems to me nevertheless to be proper.

BLACK: I would be afraid of this kind of thing, Bob, that Congress might be led into the expectation that history would repeat itself, that just as the Court took the lead in *Brown v. Board of Education* and Congress picked up that lead ten years afterwards in the Civil Rights Act of 1964, so the Court might lead as to poverty. It would be a natural and easy thing for people to continue this reliance on judicial activity, for Congress to say, "Well, someone will finally file the right kind of lawsuit, and we will get a guidance from the Court as to what is proper to do about poverty, and when that comes along, then we will think ten years about it, like we did before on race, and finally do it, finally apply congressional power." I don't think that can happen with poverty. I don't think that any of our present constitutional law can legitimately be read as requiring the relief of poverty in general, on a massive scale.

ECKHARDT: The *Brown* case was essentially a law case, it was typically a legal problem and it was decided properly under the law. The question is, did the Court not by its process, by its method of relief, did it not perhaps create this kind of false hope that you described, that the Court might engage in the administration of achieving a just end by rather complex means? The Court got into an extremely complex problem of administering the remedy.

BLACK: That is so. I also think orders of magnitude make the quantum jump here. (I'm sure I lost the physicist vote with that one.) Sure, it is true that a lot of the remedies with regard to segregation and with regard to other matters have been rather complex, and not all of them have been successfully administered by courts. I still think you get into a different world when you begin to talk about the relief of poverty.

It would be tragic for us to place reliance on the good old Supreme Court to do anything pervasive and overall significant about this *because that reliance, sure of disappointment, would lead people away from Congress.* You made the point earlier that one of the worst things about these lawsuits to stop the Vietnam war, some of them brought even by Congressmen themselves, was that they diverted attention from the forum where one *could* have stopped the Vietnam war, the forum with unquestionable jurisdiction to stop the Vietnam war, namely, Congress. I think that's true in this case of poverty, as I do, incidentally, in cases of war and peace. I think the reliance on judges to decide issues of war and peace is quite vain.

ECKHARDT: The very use of terms and the generality of them define the difference. A court can't deal with poverty, or with war, or with peace. The court can deal with antitrust violation, denial of civil rights, failure to appoint counsel, questions of this nature.

BLACK: When you come to malnutrition, generally suffered through a large portion of the population, I don't think any judicial remedy is going to suggest itself or be very helpful.

ECKHARDT: Take very pressing needs. Suppose a person needs an emergency operation or has been wounded, and goes into a private hospital and asks for relief. They ask him for his hospitalization insurance card and he can't show it, and they turn him away. Can't a court remedy this situation by granting an injunction, or granting a broad class-action injunction with respect to all persons in that same situation?

BLACK: I think you might get the court to do that in the case you state. But as to the larger problem of medical care, it wouldn't work, because now you run into one of the things that makes this area so problematic from the standpoint of the judges, the *allocation of re sources*. One man may be able to show that he needs a certain operation, but what he can't show in a lawsuit is how many other people need it, or what other operations are needed, or what other things the doctors might be doing, or how many doctors we ought to educate in medical school every year, and so on. It is determinations like that which are going to move us strategically, instead of just in piecemeal situations, toward the relief of poverty and of the consequences of poverty.

Of course, in the end, if Congress acts, undoubtedly Congress's action will in part be a set of formulated directions to the judges. That is a different question altogether.

6 CONGRESS AND THE COMMITTEE SYSTEM

ECKHARDT: Do you want me to start?

BLACK: I think so. We're going to talk about the committee structure of Congress.

ECKHARDT: The committee structure of Congress is both the chief source of strength in our congressional system, and also a source of weakness. I can't help but think of the contrast between the operation of the United States Congress, with its Committee system, and the operation of the Texas Legislature.[1] The comparison is not altogether to the advantage of Congress. The Texas Legislature had an extremely weak committee system. A bill was devised, theoretically, by the author (but in fact usually by either a lobby group or the Texas Legislative Council), and it generally was treated in the committee altogether politically, not analytically. A bill in Congress, though it may have its original genesis with some lobby group, and perhaps has passed through the processes of the White House and presidential recommendation, is nevertheless very much the creature of the Committee to which it is referred. It will be dealt with by experts on the Committee staff, who will work in conjunction with Congress's Legislative Council; and the staff working for the Committees are very bright, competent people. The relationship between Committee staff and Legislative Council is that the Legislative Council staff members generally have specific knowledge respecting the mechanics of drawing a bill, and the Committee staff members are specialists with respect to the particular subject matter involved in the bill.

Of course, all bills are marked up in Committee, after rather ex-

1. Eckhardt served for many years as a member of the Texas Legislature.

tensive hearings of testimony from persons interested and knowledgeable in the field, people who either come on their own or are requested to come.

BLACK: You say "marked up." What do you mean?

ECKHARDT: That's when Committee members get into the act and offer amendments, sometimes generated by lobbyists close to the member who offers the amendment. Bills are amended and altered, sometimes even completely reversed in direction.

BLACK: Let me interrupt to get a clarification on two things. One is the part of the President. You speak of bills having been approved by the White House, and I take it there is a regular flow of such bills, and that it has in fact been the practice for quite a while now for there to be a considerable amount of initiative of this degree of specificity coming from the White House. Is that just an exhortation from the President to do a certain thing, in general terms, in a message to Congress, or actually a bill, a draft of a bill?

ECKHARDT: Usually a draft bill. I came up here in the Ninetieth Congress, when Lyndon Johnson was President. That was just after the Eighty-ninth Congress when the Great Society legislation was passed. The Ninetieth was probably a more normal Congress than the Eighty-ninth. It was a type of Congress that we have seen in many sessions, one in which the Democrats had a nominal majority, but in which there were enough southern Democrats who would defect to make the liberal majority not a clear or safe one. An appeal had to be made to reason, and use made of various pressures and various balances and trade-offs, in order to get legislation through. It was a typical Congress.

BLACK: There were also defections in the other direction from the Republicans.

ECKHARDT: But very few.

BLACK: It would, then, be a part of the regular procedure for there to be a flow of bills in actual drafted form to come to Congress from the White House and to be introduced by members who were friendly to the objectives in the bill and perhaps had been requested by the White House?

ECKHARDT: I was getting to that. In the Ninetieth Congress the President before about April would have sent out messages to Congress setting forth his programs, in considerable detail. This is almost immediately followed by legislation, specifically drafted legislation, which by custom is introduced by the Chairman of the Committee, and perhaps also by other members of the Committee who have long been interested in the subject.

BLACK: That is to say, the Chairman of the Committee to which the bill will be referred?

ECKHARDT: That's right. Of course, you can pretty well anticipate where it is going by the subject matter, so the Chairman will introduce it. It will not bear the Committee designation on it at the time he introduces it, but as soon as he introduces it, it is then referred by the Speaker to the appropriate Committee. Actually what happens is that the Speaker very seldom has any real input, it is the Parliamentarian who does it in a more or less mechanical way.

BLACK: An important point which we probably ought to pause and make is that the constitutional mandate of this Committee system is absolutely zero. These are devices which have been elaborated by the Houses under their constitutional power to make rules for their own governance. We are dealing with matters which are in a sense "constitutional," in that they are part of the constitutive structure of the government as it now exists—but which nevertheless can be altered in any desired way, because they are not bound to any one form by the written Constitution. So we are talking about something which can usefully be criticized without any thought of a constitutional amendment.

ECKHARDT: That's right. As a matter of fact, the current system has been criticized and attacked, and sweeping reforms proposed by the Bolling Committee Report. That report did not pass, and I myself had grave doubts about it.

BLACK: Well, tell me something more about that report, because I think it may possibly be our focus.

ECKHARDT: The Bolling Committee Report did not attack the structure of the Committee system. It in no way recommended radical change. For instance, it didn't purport to eliminate standing Committees and establish *ad hoc* Committees for specific legislation, after the manner, for instance, in which the British Parliament works. It retained the power of the Committee Chairman, and the seniority structure generally, but it shifted subject matter between Committees, and purported to consolidate a single subject matter in a given Committee, without the two- or three-track possibilities of legislation in several Committees with overlapping jurisdictions.

The Bolling Report decreased the number of Committees by dismantling some of the less important ones. Post Office and Civil Service, for instance, was moved over to a new Labor Committee, which was split off from the Education and Labor Committee. The functions of the Merchant Marine and Fisheries Committee would largely have moved, in the Bolling recommendation, to the Committee on Agriculture—with respect to parks and things like that. Agriculture originally dealt with national forests anyway, and its environmental functions would be shifted to a new Committee on Energy and Environment, which is really built on the base of the old Interior Committee. However, as you see, this doesn't really change the basic structure. There is nothing radical about the proposed change; it was simply an attempt at orderly realignment of Committee functions.

BLACK: When you speak of the basic system, you speak of—I think we might talk about what actually happens to a bill. No bill except in the rarest instance would ever reach the Floor for a vote without having been considered at some length in Committee and reported out?

ECKHARDT: I don't think you even need to specify "except in the rarest situation."

BLACK: And amendment of the bill in Committee is the rule rather than the exception, isn't it? The bill is very likely to be restudied and amended by the Committee and reported out, if at all, in that form?

ECKHARDT: Yes. In contrast to the Texas Legislature. Two very important bills that I was involved with there were simply not changed by a dotting of an i or the crossing of a t; they were very important and complex bills. One was the oil-pooling bill and one was the higher education reorganization bill, both, I believe, in John Connally's administration as Governor. The reason for that was that a bill like the oil-pooling bill constituted a compromise between lobby groups, and it was feared that any change would unloose the glue by which the compromise was held together. But that is inconceivable in Congress.

BLACK: Let's go on to the next stage. These matters are not as well known to me as they are to you. I believe I do know, and ask your confirmation, that a Committee has a very wide power simply not to report a bill out at all. A Committee can hold a bill as long as it likes, unless a petition is signed with the names of the actual "constitutional" majority of 218 Representatives for a discharge—a majority of the whole House, not simply a majority of the number that happens to be present and voting. You have to have a constitutional majority of 218, which is more than half of 435, the whole House membership, to get a bill discharged.

ECKHARDT: There is one other way that can be used, particularly if the leadership or a large majority of the House has a strong feeling in favor of the legislation, and the Committee diverges from that leadership or from that majority. The Rules Committee can simply make a rule[2] bringing out a bill initially from the Rules Committee. But this is also very rare.

BLACK: So a possibility in the substantive Committees is that the bill may be held up altogether until one of these extraordinary proceedings is gone through—and I take it that is the normal way in which a disapproving Committee acts on a bill, and not by reporting it out with a recommendation that it not pass.

ECKHARDT: That's right.

BLACK: A Committee that disapproves of a bill would be enormously more likely to hold it than to report it out with a negative recommendation, because the latter course opens it up to a vote, even though the recommendation is negative. You do have these two ways

2. The special meaning of the term "rule," and the function of the Rules Committee, are explained in the text, *infra,* pp. 142–44.

to bring out a bill other than by the Committee. Both of them are somewhat difficult to put in operation. So there is still considerable Committee power over a close question, especially when there is not a lot of support for a bill either amongst the general membership or in the Rules Committee. Despite, sometimes, the possibility that legislation would pass if it were brought out on the Floor, it may simply be held in the Committee.

ECKHARDT: That's right. There is another interesting aspect. The Floor—the whole House in formal session—is the most partisan body with respect to a bill. Once brought to the Floor, a bill is likely to be treated in terms of one's being a Republican or a Democrat, or one's general conservative or liberal position.

BLACK: It's the Floor vote that the constituency is going to notice.

ECKHARDT: It is also the vote that responds to large, sweeping pressures, or to special-interest pressures that are plainly and simply for or against the bill, or an amendment to it. The further back you get from that process—at the Committee level, and even beyond that to the Subcommittee—the more reason and compromise, structure, philosophy, and technique enter into the picture. That's the good thing about the Committee system. It tends to make possible a less knee-jerky response to a national problem, because frequently compromises, or the restructuring of a bill to meet a certain need, may be made in a Subcommittee and then the full Committee may accept the Subcommittee's recommendation.

Now the *full* Committee bears a proportionate resemblance to the House itself, in its Democratic and Republican division, and it will be more likely to vote on partisan lines than the Subcommittee. For instance, I have an easy working relationship to men like Broyhill on the Subcommittee on Commerce and Finance. He is a Republican, and he is the senior minority member on the Committee. Broyhill and I have similar views with respect to fair procedure in administrative agencies, and sometimes when some other issue may be compromised in favor of bringing out a reform in this respect, he or I will give a little to achieve this common objective. Or a man like McCollister, a Republican on the Subcommittee who is quite conservative, may be convinced, as he was on the Product Safety Bill, that it is desirable for the Commission dealing with product safety to be subject to congressional Committee oversight, and therefore he would prefer to have an independent agency, instead of assigning it to the executive department, though his party took the latter position. He was willing to compromise with the Democrats on the Subcommittee. This kind of compromise helps to move a bill through the full Committee and ultimately through Congress on other than a purely partisan basis.

BLACK: The smaller a group gets, the harder it is for them to look at one another and refuse to talk sense.

ECKHARDT: That's right.

BLACK: So the actual work of consideration, recommendation, and useful amendment is a creative and important part of Committee work. There is a tendency—though a tendency that cannot entirely be realized—to have some of the partisan content reduced and defused at the level of the Committee or Subcommittee. The Committee enjoys the power not only of recommending a bill out, but also has considerable power to hold a bill and thus end action on the matter for that session of Congress.

ECKHARDT: Well, what we have been talking about up to now is the good news. Now, let me tell you the bad news.

BLACK: Some people think that the last thing I said is bad news.

ECKHARDT: No, I don't think it is. At least it is not always so.

BLACK: It all depends on what you think about the bill. There has been many a bill that has been passed with enthusiasm in the Senate, on the confident expectation that it would be held up in Committee in the House. This used to be particularly true of bills that were going to be referred to Manny Celler's Committee on the Judiciary. Those bills were often bills that you and I would have regarded as very bad bills, so this Committee system does not always work in a manner which is obstructive of *good* legislation. Sometimes it works in other ways, and actually furnishes a cooling-off period for some legislation which might be very dangerous.

ECKHARDT: The whole process, whether positive or negative, also has the good feature of having pumped into it considerable analysis and considerable reasoned judgment respecting whether the structure of the legislation is mechanically and technically sound.

Secrecy—which played a part in the drafting of our Constitution—also has a meaning in Committee work. Of course, it used to be that Committee meetings, both hearings and mark-up sessions, could be conducted secretly. I see no reason, except in the rarest cases such as those involving national security, why the public shouldn't know what the *factual input* into a Committee is. It ought to be public that, for instance, General Motors took a stand on auto safety, and what its stand was, or that the New York Stock Exchange appeared in regard to a bill involving whether or not an arrangement to underwrite failing brokerage houses should be passed. There is no argument that I can conceive of for prohibiting the public from knowing the *factual basis* upon which a Subcommittee or Committee works. That's at the *hearing* stage. But some of these hearings used to be closed. This was particularly true of the Armed Services Committee, even many times when it was not working on anything that the public ought not hear about because of security reasons. They were just working on questions of whether public money would be spent on a naval base, or something of that nature.

On the other hand, there is the process of the mark-up[3] of a bill, where there must be somewhat subtle trading, and somewhat careful stacking of the building-blocks of the legislative structure. In this process, constant public scrutiny, and the related tendency of each person on the Committee to anticipate a public reaction—and therefore perhaps to tailor his response to what will immediately appear in the newspapers as to his position on a bill—can be bad. So, in the last Congress we enacted rules that made the *hearing* open, with only the narrow exceptions of a hearing involving security or something that might affect the reputation of an individual personally. Only if the case falls within one of those narrow exceptions can a *hearing* be closed. The position is somewhat different as to *mark-up* sessions. A mark-up session will always be presumed to be open, but

3. This term is explained, *supra*, p. 131.

this presumption may be overcome by an open and recorded vote by the members to close the session.

BLACK: This separation corresponds pretty closely to the one that is followed in judicial matters. Either a trial or an appellate argument will ordinarily be open to the public, unless pressing reasons exist to the contrary—pretty much the reasons you give, some kind of pressing reason of security, or something like divorce proceedings, which may be held *in camera*, where there is no point in exposing the personal lives of individuals.

On the other hand—and I think this is a point some people refuse to meet as they deal with these questions of confidentiality in governmental communications—no group of judges are going to confer publicly when they *discuss their positions* on a judgment. No jury that is conferring for the purpose of arriving at a verdict would conceivably be open to the public, so that each position taken, and then perhaps receded from, could immediately be reported in the newspapers. The distinction you are drawing here is exactly parallel, that the knowledge of the *input* is open to the public, as it should be, but that the *deliberative* process, wherein it is important that people take positions fluidly and then alter them as reason forces them to alter them, is not necessarily open.

A certain amount of trading goes on in the legislative process, so that those need to be at least closeable. This position seems to me a moderate one. I myself would be inclined to go further, and to put the presumption the other way, so that all mark-up sessions would be closed unless voted open, but I don't claim to be in a position to teach Congress its own business, and I am not under the pressures it works under.

ECKHARDT: The Committee Chairmen tended to go the way that you suggest, because they were used to holding mark-up sessions in closed session, and as a matter of fact the rules of the Committees prior to the new rule in the House ordinarily said that mark-up sessions would be closed unless opened by vote.

Now, about the bad news, and perhaps I ought not put it in those terms, there are several problem areas. I started out by saying that there are some points in which the process of the Texas Legislature, though having a weak committee system, was superior to that of Congress, and I think this is a good way to approach this question. The fact that the Committees go through detailed deliberation tends to make the process on the Floor too perfunctory. As a matter of fact, the more detailed and the slower the mill grinds in producing the bill in the Committee, the faster the mill is likely to turn on the Floor. And the tendency, when a bill reaches the Floor, is to have in Congress, oh, maybe a half-dozen members sitting behind microphones on the Democratic side of the Committee benches, persons who are first recognized by the member in the Chair, and the same thing on the Republican side. Some of the major issues on the bill tend to be swept under the rug. As a general rule, both sides talk about the good points and the areas of agreement, and compliment each other on their joint product.

The whole House rarely if ever sits as a body which is critically examining the provisions of the bill in an analytic sense. The bill may, however, be the source of considerable criticism in a political vein. So, for instance, a lobby may have been very effective in influencing the Committee process on some bill, perhaps by working with the staff of the Committee—not corruptly but maybe by just pulling the wool over their eyes, because a lobbyist is frequently better informed about something that affects the industry affected by the bill than the staff is. In such a case, a special-interest slant can slip through without critical analysis by the whole House.

Also, this atmosphere tends to make members of the House even more political, more partisan, more shallow in their determinations. To give an example, recently we had a bill requiring that all federal agencies move toward bringing it about that twenty percent of the shipment of petroleum to and from the United States be in American ships. An amendment to that bill in Committee, seeking to exempt small refineries—refineries producing less than 30,000 barrels—had been rejected by the Committee. The amendment was then offered on the Floor. In the meantime a great number of small refineries had written members of the House, and the immediate reaction was,

"Well, there are some people who feel strongly on this, and they'll remember it against us, and isn't it a good thing to exempt small refineries?" So, the amendment passed on the Floor on a totally political basis rather than an analytical one.

BLACK: Going back over the whole business of processing legislation, you have stages of consideration, and some things tend to drop between the planks if the person in the first stage can say, "Well, after all, I'm not making the final decision," and the person at the second stage can say, "Well, this has all been processed up to now." That's something we are familiar with in all kinds of decisional processes. I suppose that's kind of unavoidable. It really is inseparable from any staged process.

ECKHARDT: That's right, and when the one stage is strengthened, the latter stage may inevitably be weakened. For instance, in the Texas Legislature, since a term was typically compressed into a period of about six months out of two years, and the committee system was weak, every member, or nearly every member, except those absent because of illness or some pressing business, was on the Floor at all times. And the debate was a debate of the whole body, and the persons who voted on the bill had heard the debate. Of course, here, in Washington, in most instances, nearly all of the debate is not heard by nearly all of the 435 members of Congress. They come over and vote on the basis of their knowledge of the bill gained in advance, or on the basis of trust in some other members' votes. Of course, much better notice of a pending vote is given in Congress than in a State legislative body.

BLACK: This is something about the Houses of Congress that many people don't understand. A member who spent a great deal of time over on the Floor would probably attract the curiosity of his colleagues. They would wonder why he wasn't busy, why he didn't have anything to do.

ECKHARDT: Well, if he were a senior member, he would almost surely be over there to frustrate the process. I would not speak ill of any of my colleagues, and I don't mean to in this case, but Mr. Gross was of that nature. He was a conservative on the Republican side. He was a watchdog over the process, and if it were attempted to get a bill through on suspension,[4]—that is without going through the Rules Committee and on short argument, twenty minutes to decide—and if Mr. Gross felt that the bill was an important bill, and that it was being slipped through, he'd start making quorum calls.[5] And by manipulating the process in this way he would force the leadership, even though it had a strong majority on the bill, to follow what he conceived to be a more careful and deliberate process. The bill would be taken off suspension so that Mr. Gross would quit throwing sand in the cogs of congressional procedure. Now his function there is understandable, sometimes commendable. The other persons who are on the Floor most of the time tend to be freshmen who are simply getting oriented in the process.

BLACK: Let's go on with this bad news. The first part of it is kind of eternal bad news that one has to guard against, but what other defects do you see in the Committee system as it now functions?

ECKHARDT: One of the defects, subjects overlapping Committee lines, was very powerfully addressed by the Bolling Report. Several Committees may be concerned with a certain subject matter of a bill, or two Committees (like one dog tugging at one part of a bone and another dog tugging on his part of the bone) may be fighting to control the bill.

BLACK: How does that work, if it's been referred by the Speaker to one of the Committees?

ECKHARDT: The other Committee will start objecting that the first Committee should not deal with matters that are subject to that second Committee's jurisdiction.

4. The Speaker can put any bill that has gone through a substantive Committee on the "suspension calendar"; it must then receive a two-thirds vote to pass.

5. There is rarely a quorum on the House Floor except when summoned for a vote. Ordinarily, nobody raises the point. A "quorum call"—starting with the suggestion of the absence of a quorum—forces all the members, or most of them, to come over from their offices for roll call. It takes a long time—and can be soon repeated. The business of the House could not get done if the members hung about on the Floor a great deal.

Take a bill dealing with drug control. That would normally go to the Committee on Interstate and Foreign Commerce, because of its health aspects, because it deals with the control of narcotics on an international scale. But it also has a tax aspect. The Ways and Means Committee has always controlled taxes and tariffs. The Ways and Means Committee insisted on dealing with one title of the bill, and ultimately we worked it out this way: The bill stayed intact, but the Ways and Means Committee heard and marked up the title dealing with taxes. Interstate and Foreign Commerce dealt with the area dealing with foreign relations. But that's an easy case.

Now let me take another kind of situation. What about a bill whose total substance falls in several Committees—for instance a bill dealing with establishing super-ports, say thirty miles off the coast of the United States, in international waters. There were three bills before Congress on this matter last term. The Public Works Committee felt it had jurisdiction over this question, because it deals with harbors and it had a bill. The Merchant Marine and Fisheries Committee contended it had jurisdiction because it deals with coastal zones and oceanography, and it had a bill. The Interior Committee felt it had jurisdiction in the matter because the issue affects many environmental concerns that that Committee ordinarily handles, and it had a bill.

So the question in the Rules Committee became, "Whose bill is going to be given preference? Which bill is to go to the Floor, and in what way?"

BLACK: I think you are assuming in your references to the Rules Committee a knowledge (which frankly I didn't possess until a few years ago) about what this Committee actually does. The layman tends to think of it as a Committee which is concerned with the continual purification and improvement of the Rules of Procedure of the House. Now, actually the word "rule" is used with respect to this Committee in the rather unusual sense of a *particular rule* applied to a *particular bill*. You go to that Committee to get a "rule" as to how that particular bill shall be considered on the Floor of the House.

ECKHARDT: Exactly.

BLACK: And since a bill, to get considered on the Floor, has to get a rule, unless some of the alternative proceedings we talked about are used, this Committee is really a second watchdog, isn't it?

ECKHARDT: It's a dispatching Committee, and a second watchdog.

BLACK: Yes, I had a vague idea that the Rules Committee was pretty powerful, but it wasn't really until you got in Congress that we began talking these things over and I began watching it more closely. But I now realize just wherein that power consists, and let's really pin it down, because I think a lot of people don't know that the power consists in operating as a traffic cop for virtually every bill that gets to the stage of being passed on the Floor. Does the Senate have a corresponding Committee?

ECKHARDT: No, it doesn't.

In the Texas Legislature one always knew that he could offer amendments, could move to recommit, to reconsider, to do all the things he did on the Floor, and in accordance with a set body of rules. There the Rules Committee was what a person would think it would be. It was concerned with drafting that basic set of rules which controls the operations of the Texas Legislature.

Now the Rules Committee here in Congress formulates the process each time. It sets up a rule that governs a specific bill as it goes through what is called the Committee of the Whole House. The Committee of the Whole House is identical in every respect, as far as personnel is concerned, with the House itself. It's a device that was originally established, in the British Parliament, to exclude the King's spies from coming in and seeing what was going on. But with us it affords flexibility, and control of process for the particular bill, removed from the rigid constraints of a set of standing rules. So, each bill goes through on its own rule. These rules are generally very similar from one bill to another, but they may vary.

BLACK: Just to get an idea, what would be an example of such rules? The Rules Committee, I take it, could send a bill to this Committee of the Whole House with a rule attached to the bill that there was to be a one-hour debate on each side and that no amendments could be offered.

ECKHARDT: That would be a closed rule.

BLACK: That would be a closed rule.

ECKHARDT: That's very unusual, for a rule to be closed.

BLACK: But it's a possibility.

ECKHARDT: It's a possibility, and it's usually applied to tax bills, or tariff bills, because to permit every special interest to attempt to get favorable tax or tariff treatment by amendment of the bill on the Floor would be undesirable. The normal rule would be an hour or two hours of debate on each side, after which an amendment period commences in which each member has five minutes to speak on an amendment or to speak in opposition to or in favor of an amendment. As a matter of fact, he has guaranteed to him five minutes to speak generally, because he may seek recognition to strike the last word. He really doesn't ever expect the last word to be stricken out. But, technically, he is proposing an amendment and therefore he is entitled to speak for five minutes.

What we've been talking about sounds like a pretty disorderly process—Committees with overlapping jurisdiction hearing the same factual testimony and coming up with separate bills; the Rules Committee acting as a dispatcher and sometimes having difficulty in being the umpire between Committees' jurisdiction; claims of jurisdiction by one Committee on a bill, so that the bill has to be treated piecemeal between several Committees, and so forth. This disorderliness is what the Bolling Report addressed. But the Report created other problems that may be much more serious than the disorderliness. After all, almost every governmental process that has been put together by the minds of Englishmen or Americans has been pretty disorderly. But it has been tested, and it works—at least works fairly well. This doesn't mean it shouldn't be reformed. But switching of jurisdiction, in the way that the Bolling Committee Report called for, creates some other problems. For instance, the Bolling Report says that about six Committees have some piece of the energy question, and since this is so, they should be consolidated into a Committee on Energy and the Environment. Therefore, the Report would shift the energy component of the Committee on Interstate and Foreign Commerce, which is dealt with in its Subcommittee on Communications and Power, to this new Committee, and would also put certain other things in that Committee, and the theory is that a single Committee could act on the whole "energy" matter.

BLACK: I fail utterly to see how that begins to solve the problem of competing and overlapping jurisdiction, because if you start talking about energy you are bound to be talking about the interstate transmission of electricity, the interstate movement of trains, trucks, and automobiles, and indeed the whole interstate . . .

ECKHARDT: You are talking about almost everything.

BLACK: It seems to me that the enterprise of reorganizing Committees so there would not be competing or overlapping jurisdiction is plainly hopeless. It can be demonstrated that this is impossible by recourse to the very simple fact that all major concerns of society have a number of facets and may involve transportation, the environment, the shoreline, the parks, and all these things together.

ECKHARDT: Anyway, I think a big conglomeration of jurisdictional power, like that in the Interstate and Foreign Commerce Committee, is beneficial rather than harmful. Compare it, for instance, to the committees in the Texas Legislature. There's an Insurance Committee; well who runs that? The insurance industry, of course. The Oil and Gas Committee in the Texas Legislature becomes a creature of oil and gas. And the more neatly you package the subject matter, and the more narrowly you divide it, the stronger is the tendency for the interest supposedly controlled by the Committee ultimately to control the Committee. It sometimes does this subtly, and in some instances blatantly. The subtle process is to go to the Committee on Committees,[6] and influence those members not to let a member on the substantive Committee that deals with oil who might for instance be antioil.

So, there's one problem in neatly packaging Committees in this way. An energy and environment Committee would have, say, Exxon and the Sierra Club vying for control, and you can imagine who would win.

6. This Subcommittee makes up rosters of the other Committees.

Another point, though, is this question of appropriateness and exclusiveness of a Committee respecting a given subject matter. If only one Committee can possibly deal with the question of offshore ports, that Committee also has the absolute authority to block all legislation on that subject. On the other hand, if several Committees could at least conceivably deal with it, you have a way of getting around the blockade, which I think is desirable. Let's say for instance a Committee on Public Works was very much partisan in favor of the present port authorities—and they naturally would be because they deal with the present port authorities—and present port authorities have conceived of an offshore oil port as depriving them of considerable tonnage. The Committee simply takes the bill and sits on it. On the other hand, let's say that the Merchant Marine and Fisheries Committee feels that we are coming to an age when the production of oil offshore, and the movement of oil, has to be related to ocean transportation, and must not be limited by the depth of the onshore ports. They have the general jurisdiction in the area so *they* can move on the bill.

BLACK: How do they get the bill? Is the bill first referred by the Speaker—and in practice that means the Parliamentarian? What is the process of re-referral? Would that go through the Speaker again or to the Rules Committee?

ECKHARDT: It goes through the Speaker. There's a certain flexibility that I think is rather healthy. You can phrase your new bill as an amendment to some Act that the Committee has previously dealt with, and then the bill will go to that Committee. For instance, I had the Open Beaches Bill. I had a strong interest in it. By phrasing it as an amendment to certain legislation involving estuarine matters, I could get my bill referred to Merchant Marine and Fisheries, because that Committee had previously processed the statute my bill amended. Had I amended certain bills dealing with land use, I could have got it referred to the Interior Committee.

BLACK: You mean by offering these things in the form of an amendment to certain sections in the present United States Code?

ECKHARDT: Right.

BLACK: I see.

ECKHARDT: Now this sounds as if you can manipulate these matters.

BLACK: Yes, it does.

ECKHARDT: You can, but this is not undesirable, I think. It gives a certain flexibility, and ultimately, of course, if you manipulate them too baldly or too obviously and blatantly, so that there's an illogic to taking the action, you tend to defeat the bill ultimately on the Floor and to attract the strong enmity of the Committee that you have taken it away from. So, it creates a flexibility with built-in limitations. Also, under the present system, if the Speaker wants to exercise his authority strongly, he can simply decide that all bills dealing with the subject matter of offshore ports are going to go to Interior or to Merchant Marine; regardless of what statutes they amend, he's got the absolute authority to send them all to the same Committee.

BLACK: Is there any way in which a recommitment, or rather a commitment to another Committee, can be procured by the whole House?

ECKHARDT: Theoretically it can be, but I don't remember a time that it has been done here. It was done in the Texas Legislature years ago to get a gas pipeline tax out of the Revenue and Taxation Committee to the Agriculture Committee and then to the Floor. I mention this because the Texas Legislature's rules are patterned after the rules of the U. S. House.

BLACK: You seem to me to be saying that it's not particularly bad news that several Committees may have some claim to jurisdiction over a bill, that this actually adds flexibility to the process. My guess from the outside would be that you don't have to worry about this no matter what a report, such as the Bolling Report, may do; it is impossible that any structure of Committees can be devised by the wit of man which will result in there not being competing jurisdiction over a large number of subject matters, because any subject of any magnitude has different aspects to it.

ECKHARDT: But there are some things, some problems that the Bolling Report points up that ought to be met.

BLACK: What are some of them?

ECKHARDT: The Speaker should be more willing to assign a given bill and its related subject matter to a given Committee, even though other Committees may have interest in that subject matter. For instance, suppose in the case of a national health insurance bill it appears most expedient to assign it and the matter of financing the program to the Interstate and Foreign Commerce Committee. In the past it has always been assigned to Ways and Means because it is financed by the Social Security tax. In this session it has been assigned to both Committees. Perhaps the Speaker should assign the whole bill and subject matter exclusively to the Committee concerned with health, the Interstate and Foreign Commerce Committee.

BLACK: It seems to me that the connection with commerce is almost as arbitrary as the connection with taxation. I take it this is a historical rather than a logical connection. It doesn't strike my mind immediately that it's appropriate to refer a bill on health to the Commerce Committee any more than to the taxation Committee, which I take is what Ways and Means actually is.

ECKHARDT: Well, I'm not really making any argument either way, but I see no reason why the Speaker ought not to exercise a rather free option to place the total subject matter in one Committee.

BLACK: Why doesn't he do that? In what you've described there is no organizational compulsion on him at all. He could assign a bill anywhere he wants to, and it's up to somebody else to try to get it away from that Committee. But there are strong built-in institutional guarantees which make it hard to take it away from the original Committee. So why doesn't the Speaker just assign the bills where he thinks they may most usefully be considered at this time?

ECKHARDT: Because he's likely to get a bitter fight from the Committee Chairmen on the Floor, and because in our institution—and this is one of its weaknesses—we've tended to divide power among a number of powerful barons who control Congress, rather than a king who directs the total course. The Speaker is weakened by the existence of the many powerful Committee Chairmen.

BLACK: Well, what's some more of the bad news on this? Are we going to reach the subject of seniority? The Bolling Report did nothing about that?

ECKHARDT: It didn't really address that question, and it should have, because if you switch great blocks of jurisdiction from one Committee to another, what do you do about shifting persons on the Committee that loses that jurisdiction to the Committee that now has the subject matter? For instance, if energy were to be shifted from Interstate and Foreign Commerce, I'd probably be more interested in the Energy and Environment Committee than I would in Interstate. Now, if the Bolling Report had been adopted, could I have exercised my full seniority to go over there, or not? The Bolling Report didn't answer that question.

BLACK: I think the public tends to think of seniority as a kind of ugly word anyway. To the person on the street it looks like an objectionable conferral of power on mere grounds of long service, and not on merit. I disagree. I think that seniority is as good a way as any to select Committee Chairmen, and to distribute other things—given the alternative, which would be a bitter politicized fight every time any position becomes vacant in Congress.

ECKHARDT: I suppose it would probably be the Speaker who would make these determinations, if they were not made by seniority.

BLACK: Well, if the Speaker were to be elected with the knowledge that he was going to make those determinations, then he would probably have to make an awful lot of deals to get elected.

ECKHARDT: That's right, and it tends to diminish the independence of the member in making a determination on ideological questions. For instance, if I know that I can be removed from a Committee, if I don't follow the Speaker's desires, then I make a decision against my better judgment.

BLACK: What we're exploring here are the eternal alternatives of organization, and I think most people are disappointed to find that to these questions of, let's say, the distribution of Committee Chairmanships, there isn't any perfect answer. There is no side of the angels to be on. I feel very sure that if seniority were totally abolished, and the Speaker given autocratic power to assign Committee Chairmen—

let's say to move you up in seniority if he were pleased to do so, or make you Chairman next term of Congress, of the whole Committee on Interstate and Foreign Commerce, and then if you didn't suit him during the succeeding year, to pull you back, take you out, and put somebody else in instead—then we would begin hearing words we've heard long ago, calling the Speaker "Czar," and "autocrat," and complaints about the lack of *independence* on the part of Committee members. If Committee Chairmen were elected by a vote, either on the Floor or in the full Committee, the process would become so politicized and be subject to such continual convulsions that I think we could look forward pretty confidently to one hell of a mess.

ECKHARDT: I've had actual experience in a system that had no seniority, in the Texas Legislature. Of course there I benefitted in my second term; I was the Chairman of a Committee because I had been one of the early supporters of the man who got elected Speaker of the House. Next term a man on the other side got elected, and I wasn't even on the Committee that I had chaired the previous term.

Some of the reforms in the congressional seniority system are most desirable. I think that we should not disturb the movement (almost mechanical in its nature) of a man to the Chairmanship on the basis of seniority, but we should not, simply because he's old in the service of the Committee, and therefore Chairman, assign to him inordinately grea*t power*. The reform movement that has occurred since I have been here (let's say it began about the Ninetieth Congress and has continued to the present) is to make the Committee Chairman amenable to rules, so that he doesn't make the rules as he goes along. The openness of the Committee hearings, and of most of the Committee mark-ups, tends to make the Chairman fair, because, if he is obviously a dictatorial Chairman he alienates the press. It may even get back to his district, to the point of defeating him. The Committee members may become a little bolder in objecting to his arbitrary rulings in public than they would be if it were in private, because they are protected to a certain extent by public opinion. Incidentally, that's the reason I would tip the scale in favor of creating a presumption in favor of openness in mark-up.

BLACK: As to the mark-up, my real objection is that a certain amount of business *will be* conducted in secret, no matter what they say about it. I tend to prefer that that secrecy be a *formal* secrecy, with a record kept, so that there is an element of responsibility, rather than having everything seem to be on parade and in the open, while the necessary confidentiality—which will always be present in any process of government—will have to take place in informal ways with no record for history, no responsibility of any kind. That's one basis for my preference for formal confidentiality.

ECKHARDT: In any instance, amendments which are offered must be a part of the record, the results of the vote must be a part of the record, and if a vote has been recorded, the way the members voted must be a part of the record.

BLACK: That's the kind of record I would think right—a public record for which a public man should be responsible. But go ahead. We're talking about the power of a Chairman, and you feel that the sociology, you might say, of this has been changed by being opened on most occasions because tyrannical action is very much more difficult to carry on in public and the members are somewhat emboldened.

ECKHARDT: That's right.

BLACK: Possibly because they don't want to appear submissive.

ECKHARDT: The openness of the hearing, the requirement of written rules subject to certain basic standards in the general rules, the assurance that members may exercise their position on their Subcommittees and retain them in accordance with the preconceived design, all of these things give the members independence and make the Chairman of the Committee more like a Speaker, or presiding officer, and less of a powerful operator writing law or amending law through his large and able staff, frequently with the connivance of the minority, through the ranking minority member. In the past, before the rules changes came into effect, there was a tendency for two powerful old cronies—the Chairman and the ranking minority member, who might become the Chairman after the next election—to get together. These men had a lot in common and frequently, with the kind of power they had through the staffs and through the fact that they could either bring up or not bring up bills, they could direct Subcommittee Chairmen to hear or not hear bills. They can still do all of that, but not so much in private. It was an enormous power that could be exercised by these two men. If there are no rules, and if the hearings can all be held in secret, these two men have enormously greater power within their sphere than the Speaker of the House has in the sphere of the whole House. I would tend to favor weakening the position of the Committee Chairmen and strengthening the position of the Speaker.

BLACK: Probably the greatest power left to the Committee Chairman, if I've followed you in this discussion, is the power to prevent a bill from coming up in his Committee, which in effect bottles it up. This, in the absence of a successful circulation of a discharge petition, or the successful application to the Rules Committee to bring it out, keeps the bill from coming to the Floor for a vote or any kind of action. What do you think of the proposition of vesting this power, not in the Chairman, but in the Committee, so that instead of a discharge petition on the Floor of the House, or—as an alternative to the discharge petition on the Floor of the House—the signatures of a majority, or some greater number, of the Committee could bring about a hearing in the Committee, and force a report on the bill?

ECKHARDT: Well, if there's a strong enough majority on a Committee, the Committee now has ways of pressuring the Chairman to do this. However, it's very difficult to do this sort of thing directly, because those who are engaged in the coup may suffer if the coup does not succeed. There are all kinds of ways that the obstreperous Committee members may be hurt. Probably the best course to break through a bill generally supported by the Democratic majority is through caucus[7] action. The caucus, for instance, may direct that a bill be treated in Committee, and its directive may be enforced on Democrats, including the Chairman and the Democratic majority on the Committee.

7. This term is defined on p. 153.

BLACK: The Democratic caucus comprises all the Democratic members of the House of Representatives?

ECKHARDT: That's right.

BLACK: Now, this again is an extraconstitutional body, and I think it's fascinating how, as we discuss the actual working structure of the House of Representatives, none of it has anything at all to do with the written Constitution, as we know it. It's all referred to in one sentence, which says that each House may make its own rules,[8] and that's it.

ECKHARDT: If the caucus ever got stomach enough to do it, and we ought to, we could direct the Ways and Means Committee to come out with tax reform. It could bring in a greater net amount of taxes, by stopping tax loopholes. When the Ways and Means Committee stops loopholes, it usually sweetens the package with some tax cuts, so that the total decrease equals or exceeds the total increase.

BLACK: I can see how caucus pressure could be useful as to *any* Committee. There are points in the flow of business in one body where what is needed to enable people to do what they want to do is some visible pressure from the *outside*. This may sometimes neutralize pressure from other quarters, and furnish them with an explanation—to those pressing for some other results—of their acting in the way that those people don't want them to do.

ECKHARDT: That's right; members of the Committee can then pressure their Chairman, if he's reluctant, on the grounds that they have been directed to do so by the Democratic caucus. They are not then put in a position of vulnerability, looking like gratuitous enemies of the Chairman.

BLACK: Have we been through all the bad news on the Committee system?

ECKHARDT: No, there's one other thing. The Committees do tend to respond to interests that have long been involved with that Committee's business, and there frequently develops an easy and informal

8. Article I, Section 5.

relationship between able lobby spokesmen and the staffs of Committees—and of course with some of the Committee members. This is a mixed curse and blessing, because persons affected by legislation also know most intimately what the legislation does and how it can be altered to avoid bad results.

BLACK: This is another one of those cases where the public is likely to see a word—in this case the word "lobbyist"—as having a totally pejorative connotation. The one lobbyist that I have known well was a lobbyist for the NAACP. He is, in the first place, a fountain of information on the problems that affect black people and on the needs and wants of black people. His access to this stream of communication is far better than that of virtually any member of Congress. The word "lobbyist" really just means somebody who has an interest in the subject, and we may agree or disagree with his recommendation, but for people who have an interest in a subject to make their views known, and to provide information, is very far from being evil.

ECKHARDT: Then another thing, lobbying at the Committee level is vastly better than lobbying at the level of action by the full body itself. For instance, in Austin, in the Texas Legislature, lobbying tended to be totally politicized, totally at the level of pressure for a decision pro or con, without any concept of accommodation or amendment, because it was at the terminal point of legislation. Either you passed the bill or defeated it, or made sweeping changes that you had no time to study. Therefore, lobbying in Austin tended to be the kind of beef and bourbon lobbying that called for an unreasoned, uncompromised result. The lobbying here tends to be the lobbying of an expert who knows the legal and technical aspects of the bill, and attempts to change its thrust to take care of certain problems that the particular interest may feel are salient. Beside that, if the change caused by lobbying occurs at an early enough stage, as in the Subcommittee, it may be undone at various stages—in full Committee, on the Floor, or in the Conference Committee.

By the way, there's one other thing that I want to mention with respect to the power of the Speaker. The Speaker has the power of appointment of all the conferees on all the Conference Committees from the House. These are the extremely important Committees that resolve the differences between the House and the Senate versions of bills, and ultimately write the final legislation. A lot of times, matters are not totally resolved by either body, and, you know, the conferees technically may not go outside the framework of difference. But corrections and improvements made at the conference stage can actually fashion the final legislation.

BLACK: And those Conference Reports usually come up to be voted up or down, don't they?

ECKHARDT: That's right. So this action is quite final. Normally the Speaker will automatically accept the Chairman of the Committee's recommendations for the conferees, and the most usual method is to put on the conference the Chairman of the Committee, the ranking minority member, and then, on down the line, several Democrats and Republicans from the Subcommittee that dealt with the subject matter.

BLACK: With conferees, then, consisting of the people who are probably most knowledgeable about the bill?

ECKHARDT: No, not necessarily. And that's a place where I think the Speaker should exercise more judgment, after consultation with the Chairman of the Committee, because the results of the Conference powerfully affects, in many instances, important programs of the majority party.

BLACK: I boggle a little bit at the idea of increasing the power of the Speaker. I'm just thinking this through aloud, but here's the trouble that I see with it. The increase of the power of the Speaker, as a general rule, would force him to make deals as to the *use* of that power.

ECKHARDT: Well, that's the reason I would not abolish the seniority system as to Committee appointments in general. But with respect to these temporary assignments to Conference Committees, there ought to be more flexibility to put knowledgeable people who are concerned with the legislation into a position in which they can control its outcome, not merely on the basis of seniority, but on the basis of knowledge, ability, and interest. I think that's a good compromise. One of the failures of our body is the failure to use its greatest talent in the areas where that talent can be most useful. What this tends to do is to remove most of the talented action, nearly all of the lawyerlike process, and all the technical action from members to staff. I think it would be well to move it a little bit more toward the members.

BLACK: Do you think the Speaker could make accurate judgments as to Conference Committee membership on the time schedule that he has to operate on? How many of these Conference Committees have to be appointed in a course of a session?

ECKHARDT: A great number. It'd be in the hundreds.

BLACK: Why don't we step back a pace, and take a look at your own conceptions as to desirable reforms?

ECKHARDT: I think there are two areas for reform in the Committee process—two primary areas. They both have to do with the question of the degree of flexibility and the means of getting around crystallized jurisdictional forms. Neither of these really calls for a change of the power either of the Speaker or of the caucus. First, with respect to a bill which may overlap the jurisdiction of several Committees, it seems patently ridiculous to divide up a single bill with related subject matter in the jurisdiction of two Committees, and not hear witnesses on all aspects of the bill together. The same persons should hear all the testimony and also devise a structure and balance for the total bill. For that reason, it seems to me, the Speaker should exercise authority quite freely to designate a single Committee to hear a single subject matter or a single bill which may contain several related subject matters, and that this should develop to the point where the traditional operations of the House will not respond adversely to such procedure, expressing a narrow jealousy with respect to jurisdictional rights in the subject matter of the bill.

BLACK: That is one of the proposals which it scarcely takes any experience in the process to evaluate favorably; it seems to me quite obvious that any bill that has any business being a single bill, has parts which react with one another. I am surprised to learn that there is a practice of splitting these bills up. It seems to me so evidently wrong to do so. A bill that lends itself readily and practically to being divided into pieces and given to different Committees shouldn't have been a single bill in the first place.

ECKHARDT: Let me say quickly that though jurisdictional jealousy between Committees is pretty deeply ingrained, nevertheless a single Committee frequently does treat subject matter overlapping the jurisdiction of another Committee without any contest from the other Committee, where the question is not one in which some strongly felt viewpoint of one Committee, or of some lobbyist influential with that Committee, has been infringed. But where there is a protest, the Speaker ought to settle it and settle it conclusively, so that the Committee may proceed in a validated process, and there is not a wrangle on the Floor at a later time as to whether the bill ought to come out at all.

BLACK: Yes. But it seems to me that for expertise it might be relevant, it might be possible, to develop some *lateral* lines of communication which would, for example, place some of the staff of one Committee at the temporary disposal of another for help in evaluating one part of the bill. That strikes me as another useful device, for ensuring enlistment of all relevant expertness.

ECKHARDT: That is something that ought to be done much more than it is now. It is not highly developed, and it should be. The other point of flexibility, which again is within the present rules of Congress, is this. Where a bill has a subject matter of grave importance, a subject matter that very likely calls for expertise from several Committees, like the question of an entire revision of the health system of the United States, such a pervasive and important subject matter would be best treated by a Special Committee devised to deal with that bill only. What I am talking about is a Committee that would act precisely as a standing Committee acts on a bill within the jurisdiction of that standing Committee, but only on the single bill; a Committee that would end with the passage of that bill.

BLACK: For example, a bill setting the overall energy policy of the United States would affect so many areas that it would be wise perhaps to refer it to a special *ad hoc* Committee—to create a Select Committee for the sole purpose of considering this bill, or perhaps a group of competing bills on the same subject, from all of which some suggestions might be drawn and among which a selection might be made.

Let's summarize here. The American people have very little knowledge—and that exceedingly inexact—of the actual processes by which law is made. You have concentrated on the House of Representatives because that is what you know best. But there are comparable functional processes in the Senate. What we find first about these processes is that they actually work smoothly in the main, and that may be why people think of them so little and know so little about them. They are entirely extraconstitutional—they are not commanded by the Constitution, and therefore are entirely malleable to change if you want to change them, and without any question of constitutional amendment. Now, it seems to me that what we find in the structure we have been exploring is not a set of contrivances which are elaborated simply for the purpose of having a complicated procedure, or for any other ulterior purpose. They are contrivances or devices which are made virtually necessary—not in their present form, because the form could be changed, but as a generic matter—by the nature of the work itself. It is impossible for the hundreds of members of the House of Representatives to get together collectively and consider, in the detail required for intelligent judgment, all the features of every bill that is needed to be passed in the session, or even to go so far as to decide which ones of them do need to be passed. There aren't that many hours in the day; there isn't that kind of capacity for deliberation in a body of that size. Reference to some kind of smaller body, a body charged with special and more intensive responsibility, is necessary. Now, given that fact, the Committee system seems to emerge as very probably the best imaginable solution. The other solution would be the use of outside people, people who are not going to have even a part in the final decision, and I don't think one needs to dwell very much on the wrongness of that.

In the staff system, with the Committees, we get the benefit of all the rightness of that; we *do* have people who are not charged with the ultimate responsibility but who are helping in all this. But the

Committees themselves are a part of the body that will finally decide. That does not require apology. I think it is self-explanatory, and in itself suffices to rebut what I think is the prevalent folk wisdom to the effect that the Committee system is sort of an unnecessary excrescence on the legislative process. It is, on the contrary, necessary in *some* form, and the general form it has taken is probably the best that it could take.

The question then becomes, "How best do you select these Committees and how best do you select the Chairmen who run them?"

ECKHARDT: Before going on to the question of the constitution of these Committees, how they are chosen, I think one of them—the Rules Committee—needs to be singled out and its necessity pinpointed. There has got to be a traffic cop. There's no way to run the business of the House of Representatives without *somebody* who will say what is to be done next. There also must be somebody who places a time limit on consideration, because the alternative to the limitation of time is the filibuster, which is indeed a feature of the life of the Senate, though not a widely admired feature. We do not have it in the House, and we do not have it precisely because there is somebody to impose a time limitation on discussion. Whether the closed rule is wise in a particular case or not—the rule that no amendments can be offered—is a question of judgment, but it does seem that in the case of a tax bill or a tariff bill it is probably very wise to impose such a rule. If it is *ever* going to be wise to do it, somebody will have to decide *when* it is going to be wise. I think these considerations make some group of people, fulfilling roughly the function of the Rules Committee, an absolute necessity to a deliberative body that does not propose to become totally bogged down in a tangled morass of business. The Rules Committee also fulfills a very important function in creating exceptions to the very strict germaneness rule[9] of the House. If one could insist on germaneness in areas where the problems

9. This rule requires that any offered amendment to a bill must be "germane," that is, relevant to that bill—must concern its very subject matter. This rule prevents use of the "rider"—a provision tacked on to a bill on another subject entirely.

may be corrected outside the formalistic area that the bill deals with, desirable alternative approaches may be blocked off. The Rules Committee can waive points of order on any point, and waiver of the germaneness rule is the most common and most important. Of course, the Senate does not have any germaneness rule.

BLACK: I am especially impressed with the point that life could not be lived in the House of Representatives without some kind of a traffic cop. Now, if you see that these functions are necessary, then the only question left is as to matters of detail, and not matters of constitutional structures. I am very much inclined to agree with you that in a world where perfection is unattainable, the least trouble is to be found in the seniority system, the system that avoids all the bloodletting and all the dealing that any of these other systems would involve. Bear in mind that this bloodletting and dealing would not be over any substantive issues, but would be strictly ancillary, or even obstructive, to the real business of the House. I don't think it is worth it.

I will just make one final remark. I think that the American people, being a quite idealistic people, tend to think (if one brought the thought out consciously and stated it explicitly) that what ought to be done is that every question be brought very promptly to the Floor of the House and immediately voted on by everybody there with all members in attendance. This is a possible system. It is possible in the sense in which it is possible that twenty million people in the United States will learn to speak fluent Japanese within the next five years. This is a possibility. We don't know any physical fact that makes this impossible. This possibility is negated, instead, by the nature of human beings in society and their necessities from an organizational point of view, from a motivational point of view, and so on. Now, in the real world of the House of Representatives, and in similar deliberative bodies, it is *in this sense* impossible that such rapid-fire, idealized progress—if it would be progress—will ever take place. There have to be more complex procedures, they are quite evidently necessary on the basis not only of the considerations we have had time to analyze but also of a great many others, and I think we have to look once again for something different from what we usually tend to look for.

I think we misdirect our attention, in this as in many other areas of American political life, when we look for the trouble in *organizational or constitutional* dispositions. If things are not going well with us, and with our government and society, this is not by and large, in my view, a result of any structural defects. The defects are of *will*. The House has the machinery *now* which, with a few adjustments such as you suggest, can be made to work exceedingly well, whenever the membership wants it to work well, toward those ends which the members, representing their constituencies, want to attain. That is all that we can ask of any political organization. That is democracy; the question now is, "What does democracy *want* to do?"

ECKHARDT: I think that sums it up well.

7 DO WE GET THE PRESIDENTS WE DESERVE?

BLACK: There is little question that at the present time one of the problems to which the political system of our nation has to address itself is the rehabilitation of the presidency. It would pay us at this time to think and talk a little bit about the most fundamental thing, constitutionally, about this office—the means by which the President is elected. This sorts itself into a number of levels. It would be more clarificatory first to talk a bit about the distinctively American institution of the Electoral College, which has been subjected, in recent times, to a great deal of criticism.

ECKHARDT: One thing that the Electoral College system does is put a great premium on the obtaining of support in those areas where great blocks of electoral votes may be obtained—New York and California, Ohio and Illinois.

BLACK: Let's not forget Texas.

ECKHARDT: And Texas. We have the winner-take-all principle. If one of those States is won by the barest majority, the total electoral votes of that State are thereby cast for the candidate. I think there's no question but this gives more clout to the States with the big blocks of electoral votes. The question arises, is this necessarily bad? I suggest that it's not necessarily bad, for two reasons. One, it affords some degree of balance in favor of these large population areas, which, as I have listed them, are areas where, perhaps, more progressive total political climate exists, as compared, for instance, to the South. It creates a kind of balance because, as is generally known, the South has an inordinately great weight in the Congress through its being composed largely of one-party States, because this results in tremendous seniority for Congressmen coming from the South. Ultimately, they end in Committee Chairmanships. Texas, for instance, has something like five Committee Chairmen at the present time. And the South at large, if I recall correctly, has about a third of the total Chairmen in the House, with the population much smaller than a third of the nation. The other point for giving a little additional weight to the big States is that it is in the big States that many extremely important problems develop first, and there is a greater sensitivity to those problems in those States, and the greatest likelihood of obtaining some solution for them. Take, for instance, the most difficult and the crying problem for us, the race question. There's no question but that men like Truman, seeking the nomination, paid more attention to the areas in which the loudest voices called for racial justice. And, I suppose they would have been at that time New York, Illinois, California, as opposed, for instance, to southern States who wanted to retain the status quo, or some of the western States in which there wasn't really any problem. So the fact that the problems of modern government frequently develop in big metropolitan areas, or in large population areas, causes the candidates to pay more attention to problems that are in the van of political development.

BLACK: It's perhaps indicative, however, of the lack of mechanical character of this, of the fact that we're dealing with an organic whole, that the *very* sparsely populated States get some advantage out of the Electoral College system, so that they are not entirely negligible in a presidential campaign. If they really were rated entirely on their population, and that alone, they probably would be disregarded altogether and there would be no necessity whatever for a candidate's even thinking about them. But the formula by which we choose the electors, that is, one for each Senator and Representative,[1] ensures that no State will have fewer than three. But still it works out that it's an advantage to the more populous States, in all likelihood, in most presidential elections. This would again depend on particular configurations. Truman, I believe, managed to put together a victory without many of the larger States. But, even so, I think, through

1. Article II, Section 1.

history, this large-State advantage is both the mathematical probability and the working assumption of all practical politicians.

ECKHARDT: I think it is interesting that a good number of representatives in Congress from the very heavily populated areas have misconceived the advantages and disadvantages of the Electoral College. Looking at the addition of the senatorial positions in calculating the Electoral College, they've actually come to the conclusion that the electoral system favors the southern States. As a matter of fact, and on the other side, on the votes concerning a constitutional amendment to bring about direct election of the President, the southerners have frequently voted against their interests, they've been the ones who have stood most staunchly for the Electoral College.

BLACK: Well, I think this is because people are living either in the past or in a present which is rapidly disappearing. In earlier times, the Electoral College was extremely advantageous to, say, Mississippi, with approximately the same population as Connecticut, as long as about half the people—the blacks—were totally disenfranchised. The *population,* including blacks, governed the number of electors, and this advantage worked not only in the Electoral College, it also worked in Congress. It really was astonishing, and to some extent still is, to look at the figures of voting in these two States. What's happening, however, is that in the peripheral South, in the border South, the groups who had been disenfranchised, of course mainly black people, are voting in greater and greater numbers, and this particular advantage is on its way out with the Voting Rights Act. The situation virtually everywhere is on its way out just as fast as black people start to vote in great numbers.

Now the alternative that is in the minds of the people who propose alternatives is direct popular election of the President. The fear that animates this is that somebody will be elected who does not have as many popular votes as his opponent. And the desideratum which has been held out is that that person shall be elected who is desired as President by the majority of the American people. The trouble with the concept of bringing it about that the person who is wanted as first choice by a majority of the American people shall be elected as

President is that ordinarily there is no such person. Where there is such a person—and it may have happened a couple of times in this century, let's say with Roosevelt in 1936, and with Eisenhower—that person is going to be elected under *any* system. He's going to get an overwhelming majority in the Electoral College, and is going to get a substantial majority of the popular vote, and there's not going to be any problem. The usual situation is that *no* person is the first choice for the presidency of a majority of the American people. And the real problem in electing the President is not to devise means to elect the person who is the first choice of a majority of the people, because he doesn't exist, but, rather, to elect, and to legitimatize in some acceptable way, somebody who is the first choice of a very substantial number of people, and who is reasonably acceptable, down a descending scale, to enough of the rest of the people that he can be a viable President.

Direct popular election is not the best means of finding that reasonably viable person, because there are only two ways to do direct popular elections, as far as I can see. There may be variations on them, but they're all going to boil down to this. Either you hold a single election, and install as President the person who receives the highest number of votes, whatever percentage of the vote that may be —electing, in other words, on a plurality basis—or you hold a runoff. The first of these obviously is a laughable method of trying to get into office the person who is preferred by a majority of the American people. It's entirely conceivable, indeed could easily happen, that the candidate who got the most votes—perhaps 25 percent—in a field of, say, five or six people, would be detested by all the people who voted for all the other five people, and would be the *last* choice of a very large majority of the American people.

A runoff doesn't really better this situation. The first campaign I remember in Texas, and you probably remember it too, took place some fifty years ago. It was in the summer of 1924, because what we called the "election" then was of course the runoff in the Democratic primary. In the first primary, a minority of the votes, a decided minority, went to Mrs. Ferguson, the wife of an impeached and removed Populist former Governor, who was himself disqualified from holding office, but who had enough popular following to ensure that he could get his candidate in the runoff, and to Felix T. Robertson, the Grand Kleagle of the Ku Klux Klan in Texas, who, in turn, had a minority of the votes, but could command the KKK votes in Texas. Now that put two minority candidates in the runoff, because they were the two highest. As I recall that election, it's very likely, certainly it's easily possible, and I think it was the case, that nearly everybody except those who had voted for Felix T. Robertson in the first primary greatly disliked the prospect of Felix T. Robertson's being in the governorship, while everybody except those who had voted as loyal Jim Ferguson followers for Ma Ferguson disliked the prospect of Ma Ferguson in the governorship. In other words, if you had had a straight yes-or-no vote on either one of those people, the no's would have prevailed, overwhelmingly. Instead, you put them both in a runoff. My people, and I imagine yours, rather reluctantly went in and voted for Mrs. Ferguson, in order to avoid having a Ku Kluxer at the head of the State government, but this, as you see, was in no way a triumph of the principle that the person who is most desired by the people should be Governor.

ECKHARDT: Nevertheless, the runoff election is a very good way of determining who is ultimately acceptable to a majority, and a very good way to give an ultimate public sanction to the winner under ordinary circumstance. It has some rather peculiar problems though, if you apply it to the presidency. In the first place, there is much more tendency to divide the public in accordance with two parties that have something like an ideological base, as each party does. It's really almost inconceivable that someone other than a Democrat or a Republican, in most of our elections, would have even a chance of winning. And, of course, if we had a runoff, the issue would be so delayed in decision that a lot of problems could arise. I don't know whether the runoff as a matter of basic philosophical principle is as bad as you depicted.

BLACK: Well, I think it is, because I think what our present system forces us to do is, normally, to cause each of the major parties to come forward with what is in effect a coalition candidate. The straight open primary, like we used to have in Texas, encourages a large number of candidacies. No one of those candidates has to make, necessarily, or is under any particular pressure to make, any broad coalition which softens viewpoints and allies them, so that they can go forward to become sort of a general government. Very often a candidate's interests are just the other way. He may see his chances of getting in the runoff as dependent on holding, let's say, 25 percent of the people very loyally to himself. That may be enough, in a field with a lot of candidates, to get you into the runoff. If we had that kind of presidential election it would change the rules of the game all down the line. We would have a lot of candidates; we could not hold it down to two, three, or four. We'd have constant pressure for smaller ideological groups, with a greater coherency of ideas and much less willingness to compromise, to put forward a candidate representing that point of view. If that possibility, or that probability as I see it, were to eventuate and become a fact, then the normal runoff would be between two representatives of rather narrow bands of the political spectrum, rather than between two people who have been forced by the process, in advance, partly by the party process, but to a great extent by the single-election winner-take-all process, to form a broad coalition of interests before they go into the race. I really think that is the arithmetic of it, and I believe that is the way it would work out.

I would point out, too, the manner in which this might impinge on congressional elections. Six, eight, or ten candidates for President might be on the ballot in the first presidential election, the one preparatory to a runoff. There is no way we could prevent that, and that there would be great deal of pressure for it to be so. If each of those people were fighting with an idea of possibly getting into the runoff, the inevitable result, it seems to me, would be that a full ticket for Senator and for Congressmen would be fielded in each State, and in each congressional district. We would tend to have, correspondingly, six, eight, or ten candidates for Congress in this first election as well. Now, how are congressional elections now managed, by plurality —or does it vary from State to State?

ECKHARDT: Congressional? In the general election it is by plurality.

BLACK: Now, if that were the system followed, and we followed a plurality system as to Congress, though not as to the presidency, and didn't have a runoff, we'd get a Congress of an immensely different complexion from what we now get. We would get Congressmen who had tagged along with perhaps a minority candidate, and who were elected at the end of the first election, even though that candidate was not going into the presidency. We might get representatives of six, eight, or ten different narrow bands in an ideological spectrum in Congress, with no allegiance to either of two major parties. In fact, the two major parties might easily go out of existence or cease to have much influence. If we had a runoff in congressional elections, we'd have much the same difficulties as in this other connection, but, since the margin between getting in the runoff and not getting in the runoff is likely to be rather narrow in a large field of candidates, it might well happen that the runoff as to *congressional* candidates would not involve representatives of the same bands in the political spectrum as were represented by the two *presidential* candidates in the State.

ECKHARDT: I would put the argument on a more directly pragmatic basis, although I'm not sure you're not doing the same thing. Looking at the presidential elections in the past, of course, the popular vote, the plurality, in every instance, except possibly one, has achieved the same result as the Electoral College. The Hayes-Tilden race might have been an exception, but it is a bad one to point up as an exception, because I think it was simply stolen from Tilden.

BLACK: Hayes-Tilden is not a good example at all, because you could steal any election, no matter what the system might be. The Jackson–John Quincy Adams election is not a good example, because it didn't fail, if indeed it failed at all, on account of the Electoral College. The election was thrown into the House of Representatives. This has to do with a different feature of the system, and nobody got a majority of the popular vote in that election. There was a plurality for Jackson, but not a majority. So, there's one other one and that's the Benjamin Harrison, the second Harrison election, where there was a slight excess of popular votes on the part of the loser. Now, this is a very small amount of failure for a system. A very small amount of failure. The difference was very small, and in fact so small that the election, for all practical purposes, could be looked on as a tie. When you look over nearly two hundred years, this is really a very small margin of failure on the part of the Electoral College system.

We have to remember on the other hand that the system has had some stunning successes. Abraham Lincoln was elected President under the Electoral College system, with some 39 percent of the popular vote. Had there been a runoff, had there been a popular vote election with a runoff, there isn't any doubt whatever that Lincoln would have lost, because any supporter, or virtually any supporter, of Douglas, Breckinridge, or Bell would have voted for any one of those three rather than for Lincoln. It would, as it happens, have been Douglas, because he was the runner-up. It's inconceivable that supporters of Breckinridge and Bell in that election would have gone into an election involving Lincoln and Douglas and voted for Lincoln.

Now that 1860 result was a good result, and the reason it was a good result was that in that election the Democratic party, by the sheer fact of its splitting up as it did, showed that it really wasn't a fit instrument to govern the country at that time. It was so badly divided in itself that the only thing Douglas could have done would be to put together a coalition government which would have begun immediately to spread apart through inherent centrifugal forces, whereas this 39 percent who were Republicans were reasonably well united, in a reasonably strong coalition, actually capable of running the government. The system worked out beautifully in that case, quite aside from the accident of the fact that we got our greatest political genius, and our greatest man—who was elected in this manner which is so repulsive to people who attack this system today.

There is one more thing about the direct popular election which seems to me very important. It's a practical problem, but it's a practical problem which is virtually insoluble. If direct popular election were the rule, the vote fraud and recount problem would be, for a nation of this size, almost insoluble. You'd have it at two points, one of them with a very exigent time-limit on it—the point where you have to decide who has made the runoff. Now some of those elections may be very close, and you notice that if it's a nationwide popular vote, it's not separated into compartments where you can say as to a large number of the compartments, we don't care whether there is a fraud there or not, except for purposes of criminal prosecution, because if the State despite minor errors went overwhelmingly for this other person it wouldn't make any difference whether 10,000 votes were stolen. But it would matter everywhere if the vote were taken nationwide.

ECKHARDT: Exactly.

BLACK: And I think it passes the wit of man to devise a system which would produce a satisfactory solution—a solution with a feeling of appeasement, of the thing's having been done right—to the question of which of two candidates went in a runoff, when perhaps the difference between them, on a nationwide basis, was 5,000 or 10,000 votes. That could easily happen in a large field of candidates.

ECKHARDT: Well, as a matter of fact, some presidential elections even now are not won by more than a few percentage points or even by only a fraction of a percentage point.

BLACK: The election as close as the Kennedy–Nixon election in 1960 would in the second stage, between the two candidates, probably never produce a satisfactory result. It would have been fought out years later whether there was a vote fraud which was decisive in the case, because you couldn't confine it to one or two states. If a vote fraud was charged in Florida on the part of one side, it's just about certain that the other side will develop the theory that there was, say, a vote fraud in Oregon that matched out against the one in Florida. The recount would have to be general—for the entire country.

ECKHARDT: There's a strong interest in finality, and a strong interest in a general feeling among the electorate that the election was valid. For some rather complex reasons, the electoral system, the way it has been set up, always, or nearly always, strongly accentuates in the electoral vote, or magnifies in the electoral vote, the majority in the popular vote. So that there is this feeling. And the fact that someone might find that a recount of the votes in Duvall County in Texas, or Cook County in Illinois, would have changed the popular vote, becomes irrelevant in the minds of the people because there was such a sweeping electoral victory, and, technically, the recount wouldn't change the results.

BLACK: Often, though not always, it wouldn't change the result even if fraud or mistake were there. Of course, it obviously can happen, under the Electoral College system, that vote miscounts, alleged vote miscounts, and frauds are so strategically located that if each one of them were resolved in favor of the apparent loser, the result would be changed. But that's going to be rather infrequent with the Electoral College system, whereas it would be an occurrence almost every time you had a close direct-vote election. And consider the motivation generated to steal votes everywhere. There are lots of places now where it wouldn't do you any good to steal a few votes, because the State is going to go one way or another anyway, so there's no motivation for it. If the total nationwide popular vote were anticipated to be close, then there would be a motive to steal votes everywhere.

ECKHARDT: And where they could be stolen most easily.

BLACK: Exactly. The places where it happened would be those where concealment was most easily possible.

I tell you that what finally happened with this Electoral College business, it seems to me, was that all the difficulties that we have been talking about, and many others, gradually entered the consciousnesses of the people who were working on this, and who were first animated by this rather naive feeling that the thing to do was to get the person whom the majority of the American people want— the person who, as I have said, doesn't normally exist. They began putting in one bill after another; each person got up a different bill. Epicycles like the Ptolemaic epicycles, were put on top of epicycles, certain percentages required to trigger this, and certain configurations required to trigger that, to the point where they looked like machines that the late Rube Goldberg might have devised. But the point was— and I think that this is what really happened—it finally became clear, as these alternatives became more and more complicated, while each particular one commanded less and less support, that there was *no acceptable alternative* to the Electoral College system. There was no alternative that could actually command support of any breadth, after it was taken out and fully examined and criticized. At that point I wrote Senator Brooke, who sent me one of these plans when I was in England a few years ago, just exactly in these terms. I said it looks to me, Senator, like now the thing is getting so complicated that what is actually being demonstrated is that we cannot now devise and get support for any good alternative to the Electoral College. And it seems to me that's the time to quit, that's what's actually been demonstrated. So, let's just go back to what we've done, without any serious problems about it, for a couple of hundred years.

ECKHARDT: I think that ultimately, the most important shortfall in justice and effectiveness is in the selection of the *nominee.*

BLACK: Let's put the grease on a squeaking wheel, and the wheel that is really squeaking is the selection of *candidates.*

ECKHARDT: Well, let me say first, that whatever defects may exist in the system of electing the President, at least it's constitutionally governed. There is no law that really governs the *selection* of candidates. There is no basis in the Constitution. As a matter of fact all the statutory law that touches on the matter, doesn't touch on the machinery, or the process of the selection, but only touches on things that are forbidden as abuses connected with convention process, or election process, and so forth. But the total structure of selecting the candidate is within the control of the political parties, almost completely unrestricted by the Constitution.

BLACK: I think it is totally unrestricted by the Constitution.

ECKHARDT: That's right, and it's only affected peripherally by law.

BLACK: Of course, that is not to say that it can't be *dealt with* by law. The recognition by Congress that this is in fact the method by which we elect the President, and Congress's operation on it by statutory means, would be entirely constitutional. Whether it would be desirable, and to what extent, and what mode would be desirable are other questions.

ECKHARDT: I think that it should be dealt with by federal statute. I don't believe that a federal statute should create a straitjacket with respect to the structure by which a convention or an election would determine the method of selecting delegates to a convention from a State. But I do think that there ought to be two things addressed by a federal statute. One is the problem of the long period of time during which the nomination process runs. For instance, there is a primary in New Hampshire, during the early period of nomination, and then in another State a convention that may occur in May, and then in another State a primary which may occur anytime before the national convention.

BLACK: There's not much necessary to say about that, because I think it is an obvious fact that presidential campaigns are enormously too long by a factor of four or five times. The whole process should be shortened up, not only in the stage of nomination, but also in the interval between nomination and election.

ECKHARDT: I think it should.

BLACK: It is an exhausting process that is entirely unnecessary.

ECKHARDT: And beside that, the process is one that focuses the attention of the press of the entire nation at any one time on a relatively small part of the country. The result is that what is being done in that corner of the country is the conducting of a kind of a circus. We have the crass and shocking spectacle of Robert Kennedy, in the midst of a parade in Chicago, having his clothes torn off in the presence of television, so that people would have souvenirs. The whole thing is done as a great circus before the national public, when it ought to relate to the serious deliberations of a particular State on the question of who their delegates will be, and who they will favor for the nomination. We invite, in that sort of situation, every kook in the country to come, not just from the electorate from which the delegates are to be chosen, but from the entire United States, to take

a pot shot at the most promising candidate. We create a totally impossible situation, it seems to me, by our present system.

BLACK: We sure do, and one of the many things about it that is
distorted. A distortion which has been demonstratively realized in
recent times is that because of the spacing of these primaries, because
they go on so long, because they are so remote in time from the
election, there is a tendency for people who are exceedingly zealous
on behalf of a particular candidate, a candidate representative of a
rather small spectrum of political possibility, to work very hard in
advancing this candidate toward becoming nominated, and to succeed
in bringing this about through very intensive activity in one primary
after another, at a time when the mass of the people are not really
stirred up at all. You get, in consequence, a candidate of the far right,
like Goldwater, or a candidate of the rather far left, like McGovern,
who hasn't got a chance in the world of winning, who has insufficient
appeal to the electorate at large for winning the presidency to be a
serious possibility. Now of all the things that could defeat the system,
it is for the *nominating* process to eventuate quite often in the production of a candidate who hasn't got a chance to be elected. The whole
system has failed at that point. We've seen that happen twice just
recently, as the primary systems have become more complicated,
proliferated more and more. I'm afraid we're going to see it again,
indeed maybe get to the point where it is rather the norm, so we might
even have the situation of two candidates representing rather small
areas in the political spectrum pitted against one another, without
the kind of formation on either side of a coalition which makes it
possible to carry on a government with a considerable amount of
consensus after one candidate is elected and in the White House.

ECKHARDT: We have the technological ability to afford wider exposure of the candidate and the platform of the candidate in a short
time—a more realistic joining of issues between candidates, a better
opportunity to frame positions and to give persons a choice on the
basis of positions than has ever existed in America in its entire history.

BLACK: And we're just not using that at all. We're using it to
produce prolonged sensation, rather than enlightenment.

ECKHARDT: Exactly. In this long spread of time the incidents are used solely as an interesting spectacle in connection with the campaign, but not as a part of the fiber of the electoral process. Now I think our problem is to try to shorten drastically the period for selection of delegates, and to try to afford a means by which these powerful media, television and radio, can afford a modern stump, a modern opportunity for the public to hear the candidates and to make realistic decisions.

BLACK: I remember one night in the late '30s my father and I went down to Wooldridge Park in Austin and sat on the grass down there and listened to a number of candidates for Governor speak in succession. I think there was more enlightenment, more chance to canvass the issues in one's mind, and to make an intuitive judgment as to the quality of these men on that occasion, than we have now with all our resources. We've got to start thinking how to bring Wooldridge Park about on a nationwide basis. We certainly won't do it by a prolonged series of sensational events like the New Hampshire victory for McCarthy in early 1968, and pulling clothes off a candidate in another State.

The old method is not good either; it's still being used. It was the method by which Mr. Nixon sewed up the nomination, and is probably being used at the present to some extent by one or more other hopefuls for the 1976 election. You go around and, by private cajolement and dealing, line up the county chairmen, and people at about that level, at a time when there is no public interest concentrated on the election at all. The pledges are taken and the hostages are given long before anybody realizes what has happened, and then the public part is just shadowboxing. That's not good either.

ECKHARDT: I'm really addressing this question of compressing the time for the selection to a limited period of time, say in the early summer. I'm applying that to the primaries, to the election of delegates to the convention, and to the election itself.

BLACK: Compression of time, and virtual simultaneity among primaries, both of which we ought to look for, would probably have the effect of concentrating public attention sufficiently that neither of these processes—neither the process of slow attrition, with the energy of real zealots being the only dominating force, nor the process of going around and sewing up bosses at a low level before anybody knows about it—would be successful. Our job in this, of course, is not to produce success; no mere system, in itself, produces successes. Success is not going to be produced by anything but the efforts of the people and the interests of the people. If they won't get interested, if nothing can make them interested, then obviously no structure is going to do any good. The job is to provide a structure which maximizes the probability that an intelligent and wide public interest in the process can be stirred. It certainly cannot be stirred if what you have to do is first go up to New Hampshire and ring door bells all over that State, and then run down to Florida and work like hell in Florida, because there aren't many people who can do that. You have to be terribly committed and dedicated to a particular candidate to do that.

ECKHARDT: It takes a lot of money, too.

BLACK: It certainly doesn't open it up, either, to have it all settled by the county chairman before the system starts to operate.

ECKHARDT: This leads to the second point. In the beginning I had said there were two points that need to be addressed, two problems. One was the question of the long-continuing circus that we have pretty well discussed here. But you have raised the second point. That is, no matter whether you compress the election period and the convention period into a short span, you still have the problem of whether or not these county chairmen and other focal points of political power, city bosses, can be sewed up, so that when the convention occurs, many months later, it is simply a farce, simply determines the outcome of the democratic process by a decision that was reached by the sleaziest fixes with local bosses.

So the second thing that needs to be done is to provide minimal fairness in convention systems. It isn't enough to say that a delegation when it goes to the national convention must be representative of those who constitute the State convention. You've got to go behind that to what happened at the district convention, and at the precinct

convention. Because if the State convention itself was not representative, if ultimately there was a fix on at the state convention, you may,
at the national convention, have a group of delegates quite representative of the *State* convention, but you may have one that has completely
squeezed out any dissenting group, or even possibly a majority group
at the grass roots.

BLACK: I would like to say one thing. It may be a triviality, but
maybe it's not. Maybe it's the thing that's hovering behind all this,
particularly since symbolism is so important in politics. I've sat and
watched these so-called conventions, quadrennium after quadrennium,
until it became no longer possible for me to do so continuously, but
I still walk in and out of the room and watch them. Now I think that
as to the balloons and the cheering sections, the contrived demonstrations of exactly forty-five prearranged minutes, and all that stuff, I
really think that we're big boys and girls now, and the time has come
to stop that. Simply to stop it. This is not a meaningful symbolism
anymore. It's nothing but a terrible, colossal bore, except that I think
it may have a more sinister aspect, in that these contrived enthusiasms,
these ridiculous vaudeville turns that are done by the convention
collectively, and by individual members, these speeches made *pro
forma* with no serious intent behind them, may conceal and divert
attention from what's really going on; selling the people on the idea,
which is often no more than fraudulent, that something of importance
is really happening there. There is nothing happening of importance
on that floor, in the normal case. The arrangements either have been
made a long time in advance, or they are being made in other places,
by other people than the ones you see on the television. Now I think
we either ought to make these conventions serious things, we ought
to regard a balloon parade on the floor of a convention in about the
light in which you would regard a balloon parade on the floor of the
House of Representatives—the business being about as serious in one
place as the other—or else take convention votes by mail and cease
to go through this ridiculous pretense that we have, in this disgusting
orgy of vulgarity, an authentic process of choice.

ECKHARDT: I've been to enough conventions to see what tends to encourage that kind of vaudeville on the floor of the convention. The big show is ordinarily done either by a group that doesn't think it has the majority and wants to excite enough people to swing a majority, or else it's done by the majority to make the people think that the majority has been fairly achieved, and that there's a near-unanimity in support of that candidate.

You can take it as a general principle that the more process there is, the fairer the process there is, the more representative the delegates will be. Take, for instance, recent conventions in Texas, which have been pretty good. If you sit down and select a certain number of representatives to go to the national convention, proportionate to those who were for Wallace at that convention, and a proportionate number for McGovern, the show is not necessary, because nobody is going to be able to demonstrate that the convention was ever homogeneous. So, the more orderly, the fairer, and the more representative the process is, the less occasion there is for the cheap demonstrations or cheerleader type shows.

BLACK: What we really need is not a show but a process, whether it be a primary or state convention or series of conventions compressed within such an interval of time as to enable the public to concentrate on it and become interested in it and participate in it, not so rigged as to make it comprehensible only to a few insiders, but so structured as to invite participation and to bring into the hall a representation which would roughly correspond with the sentiment in the party outside the convention hall. Now when we get to that point, I think the people have got to grow up again, in another way. Again, we're big boys and girls, and I think what we have to do is to realize, as a people, that what happens at the convention, or at whatever takes the place of the convention, is plain out-and-out compromise. The real attempt made invariably by serious people in politics is to form some kind of a workable coalition which will possibly win, and if it wins, will be able to govern.

I think that's something that the American people find very hard to accept. The idea of compromise seems to abrade our idealisms. We are, in fact, a nation that continually compromises. The great parties, when they have been successful, have always been built on compromise. But we dislike to admit it. I think the time has come for us to admit it, to face frankly that that's what goes on, and that that is what *ought* to go on, at the convention of a national party. Nobody who comes there, unless he be a Roosevelt in 1936, is going to have everything that he wants. The job is to form some kind of coalition, with commitments as to give and take.

ECKHARDT: Well, now you started out by saying "the convention or what may take its place," but as you present the real problem you almost declare in favor of a convention as the only way to solve it.

BLACK: There must be some kind of bringing together of people so that over a determinate period of time, by processes which are analogous to those that go on in the legislative process, some kind of compromise and coalition can be reached and formed. I think probably bringing together all these people who have been selected in a manner such as we have been discussing is the best way to do it. It could be done on the telephone, but I don't think that would be as good.

ECKHARDT: You would reject, as I would, some kind of a national polling within the parties to determine who the candidate should be?

BLACK: I think that kind of polling is subject to much the same objections as those to the popular election of the President; you run up against the same alternatives. You make more difficult, rather than easier, the process which absolutely must take place at some stage, and that is the process of compromise, of coalition, or bringing divergent points of view under a single umbrella, so that you can form a government. That is what you have to do to form a government. You either form that kind of government, or you form a government which can't govern, or you form a government which governs from one little band in the ideological spectrum by some kind of force. Those are the alternatives, that's all you have, and the best of them by far is compromise and coalition.

ECKHARDT: Besides, by that process, it seems to me you exacerbate the present tendency toward electing a nominee on a kind of popularity poll—a Miss Watermelonthump or Queen of the May—instead of on the basis of national issues and national needs. Now I don't mean to say that you can ever get away from personalities as related to the issues. I think that in the selection of a candidate for President, interest has to develop around the person or a group of people. But there should ultimately be some way that these people are called upon to present their personalities, not just as individuals with this one with more charisma, that word I hate, but rather a person who is associated with movements, with concerns, with people, with a program that he intends to put into effect.

BLACK: And putting that program into effect means, in politics, that he is going to give pledges, that he is going to commit himself.

ECKHARDT: That he makes these awful compromises. I think at least the broad standards of the kind of process must be formulated in federal law.

BLACK: I think so, too. The shortening the period of time comes first, because length is the deadly feature about the present system, making idle all other attempts of reform. Next comes opening up the system—through information and simplicity of structuring—to all the people who want to participate, to the extent that they want to participate. Then comes total reform of the convention, so that the circus element is taken out.

ECKHARDT: And so that every level of the convention results in proportionate representation the rest of the way up.

BLACK: Sure, and we don't want a winner-take-all system at the state convention either. It's not like the Electoral College, because what we want to produce in the national convention is a representation of interests in just about the proportion that they bear in the population, so that the weight of each interest, in the coalition or compromise which is finally put together, will be a fair reflection of its weight in the population at large. Now this has to do both with producing a winner and with producing a government that can govern without undue stress and strain—that can command and bring to its support widely dispersed elements of the population.

ECKHARDT: One other thing for federal legislative enactment in this connection is some means of commandeering radio and television time for the purpose of affording a forum where views are spoken out. Now this is not an easy thing. We've got the problem of determining what parties should be recognized. How should you winnow out persons who really have no chance, who are simply seeking nomination for publicity purposes? But these are not beyond legislative control, and the problems could be solved. I would like ultimately to see something involving appearance of candidates before the public, not just as candidates sold like commercial products, but as persons debating each other, subject to questions by knowledgeable members of the press.

BLACK: It just has to be that some way can be found to use these enormous assets of television and radio and all the other means of communication for the kind of enlightenment and exploration of the issues that we so badly need in the country. I would pass over as obviously soluble the problem of getting the time. I don't think there's any confiscatory or other problem about that. This could be looked on simply as a kind of a taxation-in-kind for the franchise that these stations monopolistically enjoy, precisely at the hands of the federal government. There's no difficulty about that at all. I would think, of course, that it's best to make these things interesting for every reason, including that of making the stations willing participants in such a scheme. But I think that in the last resort we have a perfect right as a people to insist that the facilities, with regard to which we have conferred a valuable monopoly, be made available for what is our absolutely vital political need in reforming the government of this country, bringing the people to a much greater extent into the processes of government.

The selection of parties to get time on TV and radio does present a certain difficulty. One is tempted to just say, "Why not just untie the Gordian knot and say the Democratic Party and the Republican Party?" That's what we're really trying to do *as of now*. That's the whole thing. But I suppose that would be wrong practically (aside from our American preference for euphemisms when dealing with matters like this) because it might at some future juncture inhibit the formation of a new party. We've had several moments in the country's history where this was very important—the most important one, of course, the formation of the Republican Party in 1856 and 1860.

ECKHARDT: But in the cases of most new parties, they really never had much chance of getting very far, but frequently have been an impetus toward change. As for instance the Populist Party around the turn of the century. And, for that matter, Norman Thomas and his Socialist Party.

BLACK: If we were being realistic, if we didn't have to worry about euphemizing these things, we could deal with the Norman Thomas problem in a realistic way. We don't need for Norman Thomas what we need for the Democratic or Republican Party. We need some decent exposure so that the point of view which may later prove to have been a fructifying point of view, as so many of the points of view of the Socialist Party actually were, would have a chance to get this continual exposure. We don't need as much exposure as we do for the candidates who actually have a chance of winning, at least so I should have thought.

ECKHARDT: I think that's right.

BLACK: We don't need much at all, I guess, for the Vegetarian Party, that's hardly at the present stage a political party.

ECKHARDT: If we had some way of determining the percentage of support in any given time I think we could pretty well be assured that the Vegetarian Party would not have as much as 2 percent of the support of the nation.

One other thing I would like to talk a little about. What we said about affording a forum which would be presumably free to the candidates and to the parties leads into this question of what to do about financing political campaigns. I would not very much like to get into financing of campaigns other than the presidential ones, because we would get into terribly technical fields.

BLACK: The major theme of our talks together has been the relations of the presidency and Congress, and the rehabilitation of the presidency. These other questions are quite important, but not really central.

ECKHARDT: Besides that, if we discuss it with respect to the presidency, analogies can later be drawn with respect to other positions. It seems to me that perhaps the best answer to what has been called public financing of campaigns is to afford one area of exposure, of extreme importance, that's available to all *without respect to money*. If this is done, the expenditure of money in the ordinary, mundane processes of candidate exposure lessens greatly in importance and, therefore, the impact of tremendously larger expenditure by one candidate than by another is greatly diminished. For instance, if the candidates for the presidency of the United States were presented, effectively, and with *enough* prime TV time, you'd have to buy a heck of a lot of billboards to make an iota of difference in the view of the people. The people driving down the street would no more look at the billboards of a candidate than they would look at the advertisements for whiskey. They would probably confuse them with advertisements for whiskey.

BLACK: That's right, and it implies again a strategic shift in our view of what we are to require of television in these matters. We have these presidential elections, of transcendent importance, once every four years, and I think we should consider ourselves to be in a position simply to use this great national asset of television, just as heavily as is necessary, for the purpose of bringing it about that the serious candidates who have a chance at election will be thoroughly exposed and the issues thoroughly canvassed on television, so that the only reason a citizen will have for not being informed as to both candidates (if there are only two as we anticipate), and as to all the principal issues, would be simply that he didn't care, that he didn't want to watch. Now if we do that, if the exposure is not looked on in terms of four hours once every two weeks but something that is a major part of television during the time concerned, then I think the importance of additional expenditures of money becomes progressively less and less important. I think we could cease to worry quite as much about it as we do now when it's the be-all and the end-all of a candidacy.

ECKHARDT: We have other means to facilitate communication without great expense through government activity. For instance, we could afford a certain franking privilege to the parties and to the candidates. These things, it seems to me, would so dilute the effect of the expenditure of money as to answer the major problems involved. Every other proposal concerning public financing of campaigns and permitting the candidates to use the money exactly as they desire presents so many difficult problems both in the magnitude of expense, and in selling the matter politically to the public at a time when they are fed up with candidates generally, with politicians.

BLACK: We are thinking affirmatively on this, and I think that's just the way to think. Notice too that this kind of affirmative action with respect to furnishing the means of achieving notice and getting one's point of view understood on television or by franking also automatically diminishes the advantage of the incumbent, in just exactly the right way. You can't take it away altogether, and I think it's a feature of every stable government that incumbency is something of an advantage. But these measures would tend to iron out this advantage to some extent, to put it in lower relief and at the same time to diminish the importance of money.

Now I'm interested in diminishing the *importance* of contributions because I don't think there is any practical way to *limit* contributions. There are so many different ways in which money can be used to make a candidate conspicuous, there are so many other things other than money that can be bought and then contributed, and can't be controlled, that you're in the position of King Canute, sweeping back the tide, when you try to deal negatively with campaign funds. Some of the limitations may be minor palliatives; that's really all they are.

ECKHARDT: I agree with that.

BLACK: On the other hand, this affirmative attack, this affording of a Wooldridge Park, as it were, a national Wooldridge Park, would do great good. Wooldridge Park was owned by the City of Austin and it was furnished for candidates. Now, we don't own television, but we own the franchises, they're public franchises.

ECKHARDT: The air waves are free.

BLACK: I think we ought to be thinking boldly about this. There would be no reason why the government itself, if all else failed—I don't think this is necessary, it isn't conceptually or practically necessary—but, if it were, it really wouldn't be too outrageous a suggestion that once every four years the government itself pay for or otherwise provide television transmission facilities for this purpose. But I don't think we have to do that. I think we're entitled to call on the beneficiaries of these monopolistic franchises that are granted by the government to furnish in the public interest whatever time we need.

ECKHARDT: One trouble with prohibitory measures in connection with political elections is the question of remedy. The only effective remedy is to deny the fruits of the election to him who has violated the rules.

BLACK: You can't do that.

ECKHARDT: You would also be denying to the people their majority choice.

BLACK: Certainly, and there's nobody who can do that, or ought to. Let's take the prohibition against corporate contributions. You enforce that, usually, by a fine on the corporation, which is just an additional contribution that they make. Putting a few people in the penitentiary for irregularities is not an affirmative solution to our problems in politics today.

ECKHARDT: It's so easy for corporations to get around this sort of thing. For instance, in Houston, to raise money for candidates favorable to their interest, they hold a big display of corporate equipment, road-building equipment, and send all their employees there on $7 tickets, which were purportedly paid to see these displays. The corporation was concerned about their employees seeing the equipment that was being used in road-building and the $7 per head was then accumulated and donated from this organization, which was not a corporation, to the political candidates.

BLACK: Money will find some way to be useful to the candidate— but its marginal utility will be much less if adequate prime exposure is furnished free.[2]

---

2. Despite the acknowledgment difficulty mentioned in the preface, one must here mention that this chapter owes much to the thought of the late Alexander Bickel.

8 KNOWLEDGE FOR GOVERNMENT IN THE TWENTY-FIRST CENTURY

BLACK: In many ways, the problem of knowledge—of public access to knowledge, of the acquisition of knowledge by those who require it for governmental decision—has come to be highly visible in our society today. We have just come out of a long national debate on executive privilege; we have before us the so-called newsman's shield laws;[1] we have the recent institution of open Committee sessions;[2] we have a great awareness of the problem involved in access to the enormous quantities of data that are now stored in our government departments and elsewhere; we are becoming on the whole keenly conscious of the fact that knowledge is power, and that access to information is one of the most important things in politics.

ECKHARDT: Congress is running into the problem of the extent to which it may command the executive department to supply it with information. It seems to me that Congress's right to demand information should be virtually unlimited with respect to knowledge about the actual result of the executive department's action, and virtually unlimited with respect to the sources of fact that the executive department has in making a decision. But the point at which a limitation seems appropriate is the point at which the function of judgment is exercised in the executive department upon these facts. Take an example collateral to the matter of executive privilege but based on similar considerations: It might be an infringement of First Amendment rights if Congress were to command the editor of a newspaper to give to the Congress that which had been rejected in the prepara-

---

1. These laws would, where enacted, protect a reporter from revealing the source of his "information."
2. See *supra*, pp. 137–38.

tion of an editorial. Similarly, if Congress should command the President to supply the discussions which occurred in the Oval Room preparatory to a presidential message to Congress because Congress wants to know what motivated the President's position on certain recommendations, such would clearly fall within executive privilege or presidential confidentiality.[3]

BLACK: Before we consider the negative side of the executive privilege, let us consider the affirmative side of the difficulty of Congress's receiving a flow of information. I think executive privilege, which I have favored within proper limits, really doesn't have much good-faith applicability with respect to the kind of hard data that you are referring to, or the source of it, and certainly not with respect to executive action. Once action is taken, then Congress very clearly has a right to know about it, except in the very few cases of exceedingly high national security considerations. I think that we can return to executive privilege and presidential confidentiality, which may be different things, later on, and consider for the moment the *affirmative* problems that any body of people, let's say in this case a Committee of Congress, faces in the acquisition of data.

There is no question that there exists in and about Washington, and elsewhere in the country, in the files and in the computer banks of governmental organizations, enormous quantities of data which would be helpful to Congress in resolving certain issues, or in considering certain proposals; this is a very important factor in congressional activity. I see some difficulties about getting at this, and I will put them up to you because I am simply imagining them and you may have had some experience with them. The first thing I would think of, the first difficulty that would occur to me is: "How do you know where it is? How do you know whom to ask for what you need?"

ECKHARDT: Ordinarily, it is done this way. Suppose we have before us a bill that affects the executive branch of the government, say, an administrative agency or even an independent agency. The first set

3. See pp. 89–93, *supra,* and the citation and brief discussion of the case of *U.S. v. Nixon,* at p. 90, footnote.

of witnesses are heard more or less as a matter of courtesy, and these are members of Congress, the person who introduced the bill, for instance, and other members who might want to record a position that would be favorable to them in their constituencies. That's not terribly important, except that the sponsor of the bill may well give an outline of the purposes of the bill and what its objectives are. The second group of witnesses nearly always come in from the governmental agency that is affected by the bill, and Congress ordinarily has before it, say, a Secretary or an Undersecretary, or an administrator at the top of an agency. Before the Committee hearing, the Chairman of the Committee will have asked for a report from this executive agency as to their view of the bill. Say, for instance, it is a bill prescribing procedures for making substantive rules to enforce the Federal Trade Commission Act. The first witness after members of Congress would be the head of the Federal Trade Commission, or perhaps the whole Commission. Prior to their appearance they would have given their view as to the bill, whether they favor it, and if they do not favor it, why they do not favor it. So this is the initial inquiry for information and opinion.

The trouble is that if the agency really does not want to give the information necessary to Congress, there are two ways to conceal it. One is simply not to furnish basic facts which constitute necessary information bearing on the bill. The other is to overwhelm the Committee with access to undigested files, which is just about as bad. That's pretty much corrected by the fact that the representatives of the agency come before the Committee, and the Committee can then ask questions about these facts, and can obtain information leading them to the type of information that might be useful. I have not had much difficulty in questioning executive agency heads on such points. They usually give an answer, or the chief of the agency bends his ear down to some knowledgeable officer of the agency or an attorney who can advise him right there, and you get the answer. Or sometimes, knowing that you are asking for highly technical information, you say that perhaps the witness would like to reply in writing, and you open up the record at this point for this information, and nearly always the agency head says, "We will be glad to furnish you that information," and it comes in within a matter of days.

BLACK: Let's hope you don't have to deal with the phenomenon of reluctance very often, but I think that if you do, the resources for concealment are pretty formidable. Sometimes the concealment is only half-conscious. It may sometimes be equally well explainable as a lack of understanding, and I suppose you've got to depend to some extent on the good faith of the people involved and on their general amenability to congressional pressure of various kinds.

A further problem is that of ascertaining and then getting an idea of what data and information might, in some manner that does not quite meet the eye, be relevant to a given proposal. For some reason the example that comes to my mind is a European example, but it could be a paradigm of very many governmental problems. When the countries of northern Europe (in the case that I actually heard of, the government in West Germany) were considering the policy with respect to the inflow of migrant workers from the southern countries of Europe, they thought of *some* of the agencies and asked questions of them, but they did not have the imagination to think of all of the agencies that turned out to be affected. For example, the need not only for expanded medical care but also for certain different kinds of medical care eventuated in a manner which had not been foreseen. The transportation problem had been pretty thoroughly canvassed as far as it concerned getting the workers there and then getting them home, but the additional load that they would put on the inner-city transportation systems had not been thought of. It seems to me that proposals concerning railroads, or energy, or a lot of other things, have effects that are likely to run beyond the expertise or knowledge or data banks of the agency that appears to be primarily concerned. Is there any procedure that one can prescribe generally to meet that problem, or is it just a matter of the exercise of the creative imagination on each problem as it arises?

ECKHARDT: It's good that you brought up a problem that may not be specifically addressed by an already formulated bill. A general problem, such as obtaining labor from outside the country, may lead to legislation, but before any legislation is enacted, facts surrounding that problem must be known. Indeed, once the facts are learned, the whole idea may be rejected. The same situation exists in the energy field. Many questions concerning, for instance, importing of oil and limitations on its import, may rest on the nature of petroleum reserves or fossil fuel reserves of the United States.

BLACK: That will turn on the question of whether they can be exploited economically; we are in the midst of a debate on that.

ECKHARDT: And environmental safety—as for instance, with strip mining.

BLACK: We don't want to do that without adequate replacement of the soil on top, if that really is a workable plan. I somewhat doubt it myself. Well, then we could go on, of course, to the transportation problems that might be created by the springing up of new communities around the strip-mining areas, and the electrical power that would be needed there, and so on. The whole set of problems that come in the wake of a solution of what seems to be a single problem constitute really one of the great knowledge problems in the formulation of policy.

ECKHARDT: Yes, and I think the question you are raising points to the reason why legislation is so frequently formulated by the executive department, because the executive department—the presidency—has access to all the agencies for data or advice, to a greater extent than Congress has.

BLACK: Then, don't we have our hands here on what really might be the main strategic problem about a flow of information and knowledge and even about what we are considering in general in these talks? We have been exploring the problem of some re-formation of the relations between the presidency and the Congress, some restoration of creative energy in Congress. The fact that this kind of overall generalized access to all sorts of possible relevant information is in the executive department rather than in Congress is something we ought to think about.

ECKHARDT: In the British Parliament and in the Canadian Parliament the question period affords some of this opportunity for the body of Parliament to understand what the government is doing, but it is much simpler there because the ministers who respond to the question period are actually members of the Parliament.

BLACK: Once again, the most important thing would be to know what questions to ask. A question period might help some, but I would think that probably if you knew what questions to ask you could probably address questions in writing to administrative agencies, or call the agencies and ask what they think about it. The much more difficult problem is the continuing awareness of the necessity of certain information.

ECKHARDT: The trouble with our system is that questioning of this nature seldom commences before the bill is actually introduced, and then when it does commence, the questions are from a single Committee, which might not have the scope or the background to envisage all the problems.

BLACK: A Committee that tends to be specialized on the very same subject matter as led to the reference of the bill. I am very interested in this problem because it seems to me that creativity, energy, and innovation is the very point at which Congress might begin the restructuring of its own position in government, precisely because, as we have discussed elsewhere, the disciplining of Congress, its being compelled to vote a certain way, is not possible under our system, while it *is* possible, with the talented energetic people in Congress, to get a whole lot done there in terms of innovation, suggestions, creative proposals, which could then go through the same kind of process that we have already discussed. I am afraid that for that change above all else, not only is knowledge power, but an apparatus that keeps Congress *continually* aware of the *need* for knowledge is necessary. I would not despair of that being developed in Congress. I think it is just a matter of some very bold thinking about the kind of staffing that Congress could provide itself for this purpose.

ECKHARDT: It just occurred to me in this discussion that the strengthening of the role of Congress doesn't mean the weakening of the role of the executive. What we're talking about now is devising means by which the Congress will be better informed, but not to the disadvantage of the executive. This is not a question of conflict of powers.

BLACK: Certainly not on this matter. There's one commodity of which there's never too much, and that is innovativeness and creativity, fruitfulness in proposal, and if any structural reforms led to a noble emulation between the executive and Congress in fruitfulness of proposal, that would be just fine; there doesn't have to be any loss by either side. When it comes to the question of who is to decide when to make war, then there will surely be some competition. But when it comes to the question of who is to come up with the right set of proposals for handling an energy crisis, there's plenty of room for initial creativity on both sides of the fence.

ECKHARDT: Besides that, the machinery we're talking about now also affords a means by which Congress could step into an executive gap at any time. Perhaps one might begin by planning for greater congressional involvement in budget formation.

BLACK: I think here of the British government and the phrase "to bring in the budget." When a British government "brings in its budget" for the year, this is equivalent to its declaring its overall total policy with respect to society, because they appreciate, as this phrase shows, more clearly than we do the dominance of resource allocation. But I think that if we reflected, we'd give it the same importance—how definitory of the total policy of the government it is when one considers how money is to be gathered and how money is to be spent. If you look over what we do, that is a very, very large part of it, and you need a kind of overall knowledge of health, transportation, demography, and all sorts of things in order to form such a budget intelligently. I don't think you can call a budget purely fiscal; it has repercussions in so many other areas. Health care is a budgetary question, but it also is a health question; it is also a question of what the population is likely to be twenty-five years from now; it is a question of what kind of a labor force is going to be available in some region of the country five years from now. Consideration of all these things goes into the making of a decent budget.

ECKHARDT: There's another thing which addresses this question in a smaller way, which might be expanded to meet some of these problems, and that is the development of the Democratic Steering Committee, a representative Committee of the caucus that works with the Speaker in designating matters of major importance and advising with him on such matters, and ultimately helping to carry out the program with activities involving the whole Democratic group. Now, if the Steering Committee could be a little bit expanded, and a little bit more formalized, so that the Steering Committee could demand information of a general nature from the executive branch, we would get by this problem I was mentioning about not being able to ask for the information until a bill has been placed in a narrow package and placed under the authority of a Committee with a specific narrow expertise.

BLACK: But I can't let the problem off that easily, and I don't think it would be very helpful if we did let it off that easily, because I think the key to the insufficiency of that plan, although it is certainly running in the right direction, lies in the word "demand."

What we really need to try to develop is some kind of relationship between the Congress and the governmental agencies—mediated perhaps by the executive branch as a whole, in order to avoid duplication —which would make it natural and almost spontaneous for the Congress to be furnished with information that it needs, and alerted as to what sort of information it really does or will need. There are really two possibilities here. First would be the development, as a congressional agency responsible to Congress, of a kind of overall and very large and omnicompetent information agency, which would develop liaison under congressional command—but, one would hope, with the development of a tradition of cooperation with all the agencies of government that have the information relevant to any particular problem under consideration. Such an agency would itself establish as imaginatively as possible—and it is at this point that imagination really becomes a tool for developing knowledge—the standard as to what type of knowledge *might be needed*. The second form—and in my mind, this would be preferable, if it is practical— would be the development of such relations between Congress and the executive branch as to make this not so much a matter of "demand" as a kind of expansion, in modern times, of the constitutional mandate of the report by the President from time to time to Congress on the State of the Union.[4] Bear in mind that it is one of the few duties which is laid on the President by the Constitution—to provide the Congress with *knowledge*. It was foreseen that they would need to know about the State of the Union, so that they might act. I would like to see a great expansion of that—enough to comprise an ongoing and copious responsibility on the part of the executive branch, with the President looking upon it as one of his principal duties to supervise a process of the furnishing of knowledge to the Congress, or the alerting of Congress to its need for certain types of knowledge, rather than of using this knowledge as a means of firming up executive power.

ECKHARDT: The trouble now is that the executive department purports to exercise that function, but it may exercise it without any inquiry, or any right to inquiry, on the part of any agency of the majority party in Congress. Now that's the problem.

BLACK: The executive branch also furnishes information only in connection with a specific proposal or with a specific position. It's unfortunately true—and it isn't a matter of bad faith, but just the dynamics of the human mind—that if you have committed yourself to a particular proposal, you are likely to see both the tenor of the knowledge, the tendency of the knowledge, and the type of knowledge that is necessary in a manner which tends to support that proposal. I am thinking of a stream of communication very different from that.

ECKHARDT: I think that there needs to be some knowledge-gathering structure, and the structure should be built not around Congress, and not within Congress as a body, but within the majority party. As to who is to obtain this information, I would suggest that it be the Speaker—as both the presiding officer of the whole House and the leader of the majority party—and the Steering Committee as a representative group of the majority party. We already have the facilities of the Library of Congress in many areas. That could afford the staffing for such a proposal.

4. Article II, Section 3. Cf. *supra*, p. 15.

BLACK: It's not spacious enough for staffing, because you need far more power of imagination.

ECKHARDT: There is no reason why within the institution of the Library of Congress you couldn't get that kind of personnel. You get very excellent personnel as staff for Committees. You could utilize something similar to or an expansion of the American Law Division of the Library. The American Law Division is a kind of misnomer; it doesn't just deal with law, it deals in every problem affected by legislation.

BLACK: Well, maybe that's because law doesn't deal with law.

ECKHARDT: I guess that's right.

BLACK: Law doesn't deal with law anymore than a knife deals with a knife. A knife deals with cutting.

ECKHARDT: I think in the first place we ought to decide whether or not this ought to be a function of the majority party at this stage, or the function of the House as a whole.

BLACK: Now are those two things really contradictory? What we are really looking for is a change in attitude that would make the flow of information, and the offering of suggestions as to the need for information, a natural part of the duties of the executive branch. I recur here to my concept of the expansion and modernization of the State of the Union Message. What we are really trying to develop is a situation in which it would be the done thing, the expectation quite outside the category of either constitutional or statutory compulsion, that the executive branch would copiously assist Congress in respect of information, and in respect of the even more vital preliminary business of knowing what information you need.

ECKHARDT: But if it's to be the done thing, there must first be somebody to do it with. And presently, the only person to do it with is the Congress, as a sort of an amorphous institution to which the President has a duty to give certain messages. What he's really doing, frequently, is to throw down a gauntlet rather than to afford information.

BLACK: That's the problem. As a matter of fact, when you stated that there were two problems, the second one is far more difficult than the first. I think that in principle we could probably agree that it would be possible to devise some congressional agency for this kind of liaison, perhaps an agency which was operated in common, both as a part, in one sense, of the executive branch, and as a part, in another sense, of the congressional staffing, as a contact—a junction point.

ECKHARDT: There is also the question, should such an agency of Congress, such an implement of Congress, be an implement of the Senate and the House, or only of the House, or should there be one in each body?

BLACK: I think one in each body is a little bit too tricky. Probably some attempt ought to be made first to make it a congressional agency. Above all, let's not worry about how much this is going to cost. I don't know how many billions of dollars we have spent in getting to the moon. We can spend a whole lot more than that, whatever it takes, to straighten this government out and send it on a path that will fit it to the twenty-first century.

ECKHARDT: The cost of implementing Article I of the Constitution is minuscule compared to the cost of implementing Articles II and III. The legislative function is cheap; it's a low-budget function, certainly compared to the executive branch, and even to the judiciary.

BLACK: That's a very interesting point. We can easily agree we can afford anything that it takes to develop such channels, if they are possible.

Now, I think at that point we probably ought to call in the people who have themselves studied problems in communication and the sociology of knowledge, problems in the hierarchic structure of institutions and so on, for their suggestions. In the end what we will have to do is make a commonsense choice, and then cut and try. But there are people who are at least in a position to offer suggestions along these lines; we ought to be looking for them.

ECKHARDT: There is another advantage to creating some institution of Congress with which the executive department would work, and to which the executive department would furnish information. The President can command an extremely high level of talent from every area of expertise in the United States—from the universities, from the business society, scientists, from every type of thinker. Men and women like that gladly go to work for the President for really extensive periods of time, at a loss in earnings, because of the prestige of it, and because of the fact that they anticipate having some input in the mainstream of government, while on the other hand, it is very difficult for Congress to command that sort of expertise. We should be able to use quite freely the assemblage of talent and expertise which the President can attract.

BLACK: But the kind of project that we are now very hazily fore-shadowing ought to appeal to the finest minds in America—young and old. I envisage all kinds of collateral benefits. It seems to me that if people need to start cooperating, need to start forming new ways of working together—and that surely is the need of Congress and the presidency—then the level of *knowledge* is an excellent level on which to start, because it doesn't intrinsically and immediately raise political issues. Political issues will be there, and they will have to be dealt with, and the knowledge problem may raise some of them collaterally, but, in the main, honest people can cooperate on questions of knowledge, or of what knowledge is needed. Then when you get down to the concrete question of what is the case, what are the data, and so on, people can cooperate in a way which may be much more difficult to attain when the immediate problem is one of *action* rather than of knowledge.

Of course, knowledge would be sure to lead to action, but both the President and Congress, within the constitutional scheme, have their parts to play in the action, and neither one needs to feel put down. The President with his veto power, and with his power as executor of the laws, and with his independent constitutional power as Com-mander-in-Chief, and in some other respects, possibly would not need to feel put down even in the action stage, but it's in the stage of the development and exchange of knowledge, insight, and ideas where it seems to me cooperation could become easy habit.

ECKHARDT: Here's a specific area in which this is badly needed. This energy problem should have been anticipated long before it be-gan to surface. But, assuming that that was for some reason imprac-tical, at any rate, we finally ended up with something like a crash program. At the time the Interstate and Foreign Commerce Committee was called upon to do something about a broad energy bill, the President had not formulated any specific policies or specific legislation for the Committee to work on. What had to be done was to improvise a number of programs, including energy-saving methods and a statutory structure to implement this, ways of rationing or the authority to ration, coal conversion, certain relaxations of environmental standards, and many other things that cover a great number of fields, and they had to be done quickly. These measures had to be devised by a limited staff, serving on a Committee that was already heavily occupied with specific legislation before it. But we did it. We didn't have a very good bill, but by the time we had acted on it for a couple of weeks in the full Committee, with about 100 amendments, we had at least some workable structure, though certainly not the kind of thing that we could have had with the type of institutionalized knowledge-producing function that we are discussing here. The bill went to conference, and in conference, Senator Jackson proposed an oil rollback which was very hastily devised, overlooking certain basic needs such as encouragement of oil production. And, also, it didn't really address the question with technical accuracy. Now it's shocking that in times of such immediate need there was no real structure to meet that need quickly.

BLACK: It's even more shocking that our government is now so divided into these two branches, tending to take an adversary position, that the energy crisis, for example, should have stolen upon us. Nobody seems to know now whether the eastern electrical grid is going to go out next summer or not. Of course, nobody could know it for sure; but nobody I know of is studying this question, collecting the data. If they are, it's in some place where you would have to dig it out and find out about it and get them to tell you about it. Now, I have in mind a new relation, as to *knowledge,* between the two great political branches of government, a relation which would for one thing involve constant study of problems of that kind, problems like the energy problem, so that suggestions of policy could emerge in Congress, or be initiated by the executive and suggested to Congress

—either one—whichever branch happened to have the burst of creativity about the problem, on the basis of an ongoing flow of knowledge. I am inclined to think that we have our hands on something here that is really of tremendous importance. Our society is to a great extent flying blind without adequate instruments; perhaps a great many of our problems would turn out to be far more tractable of solution if we just had the knowledge flowing in about these things, and available to the people who have to decide.

ECKHARDT: Instead, there is a lack of that knowledge, and lack of the knowledge at a level where broad programs can be formulated, and then farmed out to Committees of specific jurisdiction or to that kind of special Committee I was discussing before. Without that kind of machinery, we deal with small issues, peripheral issues, little parts of the total problem.

We have great difficulty with the big issues. For instance, in a recent session of Congress, our Committee worked for about three weeks in a mark-up session on a power plant siting bill. There were three versions: one was the President's version, which was pretty good, actually. The Subcommittee's version was much less sensitive to environmental concerns and much less comprehensive. I had a third alternative, supported by conservationists. So there were three approaches. The Administration didn't support its own approach, and all the Republicans on the Committee were willing to let it die, because they thought it would interfere too much with the power industry. The Subcommittee's approach was not acceptable to pro-conservationists on the Committee like myself, Moss, and Dingell, and others, because of its lack of any sensitivity to the environmental interest, and of course it was opposed by some of the Republicans because they preferred the Administration's approach. And the position that Dingell, Moss, and I took was again a minority position. So, none of the three proposals were adopted. And after about three weeks, we just let the whole subject drop. It addressed the question of the energy crisis, but it was completely sidetracked.

BLACK: I don't want just to panegyrize knowledge; we ought to think about structures by which it can be acquired. But, I want to interject here one parenthetical remark, although I don't want to make it less important because it's parenthetical. I think it's preposterous that we have come down into modern times with such a mythology of the "privacy" of private enterprise that we regard as even close to acceptable that these great aggregations of corporate and industrial power should be in any way immunized from furnishing to the government as complete as possible a flow of knowledge about their operations. I have in mind specifically the close guarding by the oil industry of how many gallons more of diesel fuel or gasoline it actually has in reserve in the United States. It seems to me that a society that doesn't put itself in a position to find out during an energy crisis, for absolute sure, what that situation is, is very sick. Those people have no right at all to take the attitude that this is their private business, just as it is my private business how many Louis Armstrong records I have in my attic. This is *public* business, and one of the ancillary steps that ought to be taken in developing a knowledge system, if I may call it that, is leveling to the ground the idea that this kind of so-called business intelligence has any claim whatever to nondisclosure.

ECKHARDT: With respect to energy resources and information from the oil companies, we addressed that in the second part of the federal energy bill package. In April we passed the Dingell Amendment that commands such information to be divulged by the oil companies.

BLACK: I am glad to hear it, but that addresses itself to only one specific case of a misconception which is thoroughly general and which really ought to be destroyed once and for all. There is no moral or equitable claim on the part of a huge enterprise, which in fact controls a very considerable portion of the economic and strategic assets of the country, to keep from government the knowledge of what it's got, or what it's doing. We have this mythology of the privacy of private enterprise. It started, I think, with cartoons of Nicholas Biddle rocking in a rocker on his porch in Philadelphia, as a representation of the Bank of the United States. The cartoon invited the reader to treat the Bank of the United States as it would treat a man rocking on his porch in his rocker—to have the same respect for its existence, for its privacy and rights, as it would have for a man. General Motors some years ago had a set of ads which really worked out about that same way. It showed a man who was born the day that General Motors was founded, and he's looking in a window where some cars are made by General Motors and talking about how the two of them have grown up together. You are invited to look on General Motors as you would look on a man.

Now that's totally fallacious. The question of the capacity of General Motors to manufacture cars, the question what the capacity is of the eastern electrical grid, are not private matters. They have nothing whatsoever in common with the sort of private information to which we give the protection of confidentiality. And, if we are going to allow these people to a limited extent to operate segments of a profit-motivated economy, then we ought at least to insist on promptly knowing, without a lot of formal procedure, everything we want to know about what they are doing and how much they have got of everything. That would certainly be a part of any good new knowledge regime that we could devise.

But I think the more difficult problem remains, and it is central to our enterprise here, the problem of devising a structure of some kind for this ready and easy flow of information between the executive branch and the legislative branch, for purposes of policy formation on both sides.

ECKHARDT: In this respect, there must be someone, some agency, some machinery of Congress to ask for it in a broader way and for broader purposes and for more preliminary purposes of planning than what can presently be done through the Committees after a bill is in progress. We have a congressional agency which checks on whether or not the executive department is properly carrying out the laws, the General Accounting Office. But its function occurs after the fact of the passage of legislation. It is a watchdog, not a pointer.

BLACK: A good exploratory way of dealing with this would be exactly in connection with the budget, in view of the importance of the budget. I would think of a congressional agency, of some size and versatility, which was in charge—not just once a year or once every two years, but continuously—of receiving, processing, asking for, scanning for, the kind of information that it takes to construct a decent budget, a budget with proper balance between expenditure and income, and a budget with proper priority as to expenditures. I think that once you've got that, it could be expanded very easily to comprise a tool for finding out information as to other things. This is a revolutionary idea, but there's no reason in the world why the best experts in the United States shouldn't be working for Congress.

ECKHARDT: It isn't really revolutionary or even precedent-breaking in concept, though it may be in scope. In this session, we passed a bill that dealt with presidential impoundment of funds and with the creation of a Congressional Budget Committee. The two quite different subjects were seen to balance each other. The anti-impoundment provisions call on the President to spend the money that Congress says should be spent. The other part calls on Congress not to order the expenditure of money until it has prepared a budget and considered priorities for programs and appropriations. Before this, we had proceeded without an original plan. We had various Committees of substantive jurisdiction that considered bills and made authorizations for appropriations, and then we had the Appropriations Committee more or less formulate a budget out of the suggestions of the substantive Committees. Authorization bills are really mere suggestions; the Appropriations bill is what puts the program into effect. So, priorities were developed at that later stage, the appropriations stage. Now a budget Committee in each House establishes priorities early in the process. We still have the authorization and appropriation process, but we add a prior planning stage to develop an overall policy of government spending, which of course implies an overall economic policy. A continuing agency of the Congress, not composed of members but of economists primarily, aids the Committees of both Houses in defining and refining economic policy.

But this process is not quite enough to get at the problem you and I are talking about. These budget Committees are a part of the ongoing processes of Congress, and they can refine budgetary processes and economic policy, but they don't afford a sufficient means for the majority party to innovate—to develop its program initially, like British cabinet members do. When the presidency is in the hands of the other party, it is necessary to have some way of doing this. There should be some machinery controlled by the majority party which could perform this function.

BLACK: Well, I'm not resolute on that, but there are things about it that bother me. I really think that I would foresee from such a party-oriented structure the almost instantaneous development of political reluctancies and animosities.

ECKHARDT: But if the President is of one party and the Congress is of the same party, this result would be diminished.

BLACK: True. But I was thinking internally, of the Congress itself. There are two possibilities there: One is that the same majority party has both Houses, which is the usual situation, and there it seems to me that the making of a knowledge-gathering enterprise a tool to be used by the majority party would almost certainly have the unfortunate effect of alienating the minority party from support of that enterprise. If knowledge is power, then any monopoly on the relevant knowledge on the part of the majority party would be very properly resented by the minority party. I would much rather see this as something cooperative. Just as cooperation probably could develop best between executive and Congress on the knowledge level, so cooperation, understanding, and fruitful interchange might best develop between the two parties on the level of knowledge. I would hate to see a situation where the minority felt that it was actually being shut off from knowledge.

ECKHARDT: Well, it is a question of the purpose of such a gathering of knowledge. Of course, it is not the only area in which knowledge can be gathered. Ultimately, of course, when a bill is considered, the action would be by the Committee with both parties present. It seems to me what is lacking at the present time is the capability of the majority party to propose a program, and it is its duty to propose a program. And the program may not win, it may be rejected because the minority party may get adherents from the majority party to defeat it.

BLACK: That's right.

ECKHARDT: But, there needs to be movement.

BLACK: We are right on the same wave length. The difficulty we face with Congress, and with its utility as a moving and active body, lies in the impossibility under our constitutional system of disciplining the members with respect to their votes. That we can't help; we have to put that aside. But that in turn has no effect, at least a very diffuse and slight effect, on the innovative and creative power of individual Congressmen and groups of Congressmen or on the majority party caucus or on any other body. And so I think that where we want to concentrate in the formation of a Congress, and of a conception of Congress for the twenty-first century, is at the level of innovation and formation of program. Now, what I don't see is that the knowledge we would attempt to develop by these new communication devices would be of utility principally to the majority party. I don't see any reason why their greater need for and use of it would not just flow naturally from their positions in the majority party, or why the minority should in any way be shut out from access to all this.

ECKHARDT: I think that is debatable, and it could be resolved either way, and I don't mean to preclude that possibility. It might be the best practicable way to work it out. I envisage Congress as it presently exists as a great diesel engine that has to be heated up before it will run and which has no device for preheating or for ignition, except the presidency. Now, I think that is bad. I think that there is a necessary relationship between the President and Congress—that no great progress will ever occur, nor will government operate with reasonable efficiency for any long period of time, when the presidency and the Congress are not in the hands of the same party. But Congress ought to have a preheating device, or an ignition system. When the President affords initiative and innovation, it does not hurt. It implements the effectiveness of government if Congress also has it. In the instance where the presidency is defused and not working, it is almost essential. There's grave fear for the continuation of the American government in anything like the form we have known in the past, unless such a device is begun.

BLACK: Let's face it. The emergency of the next few years will have to be met by improvisation, and perhaps by some considerable chance-taking. Those few years are not years in which new informational staffing in the broad sense is going to be developed in Congress. It might be a job that's started on, but it can't be put together in that amount of time.

ECKHARDT: I'm not sure of that. I'm inclined to think that because of this need, the best climate for a powerful movement in that direction is possible.

BLACK: Certainly one should make a start.

I said in a former talk that our *constitutional* structures are all right, perfectly capable of giving effect to what is willed, and that any defect is one of will. I would amend or extend that by saying that the will cannot be formed to any good effect without knowledge.

ECKHARDT: And the hope of beginning cooperation between Congress and the President is nowhere better than at the level of gathering and sharing knowledge. The joint enterprise of developing shared insights into our problems would, aside from its more immediate benefits, set up a pattern of cooperation. What would come from that we cannot now foresee. But it looks to me like the most hopeful way to begin preparing for the twenty-first century.

APPENDIX: THE CONSTITUTION OF THE UNITED STATES AND AMENDMENTS

We the People of the United States, in Order to form a more perfect Union, establish Justice, insure domestic Tranquillity, provide for the common defence, promote the general Welfare, and secure the Blessings of Liberty to ourselves and our Posterity, do ordain and establish this Constitution for the United States of America.

Article. I.

SECTION. 1. All legislative Powers herein granted shall be vested in a Congress of the United States, which shall consist of a Senate and House of Representatives.

SECTION. 2. The House of Representatives shall be composed of Members chosen every second Year by the People of the several States, and the Electors in each State shall have the Qualifications requisite for Electors of the most numerous Branch of the State Legislature.

No Person shall be a Representative who shall not have attained to the age of twenty five Years, and been seven Years a Citizen of the United States, and who shall not, when elected, be an Inhabitant of that State in which he shall be chosen.

Representatives and direct Taxes shall be apportioned among the several States which may be included within this Union, according to their respective Numbers, which shall be determined by adding to the whole Number of free Persons, including those bound to Service for a Term of Years, and excluding Indians not taxed, three fifths of all other Persons. The actual Enumeration shall be made within three Years after the first Meeting of the Congress of the United States, and within every subsequent Term of ten Years, in such Manner as they shall by Law direct. The number of Representatives shall not exceed one for every thirty Thousand, but each State shall have at Least one Representative; and until such enumeration shall be made, the State of New Hampshire shall be entitled to chuse three,

Massachusetts eight, Rhode-Island and Providence Plantations one, Connecticut five, New-York six, New Jersey four, Pennsylvania eight, Delaware one, Maryland six, Virginia ten, North Carolina five, South Carolina five, and Georgia three.

When vacancies happen in the Representation from any State, the Executive Authority thereof shall issue Writs of Election to fill such Vacancies.

The House of Representatives shall chuse their Speaker and other Officers; and shall have the sole Power of Impeachment.

SECTION. 3. The Senate of the United States shall be composed of two Senators from each State, chosen by the Legislature thereof, for six Years; and each Senator shall have one Vote.

Immediately after they shall be assembled in Consequence of the first Election, they shall be divided as equally as may be into three Classes. The Seats of the Senators of the first Class shall be vacated at the Expiration of the second Year, of the second Class at the Expiration of the fourth Year, and of the third Class at the Expiration of the sixth Year, so that one third may be chosen every second Year; and if Vacancies happen by Resignation, or otherwise, during the Recess of the Legislature of any State, the Executive thereof may make temporary Appointments until the next Meeting of the Legislature, which shall then fill such Vacancies.

No Person shall be a Senator who shall not have attained to the Age of thirty Years, and been nine Years a Citizen of the United States, and who shall not, when elected, be an Inhabitant of that State for which he shall be chosen.

The Vice President of the United States shall be President of the Senate but shall have no vote, unless they be equally divided.

The Senate shall chuse their other Officers, and also a President pro tempore, in the Absence of the Vice President, or when he shall exercise the Office of President of the United States.

The Senate shall have the sole Power to try all Impeachments. When sitting for that Purpose, they shall be on Oath or Affirmation. When the President of the United States is tried the Chief Justice shall preside: And no Person shall be convicted without the Concurrence of two thirds of the Members present.

Judgment in Cases of Impeachment shall not extend further than to removal from Office, and disqualification to hold and enjoy any Office of honor, Trust or Profit under the United States: but the Party convicted shall nevertheless be liable and subject to Indictment, Trial, Judgment and Punishment, according to Law.

SECTION. 4. The Times, Places and Manner of holding Elections for Senators and Representatives, shall be prescribed in each State by the Legislature thereof; but the Congress may at any time by Law make or alter such Regulations, except as to the Places of chusing Senators.

The Congress shall assemble at least once in every Year, and such Meeting shall be on the first Monday in December, unless they shall by Law appoint a different Day.

SECTION. 5. Each House shall be the Judge of the Elections, Returns and Qualifications of its own Members, and a Majority of each shall constitute a Quorum to do Business; but a smaller Number may adjourn from day to day, and may be authorized to compel the Attendance of absent Members, in such Manner, and under such Penalties as each House may provide.

Each House may determine the Rules of its Proceedings, punish its Members for disorderly Behaviour, and, with the Concurrence of two thirds, expel a Member.

Each House shall keep a Journal of its Proceedings, and from time to time publish the same, excepting such Parts as may in their Judgment require Secrecy; and the Yeas and Nays of the Members of either House on any question shall, at the Desire of one fifth of those Present, be entered on the Journal.

Neither House, during the Session of Congress, shall, without the Consent of the other adjourn for more than three days, nor to any other Place than that in which the two Houses shall be sitting.

SECTION. 6. The Senators and Representatives shall receive a Compensation for their Services to be ascertained by Law, and paid out of the Treasury of the United States. They shall in all Cases, except Treason, Felony and Breach of Peace, be privileged from Arrest during their Attendance at the Session of their respective Houses, and in going to and returning from the same; and for any Speech or Debate in either House, they shall not be questioned in any other Place.

No Senator or Representative shall, during the Time for which he was elected, be appointed to any civil Office under the Authority of the United States, which shall have been created, or the Emoluments whereof shall have been encreased during such time; and no Person holding any Office under the United States, shall be a Member of either House during his Continuance in Office.

SECTION. 7. All Bills for raising Revenue shall originate in the House of

Representatives; but the Senate may propose or concur with amendments as on other Bills.

Every Bill which shall have passed the House of Representatives and the Senate, shall, before it becomes a law, be presented to the President of the United States: If he approve he shall sign it, but if not he shall return it, with his Objections to that House in which it shall have originated, who shall enter the Objections at large on their Journal, and proceed to reconsider it. If after such Reconsideration two thirds of that House shall agree to pass the Bill, it shall be sent, together with the Objections, to the other House, by which it shall likewise be reconsidered, and if approved by two thirds of that House, it shall become a Law. But in all such Cases the Votes of both Houses shall be determined by yeas and Nays, and the Names of the Persons voting for and against the Bill shall be entered on the Journal of each House respectively. If any Bill shall not be returned by the President within ten Days (Sunday excepted) after it shall have been presented to him, the Same shall be a Law, in like Manner as if he had signed it, unless the Congress by their Adjournment prevent its Return, in which Case it shall not be a Law.

Every Order, Resolution, or Vote to which the Concurrence of the Senate and House of Representatives may be necessary (except on a question of Adjournment) shall be presented to the President of the United States; and before the Same shall take Effect, shall be approved by him, or being disapproved by him, shall be repassed by two thirds of the Senate and House of Representatives, according to the Rules and Limitations prescribed in the Case of a Bill.

SECTION. 8. The Congress shall have Power To lay and collect Taxes, Duties, Imposts and Excises, to pay the Debts and provide for the common Defence and general Welfare of the United States; but all Duties, Imposts and Excises shall be uniform throughout the United States;

To borrow Money on the credit of the United States;

To regulate Commerce with foreign Nations, and among the several States, and with the Indian Tribes;

To establish an uniform Rule of Naturalization, and uniform Laws on the subject of Bankruptcies throughout the United States;

To coin Money, regulate the Value thereof, and of foreign Coin, and fix the Standard of Weights and Measures;

To provide for the Punishment of counterfeiting the Securities and current Coin of the United States;

To establish Post Offices and post Roads;

To promote the Progress of Science and useful Arts, by securing for limited Times to Authors and Inventors the exclusive Right to their respective Writings and Discoveries;

To constitute Tribunals inferior to the supreme Court;

To define and punish Piracies and Felonies committed on the high Seas, and Offenses against the Law of Nations;

To declare War, grant Letters of Marque and Reprisal, and make Rules concerning Captures on Land and Water;

To raise and support Armies, but no Appropriation of Money to that Use shall be for a longer Term than two Years;

To provide and maintain a Navy;

To make Rules for the Government and Regulation of the land and naval Forces;

To provide for calling forth the Militia to execute the Laws of the Union, suppress Insurrections and repel Invasions;

To provide for organizing, arming, and disciplining, the Militia, and for governing such Part of them as may be employed in the Service of the United States, reserving to the States respectively, the Appointment of the Officers, and the Authority of training the Militia according to the discipline prescribed by Congress;

To exercise exclusive Legislation in all Cases whatsoever, over such District (not exceeding ten Miles square) as may, by Cession of Particular States, and the Acceptance of Congress, become the Seat of the Government of the United States, and to exercise like Authority over all Places purchased by the Consent of the Legislature of the State in which the Same shall be, for the Erection of Forts, Magazines, Arsenals, dock-Yards and other needful Buildings;—And

To make all Laws which shall be necessary and proper for carrying into Execution the foregoing Powers and all other Powers vested by this Constitution in the Government of the United States, or in any Department or Officer thereof.

Section. 9. The Migration or Importation of such Persons as any of the States now existing shall think proper to admit, shall not be prohibited by the Congress prior to the Year one thousand eight hundred and eight, but a Tax or duty may be imposed on such Importation, not exceeding ten dollars for each Person.

The Privilege of the Writ of Habeas Corpus shall not be suspended, unless when in Cases of Rebellion or Invasion the public Safety may require it.

No Bill of Attainder or ex post facto Law shall be passed.

No Capitation, or other direct, Tax shall be laid, unless in Proportion to the Census of Enumeration herein before directed to be taken.

No Tax or Duty shall be laid on Articles exported from any State.

No Preference shall be given by any Regulation of Commerce or Revenue to the Ports of one State over those of another; nor shall Vessels bound to, or from, one State, be obliged to enter, clear or pay Duties in another.

No Money shall be drawn from the Treasury, but in Consequence of Appropriations made by Law; and a regular Statement and Account of the Receipts and Expenditures of all public Money shall be published from time to time.

No Title of Nobility shall be granted by the United States: And no Person holding any Office of Profit or Trust under them, shall, without the Consent of the Congress, accept of any present, Emolument, Office, or Title, of any kind whatever, from any King, Prince or foreign State.

SECTION. 10. No State shall enter into any Treaty, Alliance, or Confederation; grant Letters of Marque and Reprisal; coin Money; emit Bills of Credit; make any Thing but gold and silver Coin a Tender in Payment of Debts; pass any Bill of Attainder, ex post facto Law, or Law impairing the Obligation of Contracts, or grant any Title of Nobility.

No State shall, without the Consent of the Congress, lay any Imposts or Duties on Imports or Exports, except what may be absolutely necessary for executing it's inspection Laws: and the net Produce of all Duties and Imposts, laid by any State on Imports or Exports, shall be for the Use of the Treasury of the United States; and all such Laws shall be subject to the Revision and Controul of the Congress.

No State shall, without the Consent of Congress, lay any Duty of Tonnage, keep Troops, or Ships of War in time of Peace, enter into any Agreement or Compact with another State, or with a foreign Power, or engage in War, unless actually invaded, or in such imminent Danger as will not admit of delay.

Article II.

SECTION. 1. The executive Power shall be vested in a President of the United States of America. He shall hold his Office during the Term of four Years, and, together with the Vice President, chosen for the same Term, be elected, as follows:

Each State shall appoint, in such Manner as the Legislature thereof may direct, a Number of Electors, equal to the whole Number of Senators and Representatives to which the State may be entitled in the Congress: but no Senator or Representative, or Person holding an Office of Trust or Profit under the United States, shall be appointed an Elector.

The Electors shall meet in their respective States, and vote by Ballot for two Persons, of whom one at least shall not be an Inhabitant of the same State with themselves. And they shall make a List of all the Persons voted for, and of the Number of Votes for each; which List they shall sign and certify, and transmit sealed to the Seat of the Government of the United States, directed to the President of the Senate. The President of the Senate shall, in the Presence of the Senate and House of Representatives, open all the Certificates, and the Votes shall then be counted. The Person having the greatest Number of Votes shall be the President, if such Number be a Majority of the whole Number of Electors appointed; and if there be more than one who have such Majority, and have an equal Number of Votes, then the House of Representatives shall immediately chuse by Ballot one of them for President; and if no Person have a Majority, then from the five highest on the List the said House shall in like Manner chuse the President. But in chusing the President, the Votes shall be taken by States, the Representatives from each State having one Vote; a quorum for this Purpose shall consist of a Member or Members from two thirds of the States, and a Majority of all the States shall be necessary to a Choice. In every Case, after the Choice of the President, the Person having the greatest Number of Votes of the Electors shall be the Vice President. But if there should remain two or more who have equal Votes, the Senate shall chuse from them by Ballot the Vice President.

The Congress may determine the Time of chusing the Electors, and the Day on which they shall give their Votes; which Day shall be the same throughout the United States.

No person except a natural born Citizen, or a Citizen of the United States, at the time of the Adoption of this Constitution, shall be eligible to the Office of President; neither shall any person be eligible to that Office who shall not have attained to the Age of thirty five Years, and been fourteen Years a Resident within the United States.

In Case of the Removal of the President from Office, or of his Death, Resignation, or Inability to discharge the Powers and Duties of the said

Office, the Same shall devolve on the Vice President, and the Congress may by Law provide for the Case of Removal, Death, Resignation or Inability, both of the President and Vice President, declaring what Officer shall then act as President, and such Officer shall act accordingly, until the Disability be removed or a President shall be elected.

The President shall, at stated Times, receive for his Services, a Compensation, which shall neither be increased nor diminished during the Period for which he shall have been elected, and he shall not receive within that Period any other Emolument from the United States, or any of them.

Before he enter on the Execution of his Office, he shall take the following Oath or Affirmation:—"I do solemnly swear (or affirm) that I will faithfully execute the Office of President of the United States, and will to the best of my Ability, preserve, protect and defend the Constitution of the United States."

SECTION. 2. The President shall be Commander in Chief of the Army and Navy of the United States, and of the Militia of the several States, when called into actual Service of the United States; he may require the Opinion, in writing, of the principal Officer in each of the executive Departments, upon any Subject relating to the Duties of their respective Offices, and he shall have Power to grant Reprieves and Pardons for Offenses against the United States, except in Cases of Impeachment.

He shall have Power, by and with the Advice and Consent of the Senate, to make Treaties, provided two thirds of the Senators present concur; and he shall nominate, and by and with the Advice and Consent of the Senate, shall appoint Ambassadors, other public Ministers and Consuls, Judges of the supreme Court, and all other Officers of the United States, whose Appointments are not herein otherwise provided for, and which shall be established by Law: but the Congress may by Law vest the Appointment of such inferior Officers, as they think proper, in the President alone, in the Courts of Law, or in the Heads of Departments.

The President shall have Power to fill up all Vacancies that may happen during the Recess of the Senate, by granting Commissions which shall expire at the End of their next Session.

SECTION. 3. He shall from time to time give to the Congress Information on the State of the Union, and recommend to their Consideration such Measures as he shall judge necessary and expedient; he may, on extraordinary Occasions, convene both Houses, or either of them, and in Case of Disagreement between them, with Respect to the Time of Adjournment, he may adjourn them to such Time as he shall think proper; he shall receive

Ambassadors and other public Ministers; he shall take Care that the Laws be faithfully executed, and shall Commission all the Officers of the United States.

SECTION. 4. The President, Vice President and all Civil Officers of the United States, shall be removed from Office on Impeachment for, and Conviction of, Treason, Bribery, or other high Crimes and Misdemeanors.

Article. III.

SECTION. 1. The judicial Power of the United States, shall be vested in one supreme Court, and in such inferior Courts as the Congress may from time to time ordain and establish. The Judges, both of the supreme and inferior Courts, shall hold their Offices during good Behaviour, and shall, at stated Times, receive for their Services, a Compensation, which shall not be diminished during their Continuance in Office.

SECTION. 2. The judicial Power shall extend to all Cases, in Law and Equity, arising under this Constitution, the Laws of the United States, and Treaties made, or which shall be made, under their Authority;—to all Cases affecting Ambassadors, other public ministers and Consuls;—to all Cases of admiralty and maritime Jurisdiction;—to Controversies to which the United States shall be a Party;—to Controversies between two or more States;—between a State and Citizens of another State;—between Citizens of different States;—between Citizens of the same State claiming Lands under Grants of different States, and between a State, or the Citizens thereof, and foreign States, Citizens or Subjects.

In all Cases affecting Ambassadors, other public Ministers and Consuls, and those in which a State shall be Party, the supreme Court shall have original Jurisdiction. In all the other Cases before mentioned, the supreme Court shall have appellate Jurisdiction, both as to Law and Fact, with such Exceptions, and under such Regulations as the Congress shall make.

The Trial of all Crimes, except in Cases of Impeachment, shall be by Jury; and such Trial shall be held in the State where the said Crimes shall have been committed; but when not committed within any State, the Trial shall be at such Place or Places as the Congress may by Law have directed.

SECTION. 3. Treason against the United States, shall consist only in levying War against them, or in adhering to their Enemies, giving them Aid and Comfort. No Person shall be convicted of Treason unless on the Testimony of two Witnesses to the same overt Act, or on Confession in open Court.

The Congress shall have Power to declare the Punishment of Treason, but no Attainder of Treason shall work Corruption of Blood, or Forfeiture except during the Life of the Person attainted.

Article. IV.

SECTION. 1. Full Faith and Credit shall be given in each State to the public Acts, Records, and judicial Proceedings of every other State. And the Congress may by general Laws prescribe the Manner in which such Acts, Records and Proceedings shall be proved, and the Effect thereof.

SECTION. 2. The Citizens of each State shall be entitled to all Privileges and Immunities of Citizens in the several States.

A Person charged in any State with Treason, Felony, or other Crime, who shall flee from Justice, and be found in another State, shall on Demand of the executive Authority of the State from which he fled, be delivered up, to be removed to the State having Jurisdiction of the Crime.

No Person held to Service or Labour in one State, under the Laws thereof, escaping into another, shall, in Consequence of any Law or Regulation therein, be discharged from such Service or Labour, but shall be delivered up on Claim of the Party to whom such Service or Labour may be due.

SECTION. 3. New States may be admitted by the Congress into this Union; but no new State shall be formed or erected within the Jurisdiction of any other State; nor any State be formed by the Junction of two or more States, or Parts of States, without the Consent of the Legislatures of the States concerned as well as of the Congress.

The Congress shall have Power to dispose of and make all needful Rules and Regulations respecting the Territory or other Property belonging to the United States; and nothing in this Constitution shall be so construed as to Prejudice any Claims of the United States, or of any particular State.

SECTION. 4. The United States shall guarantee to every State in this Union a Republican Form of Government, and shall protect each of them against Invasion; and on Application of the Legislature, or of the Executive (when the Legislature cannot be convened) against domestic Violence.

Article. V.

The Congress, whenever two thirds of both Houses shall deem it necessary, shall propose Amendments to this Constitution, or, on the Application of the Legislatures of two thirds of the several States, shall call a Convention for proposing Amendments, which, in either Case, shall be valid to all Intents and Purposes, as Part of this Constitution, when ratified by the Legislatures of three fourths of the several States, or by Conventions in three fourths thereof, as the one or the other Mode of Ratification may be proposed by the Congress; Provided that no Amendment which may be made prior to the Year One thousand eight hundred and eight shall in any Manner affect the first and fourth Clauses in the Ninth Section of the first Article; and that no State, without its Consent, shall be deprived of it's equal Suffrage in the Senate.

Article. VI.

All Debts contracted and Engagements entered into, before the Adoption of this Constitution, shall be as valid against the United States under this Constitution, as under the Confederation.

This Constitution, and the Laws of the United States which shall be made in Pursuance thereof; and all Treaties made, or which shall be made, under the Authority of the United States, shall be the supreme Law of the Land; and the Judges in every State shall be bound thereby, any Thing in the Constitution or Laws of any State to the Contrary notwithstanding.

The Senators and Representatives before mentioned, and the Members of the several State Legislatures, and all executive and judicial Officers, both of the United States and of the several States, shall be bound by Oath or Affirmation, to support this Constitution; but no religious Test shall ever be required as a Qualification to any Office or public Trust under the United States.

Article. VII.

The Ratification of the Conventions of nine States, shall be sufficient for the Establishment of this Constitution between the States so ratifying the Same.

AMENDMENTS TO THE CONSTITUTION

Amendment I.

Congress shall make no law respecting an establishment of religion, or prohibiting the free exercise thereof; or abridging the freedom of speech, or of the press; or the right of the people peaceably to assemble, and to petition the Government for a redress of grievances.

Amendment II.

A well regulated Militia, being necessary to the security of a free State, the right of the people to keep and bear Arms, shall not be infringed.

Amendment III.

No Soldier shall, in time of peace be quartered in any house, without the consent of the Owner, nor in time of war, but in a manner to be prescribed by law.

Amendment IV.

The right of the people to be secure in their persons, houses, papers, and effects, against unreasonable searches and seizures, shall not be violated, and no Warrants shall issue, but upon probable cause, supported by Oath or affirmation, and particularly describing the place to be searched, and the persons or things to be seized.

Amendment V.

No person shall be held to answer for a capital, or otherwise infamous crime, unless on a presentment or indictment of a Grand Jury, except in cases arising in the land or naval forces, or in the Militia, when in actual service in time of War or public danger; nor shall any person be subject for the same offence to be twice put in jeopardy of life or limb; nor shall be compelled in any criminal case to be a witness against himself, nor be deprived of life, liberty, or property, without due process of law, nor shall private property be taken for public use, without just compensation.

Amendment VI.

In all criminal prosecutions, the accused shall enjoy the right to a speedy and public trial, by an impartial jury of the State and district wherein the crime shall have been committed, which district shall have been previously ascertained by law, and to be informed of the nature and cause of the accusation; to be confronted with the witnesses against him; to have compulsory process for obtaining witnesses in his favor, and to have the Assistance of Counsel for his defence.

Amendment VII.

In Suits at common law, where the value in controversy shall exceed twenty dollars, the right of trial by jury shall be preserved, and no fact tried by a jury, shall be otherwise re-examined in any Court of the United States, than according to the rules of the common law.

Amendment VIII.

Excessive bail shall not be required, nor excessive fines imposed, nor cruel and unusual punishments inflicted.

Amendment IX.

The enumeration in the Constitution, of certain rights, shall not be construed to deny or disparage others retained by the people.

Amendment X.

The powers not delegated to the United States by the Constitution, nor prohibited by it to the States, are reserved to the States respectively, or to the people.

Amendment XI.

The Judicial power of the United States shall not be construed to extend to any suit in law or equity, commenced or prosecuted against one on the United States by Citizens of another State, or by Citizens or Subjects of any Foreign State.

Amendment XII.

The Electors shall meet in their respective states and vote by ballot for President and Vice President, one of whom, at least, shall not be an inhabitant of the same state with themselves; they shall name in their ballots the person voted for as President, and in distinct ballots the person voted for as Vice-President, and they shall make distinct lists of all persons voted for as President, and of all persons voted for as Vice-President, and of the number of votes for each, which lists they shall sign and certify, and transmit sealed to the seat of the government of the United States, directed to the President of the Senate;—The President of the Senate shall, in the presence of the Senate and House of Representatives, open all the certificates and the votes shall then be counted;—The person having the greatest number of votes for President, shall be the President, if such number be a majority of the whole number of Electors appointed; and if no person have such majority, then from the persons having the highest numbers not exceeding three on the list of those voted for as President, the House of Representatives shall choose immediately, by ballot, the President. But in choosing the President, the votes shall be taken by states, the representation from each state having one vote; a quorum for this purpose shall consist of a member or members from two-thirds of the states, and a majority of all the states shall be necessary to a choice. And if the House of Representatives shall not choose a President whenever the right of choice shall devolve upon them, before the fourth day of March next following, then the Vice-President shall act as President, as in the case of the death or other constitutional disability of the President—The person having the greatest number of votes as Vice-President, shall be the Vice-President, if such number be a majority of the whole number of Electors appointed, and if no person have a majority, then from the two highest numbers on the list, the Senate shall choose the Vice-President; a quorum for the purpose shall consist of two-thirds of the whole number of Senators, and a majority of the whole number shall be necessary to a choice. But no person constitutionally ineligible to the office of President shall be eligible to that of Vice-President of the United States.

Amendment XIII.

SECTION. 1. Neither slavery nor involuntary servitude, except as a punishment for crime whereof the party shall have been duly convicted, shall exist within the United States, or any place subject to their jurisdiction.

SECTION. 2. Congress shall have power to enforce this article by appropriate legislation.

Amendment XIV.

SECTION. 1. All persons born or naturalized in the United States and subject to the jurisdiction thereof, are citizens of the United States and of the State wherein they reside. No State shall make or enforce any law which shall abridge the privileges or immunities of citizens of the United States; or shall any State deprive any person of life, liberty, or property, without due process of law; nor deny to any person within its jurisdiction the equal protection of the laws.

SECTION. 2. Representatives shall be apportioned among the several States according to their respective numbers, counting the whole number of persons in each State, excluding Indians not taxed. But when the right to vote at any election for the choice of electors for President and Vice President of the United States, Representatives in Congress, the Executive and Judicial Officers of a State, or the members of the Legislature thereof, is denied to any of the male inhabitants of such State, being twenty-one years of age, and citizens of the United States, or in any way abridged, except for participation in rebellion, or other crime, the basis of representation therein shall be reduced in the proportion which the number of such male citizens shall bear to the whole number of male citizens twenty-one years of age in such State.

SECTION. 3. No person shall be a Senator or Representative in Congress, or elector of President and Vice President, or hold any office, civil or military, under the United States, or under any State, who, having previously taken an oath, as a member of Congress, or as an officer of the United States, or as a member of any State legislature, or as an executive or judicial officer of any State, to support the Constitution of the United States, shall have engaged in insurrection or rebellion against the same, or given aid or comfort to the enemies thereof. But Congress may by a vote of two-thirds of each House, remove such disability.

SECTION. 4. The validity of the public debt of the United States, authorized by law, including debts incurred for payment of pensions and bounties for services in suppressing insurrection or rebellion, shall not be questioned. But neither the United States nor any State shall assume or pay any debt or obligation incurred in aid of insurrection or rebellion against the United States, or any claim for the loss or emancipation of any slave; but all such debts, obligations and claims shall be held illegal and void.

SECTION. 5. The Congress shall have power to enforce, by appropriate legislation, the provisions of this article.

Amendment XV.

SECTION. 1. The right of citizens of the United States to vote shall not be denied or abridged by the United States or by any State on account of race, color, or previous condition of servitude.

SECTION. 2. The Congress shall have power to enforce this article by appropriate legislation.

Amendment XVI.

The Congress shall have power to lay and collect taxes on incomes, from whatever source derived, without apportionment among the several States, and without regard to any census or enumeration.

Amendment XVII.

The Senate of the United States shall be composed of two Senators from each State, elected by the people thereof, for six years; and each Senator shall have one vote. The electors in each State shall have the qualifications requisite for electors of the most numerous branch of the State legislatures.

When vacancies happen in the representation of any State in the Senate, the executive authority of such State shall issue writs of election to fill such vacancies: *Provided*, That the legislature of any State may empower the executive thereof to make temporary appointments until the people fill the vacancies by election as the legislature may direct.

This amendment shall not be so construed as to affect the election or term of any Senator chosen before it becomes valid as part of the Constitution.

Amendment XVIII.

SECTION. 1. After one year from the ratification of this article the manufacture, sale, or transportation of intoxicating liquors within, the importation thereof into, or the exportation thereof from the United States and all territory subject to the jurisdiction thereof for beverage purposes is hereby prohibited.

SECTION. 2. The Congress and the several States shall have concurrent power to enforce this article by appropriate legislation.

SECTION. 3. This article shall be inoperative unless it shall have been ratified as an amendment to the Constitution by the legislatures of the several States, as provided in the Constitution, within seven years from the date of the submission hereof to the States by the Congress.

Amendment XIX.

The right of citizens of the United States to vote shall not be denied or abridged by the United States or by any State on account of sex.

Congress shall have power to enforce this article by appropriate legislation.

Amendment XX.

SECTION. 1. The terms of the President and Vice President shall end at noon on the 20th day of January, and the terms of Senators and Representatives at noon on the 3d day of January, of the years in which such terms would have ended if this article had not been ratified; and the terms of their successors shall then begin.

SECTION. 2. The Congress shall assemble at least once in every year, and such meeting shall begin at noon on the 3d day of January, unless they shall by law appoint a different day.

SECTION. 3. If, at the time fixed for the beginning of the term of the President, the President elect shall have died, the Vice President elect shall become President. If a President shall not have been chosen before the time fixed for the beginning of his term, or if the President elect shall have failed to qualify, then the Vice President elect shall act as President until a President shall have qualified; and the Congress may by law provide for the case wherein neither a President elect nor a Vice President elect shall have qualified, declaring who shall then act as President, or the manner in which one who is to act shall be selected, and such person shall act accordingly until a President or Vice President shall have qualified.

SECTION. 4. The Congress may by law provide for the case of the death of any of the persons from whom the House of Representatives may choose a President whenever the right of choice shall have devolved upon them, and for the case of the death of any of the persons from whom the Senate may choose a Vice President whenever the right of choice shall have devolved upon them.

SECTION. 5. Sections 1 and 2 shall take effect on the 15th day of October following the ratification of this article.

SECTION. 6. This article shall be inoperative unless it shall have been ratified as an amendment to the Constitution by the legislatures of three-fourths of the several States within seven years from the date of its submission.

Amendment XXI.

SECTION. 1. The eighteenth article of amendment to the Constitution of the United States is hereby repealed.

SECTION. 2. The transportation or importation into any State, Territory or possession of the United States for delivery or use therein of intoxicating liquors, in violation of the laws thereof, is hereby prohibited.

SECTION. 3. This article shall be inoperative unless it shall have been ratified as an amendment to the Constitution by conventions in the several

States, as provided in the Constitution, within seven years from the date of the submission hereof to the States by the Congress.

Amendment XXII.

SECTION. 1. No person shall be elected to the office of the President more than twice, and no person who has held the office of President, or acted as President, for more than two years of a term to which some other person was elected President shall be elected to the office of the President more than once. But this Article shall not apply to any person holding the office of President, when this Article was proposed by the Congress, and shall not prevent any person who may be holding the office of President, or acting as President, during the term within which this Article becomes operative from holding the office of President or acting as President during the remainder of such term.

SECTION. 2. This Article shall be inoperative unless it shall have been ratified as an amendment to the Constitution by the legislatures of three-fourths of the several States within seven years from the date of its submission to the States by the Congress.

Amendment XXIII.

SECTION. 1. The District constituting the seat of Government of the United States shall appoint in such manner as the Congress may direct:

A number of electors of President and Vice President equal to the whole number of Senators and Representatives in Congress to which the District would be entitled if it were a State, but in no event more than the least populous State; they shall be in addition to those appointed by the States, but they shall be considered, for the purposes of the election of President and Vice-President, to be electors appointed by a State; and they shall meet in the District and perform such duties as provided by the twelfth article of amendment.

SECTION. 2. The Congress shall have power to enforce this article by appropriate legislation.

Amendment XXIV.

SECTION. 1. The right of citizens of the United States to vote in any primary or other election for President or Vice President, for electors for President or Vice President, or for Senator or Representative in Congress, shall not be denied or abridged by the United States or any State by reason of failure to pay any poll tax or other tax.

SECTION. 2. The Congress shall have power to enforce this article by appropriate legislation.

Amendment XXV.

SECTION. 1. In case of the removal of the President from office or of his death or resignation, the Vice President shall become President.

SECTION. 2. Whenever there is a vacancy in the office of the Vice President, the President shall nominate a Vice President who shall take office upon confirmation by a majority vote of both Houses of Congress.

SECTION. 3. Whenever the President transmits to the President pro tempore of the Senate and the Speaker of the House of Representatives his written declaration that he is unable to discharge the powers and duties of his office, and until he transmits to them a written declaration to the contrary, such powers and duties shall be discharged by the Vice President as Acting President.

SECTION. 4. Whenever the Vice President and a majority of either the principal officers of the executive departments or of such other body as Congress may by law provide, transmit to the President pro tempore of the Senate and the Speaker of the House of Representatives their written declaration that the President is unable to discharge the powers and duties of his office, the Vice President shall immediately assume the powers and duties of the office as Acting President.

Thereafter, when the President transmits to the President pro tempore of the Senate and the Speaker of the House of Representatives his written declaration that no inability exists, he shall resume the powers and duties of his office unless the Vice President and a majority of either the principal officers of the executive department or of such other body as Congress may by law provide, transmit within four days to the President pro tempore of the Senate and the Speaker of the House of Representatives their written declaration that the President is unable to discharge the powers and duties of his office. Thereupon Congress shall decide the issue, assembling within forty-eight hours for that purpose if not in session. If the Congress, within twenty-one days after receipt of the latter written declaration, or, if Congress is not in session, within twenty-one days after Congress is required to assemble, determines by two-thirds vote of both Houses that the President is unable to discharge the powers and duties of his office, the

Vice President shall continue to discharge the same as Acting President; otherwise, the President shall resume the powers and duties of his office.

Amendment XXVI.

SECTION. 1. The right of citizens of the United States, who are eighteen years of age or older, to vote shall not be denied or abridged by the United States or by any State on account of age.

SECTION. 2. The Congress shall have power to enforce this article by appropriate legislation.